Bottom Line Writing

REPORTING THE SENSE OF DOLLARS

Bottom Line
Writing

REPORTING THE SENSE OF DOLLARS

Conrad C. Fink

Iowa State University Press • AMES

CONRAD C. FINK is a William S. Morris Professor of Newspaper Strategy and Management, Henry G. Grady College of Journalism and Mass Communication, and director of the James M. Cox Jr. Institute for Newspaper Management Studies, University of Georgia, Athens. He was a reporter, editor, foreign correspondent and vice president of The Associated Press before becoming an award-winning teacher. Professor Fink has written six other books on journalism, reporting and writing.

© 2000 Iowa State University Press, Ames, Iowa 50014
All rights reserved

Iowa State University Press
2121 South State Avenue, Ames, Iowa 50014

Orders: 1-800-862-6657
Office: 1-515-292-0140
Fax: 1-515-292-3348
Web site: www.isupress.edu

Authorization to photocopy items for internal or personal use, or the internal or personal use of specific clients, is granted by Iowa State University Press, provided that the base fee of $.10 per copy is paid directly to the Copyright Clearance Center, 222 Rosewood Drive, Danvers, MA 01923. For those organizations that have been granted a photocopy license by CCC, a separate system of payments has been arranged. The fee code for users of the Transactional Reporting Service is 0-8138-2286-6/2000 $.10.

♾ Printed on acid-free paper in the United States of America

First edition, 2000

Library of Congress Cataloging-in-Publication Data

Fink, Conrad C.
    Bottom line writing : reporting the sense of dollars / Conrad C. Fink.—1st ed.
        p. cm.
    Includes indexes.
    ISBN 0-8138-2286-6
        1. Journalism, Commercial.   I. Title.

PN4784.C7 F49 2000
070.4'4933—dc21   99-053360

The last digit is the print number: 9 8 7 6 5 4 3 2 1

In memory of
Wes Gallagher

Contents

Introduction

EVER DREAM OF A JOURNALISM career that can take your writing—*your byline*—to the front page of *The New York Times* or *The Washington Post*? Or to prominent display on section fronts of *The Philadelphia Inquirer, The Chicago Tribune, The Dallas Morning News, Los Angeles Times*? Or into community newspapers across America?

Ever dream of a truly meaningful career in news that's crucial to *millions* of people? A career in newspapers or magazines, broadcast or electronic media that can help those millions lead better, more rewarding lives?

All that is possible through the journalism we'll study in this book—the reporting and writing of economic, business and financial news.

Clearly, career success and true public service are wide open for you through *business writing,* just as through covering politics, foreign affairs, arts and entertainment, sports or any other career track open to young journalists.

Interest in our subject is exploding among readers, viewers and listeners. All want, all *need,* to understand economic power and money—where both come from and how they touch everyone's life every day.

For all media, such news draws attractive audiences: Readers generally upscale in education and income, the sort of audiences pursued by advertisers who, in turn, provide the financial support all media need.

Editors are responding by allocating ever more resources (including higher salaries) to reporters who can collect and accurately analyze business, economic and financial news, then write it in precise, attractive language. This journalistic effort extends far beyond the old-fashioned "business page" and deeply into all sectors of journalism.

Indeed, look again at those journalistic stars you perhaps hope to emulate—the foreign correspondents, Washington reporters, the arts critics, columnists, sports writers. All devote much of their reporting and writing to economic, business and financial news.

Why has American journalism made this turn? Because U.S. foreign and domestic policies revolve around *economic forces.* Indeed, much of American life itself is shaped, moved, molded by business, economic and financial forces. For example, our arts and entertainment move on public and private funding—the money of the arts. And check even the sports pages: Many cover off-field subjects, prominent among them player salaries, contract negotiations, the *business* of sports.

So, as you move ahead in *Bottom Line Writing:*

REALITY #1

We're not looking here at a narrow, deadend career; instead, we're studying cutting-edge journalism that defines "business news" very broadly, journalism that's crucial to every form of print or electronic media, from front pages to back, from general broadcast news to highly specific all-business news services delivered electronically. Among them are a world of career options for you.

REALITY #2

There is no impenetrable mystery in economic, financial and business news reporting and writing. Despite what may be your uneasiness about "business" (and perhaps a little math fright?), this isn't an arcane art cloaked in secret formulas open only to geniuses. This journalism is open and inviting to any careful, painstaking reporter who knows how to determine what the public wants and needs to know, and who then can find it and write it—*translate* it—in terms the public can understand.

REALITY #3

This journalism can be fun. You can meet fascinating people and report incredibly interesting interlockings of money and other economic forces that drive our society—and you can (you *must*) write with all the dash, vigor and, even at times, the wit so sought after in any form of journalism.

REALITY #4

You carry enormous responsibilities in business journalism. Cover a football game and misspell Bill's last name or misreport Alice's official title in the garden club and you've committed serious errors. But entice Bill and Alice into disastrous investments or otherwise lead them astray on how to make, spend or save money, and you've committed *journalistic felony.* Whatever else you take from *Bottom Line Writing,* understand this: ***You must be completely accurate in your reporting and precise in your writing.***

And note: This book isn't aimed at making you an expert in economics or the inner workings of high finance or business methodology. Rather, the intent is to help you develop reporting skills needed to find people who *are* experts in those subjects and extract from them crucial information. Then we'll work on writing it engagingly and accurately.

That is, we'll develop reporting and writing techniques applicable to *all* journalism, but concentrate on their specialized use in the fascinating world of economics, business and finance.

I've organized *Bottom Line Writing* to edge you gradually into such concepts. Early chapters assume much about this topic is new to you, that you're a student trying to get started in journalism and that reporting mostly for college newspapers or magazines is your immediate goal. The book then gradually escalates toward preparing you for entry-level professional jobs and, perhaps, a career one day covering economic, business and financial news.

Organization of This Book

PART ONE: MARKETPLACE REALITIES

is a single chapter, Your Readers: Their Wants and Their Needs, explaining how all media target audiences by demography (age, income, education) and geography (the "market"). Know your target readers before you touch a keyboard.

PART TWO: REPORTING AND NUMBERS: KEYS TO SUCCESS

is a two-chapter discussion of reporting, interviewing and writing, with hints on getting and using authoritative details so essential to business news.

Chapter 2, Reporting: Sources Are Your Gold, covers finding and interviewing authoritative sources, both the human and electronic kinds.

Chapter 3, Making Facts and Numbers Sing, addresses the crucial question of how to obtain facts and numbers that will strengthen your writing but not overpower your readers.

PART THREE: WRITING FORMS AND STRUCTURES

is a two-chapter examination of tricks of the writing trade you can use to be accurate yet lively, complete yet engaging.

Chapter 4, The Straight Stuff: Five Ws and How, examines hard-news story forms that are the backbone of any news medium.

Chapter 5, Capturing the Human Element, looks at ways to emphasize the human element in business news and thus capture readers.

PART FOUR: THREE MAJOR NEWS SECTORS

is a three-chapter discussion of covering economic, business and financial news.

Chapter 6, Economics: Bringing the Big Picture Home, discusses how to watch distant news horizons for signals on the production, distribution and consumption of wealth—and how to translate that for your non-expert home audience.

Chapter 7, Business: Walking the Main Street Beat, probes the fascinating news beats of Hometown America, close to your readers' everyday lives.

Chapter 8, Finance: It's Their Pocketbooks That Count, shows you how to cover the management of money, credit and capital in terms meaningful to your readers' pocketbooks.

PART FIVE: YOU, THE LAW AND ETHICS

looks at doing what's morally right and also staying within the law (there sometimes is a difference).

Chapter 9, Be Fair, Be Accurate, examines standards of ethics generally accepted among journalists, then focuses on press law. There are traps in both for the unwary.

PART SIX: YOUR FUTURE ON CAMPUS AND BEYOND

sorts through campus journalism as it's practiced today for clues on how you can get started on a career tomorrow.

Chapter 10, Starting Today Toward Tomorrow, looks at business coverage—particularly consumerism—in campus newspapers nationwide. You'll gain clues on how to start today at your campus newspaper on a path toward a professional career in this exciting news sector.

APPENDIX: TERMS TO LEARN

is a glossary of terms often used in reporting business, economic and financial news.

Acknowledgments

My thanks to all the professionals whose work I cited in this book. I can't list you here by name—but I've saluted each of you with a byline on your work.

A very low bow to two former students who contributed special columns for the book: Mickey H. Gramig, business news writer for *The Atlanta Journal and Constitution,* and Steven M. Sears, senior writer for Dow Jones News Service.

Thanks to Judi Brown and Janet Hronek of Iowa State University Press and Carla Tollefson, who know how to help an author through the book-birthing experience.

Thanks, also, to Sophie Barnes for her keyboarding skills that produced a cleanly typed manuscript.

CONRAD FINK
ATHENS, GA.

Bottom Line Writing

REPORTING THE SENSE OF DOLLARS

PART ONE

Marketplace Realities

TO UNDERSTAND BUSINESS news writing you first must understand the business of the media you'll write for.

For newspapers, magazines, radio and broadcast television, the ***business goal*** is gaining audiences attractive to advertisers. Your news reporting and writing will be in a package of information offered to pull in readers, listeners and viewers that your newspaper, magazine or broadcast station then will sell to advertisers.

Why are media so advertiser driven? Because advertisers pay most of the bills.

About 80 percent of all newspaper revenue comes from advertisers. The readers' 20 percent barely covers the cost of the newsprint on which your news will be printed.

For magazines, advertisers contribute about 50 percent of total revenue. Of course, radio and broadcast television get 100 percent of theirs from advertisers.[1]

The only major news media not advertiser driven in this way are some cable channels and private subscriber electronic services whose customers—brokers, bankers, business executives—pay high fees for news.

So, you will define your work, and your editors will judge it and display it against a backdrop of your ***audience***'s wants and needs.

What is news and what isn't must be decided against your understanding of what news your audience needs. Your reporting approach and your writing "angle" must respond to the same test, as must how your editors "play" your story on the front page or inside.

Clearly, you've got to understand how the media define their markets and audiences before you hit the keyboard. Let's turn to that in Chapter 1.

1

Your Readers:
Their Wants and Their Needs

HERE'S A scenario for you:

You're reporting business news for *The Atlanta Journal-Constitution,* jointly-owned morning and afternoon papers with combined circulation of about 460,000 serving Atlanta and north Georgia.

Coca-Cola Enterprises, an Atlanta-based bottler, announces unexpectedly high net income and says it will acquire six independent bottlers for $770 million.

Is that news?

You bet.

Big news?

So big it's assigned to a *Constitution* staff writer, Mickey H. Gramig, a specialist in reporting on the soft drink industry. Her story is spread under a three-column headline across the business section's front page.

Her first three paragraphs:

> Coca-Cola Enterprises surpassed Wall Street expectations with third-quarter net income of 21 cents per share, excluding a 7-cent tax-related gain.
>
> The showing was roughly 60 percent better than the previous third-quarter result of 13 cents per share, excluding a 15-cent gain also related to a tax rate reduction in the United Kingdom.
>
> Also Wednesday, the Atlanta-based bottler said it will buy six independent bottlers for $770 million. CCE, already the world's largest soft drink bottler, will acquire the nation's 10th-largest bottler, Cameron Coca-Cola Bottling Co., which has operations in Pennsylvania, Ohio, and West Virginia.
>
> —Mickey H. Gramig, *Journal-Constitution* [2]

Now, let's say you're 900 miles to the north, on the business desk of *The New York Times* national edition. This edition is put together in

New York City, then transmitted via satellite to eight printing plants throughout the United States. Its readers are scattered coast to coast.

Is the Coca-Cola Enterprise announcement news to you now?

Yes, but with a big difference.

On the same day the *Journal-Constitution* splashed the story, the *Times'* national edition played it deep inside, on page 4 of its business section, in a column of 13 "company news" briefs. The item was not from a staff writer, but, rather, from Reuters, a business news service. This is it:

> Coca-Cola Enterprises Inc., the world's largest soft drink bottler, said yesterday that it agreed to buy six domestic bottlers in deals worth a total of $770 million, including assumption of debt. The bottlers, operating in seven states, sold 80 million cases of soda last year and had 1997 revenue of $365 million, the company said.
>
> The acquisitions were announced after the markets closed; Coca-Cola Enterprises shares rose $1.3625, to $34. Coca-Cola Enterprises sells about two-thirds of Coca-Cola in bottles and cans in North America.
>
> Reuters[3]

Why did these two newspapers treat the same news item so differently? Because they serve different markets and audiences with differing characteristics and needs, and it is those differences which establish how editors judge an item's newsworthiness and how it is written and displayed.

To explain: Coca-Cola Co. and the bottling company (they're separate) have headquarters in Atlanta. They employ thousands of Atlantans and throw millions of payroll dollars into the community. Many local stock investors are "Coke millionaires."

Coca-Cola and fortunes built on it support Atlanta's growth and many of its arts and charitable organizations. Coke is to Atlanta what Ford is to Detroit, Microsoft to Seattle, Mickey Mouse to Disney World.

That is, for *The Atlanta Journal-Constitution,* the Coca-Cola Enterprises story was compellingly important ***local*** news specially meaningful to readers—the upscale and affluent spenders—and eagerly sought by advertisers.

For *The New York Times* national edition, the story was not local and, further, had strong competition for space. The *Times* business section front page was dominated by a Microsoft anti-trust story, a $5.8 billion merger of Rubbermaid Inc. and Newell Co., a stock sale by Conoco and a feature about television advertising—all ***national*** stories—and a fifth story, about Dow Jones & Co., a ***New York–based*** media firm (and competitor of Times Co.).[4]

Note in the examples above how the *Journal-Constitution* and *Times* even took different writing angles on the story: The *Journal-Constitution* led with unexpectedly high earnings, important to those many local Atlanta investors, and the *Times* with the agreement to buy six bottlers nationwide, important to readers of the national edition.

On one business news story that day both newspapers agreed: Both played on page A-1 a story from Washington that the Environmental Protection Agency would fine manufacturers of heavy-duty diesel truck engines for violating clean air standards. For both papers, that story was "local" because even though it originated in Washington, it affected every village and city in their circulation territories—and, indeed, all of us who breathe![5]

Obviously, such shrewd, discerning news evaluation affects everyone in the news production process—assignment editors, reporters, copy editors, layout editors.

To succeed in business news, you'll need to develop such evaluation skills. Let's walk through a process you can use.

Know Your Market's Geography

Editors of all media define their ***coverage-area's geography*** and evaluate news on its importance to people in that area.

Simply put, the closer to home news breaks, the more intently you must examine its newsworthiness.

However, this "hometown test" is only one standard for judging news. You must examine all news, from home or afar, for whether it's valuable to your hometown readers.

The *Journal-Constitution,* to cite one example, define their principal market ("newspaper designated market") as two counties, Fulton and Dekalb, essentially the city of Atlanta.

The papers also seek readers and advertisers in a much wider area stretching miles from downtown Atlanta. But the papers' basic business mission is to gather readers attractive to advertisers in the city and its affluent suburbs.

If you were writing for the *Journal-Constitution* that geography would guide your news judgment and how you write business, economic and financial news.

Note: On a Saturday, AirTran Airlines, with headquarters in Atlanta, and one of its unions reach an agreement averting a strike. That story is splashed across the top of A-1, the front page of the first section of the Sunday *Journal-Constitution*, under a four-column headline. The lead shows why:

> AirTran Airlines and its flight attendants reached a tentative agreement Saturday, ending a threat of walkouts that could have canceled flights at Atlanta's second-busiest carrier during the robust Labor Day weekend.
>
> —Sophia Lezin, *Journal-Constitution*[6]

Meanwhile, a worrisome story is brewing from afar—on Wall Street. This also makes that same front page:

> Investors will find little to feel festive about this Labor Day, the last holiday of a dismal summer in the stock market.
>
> As they prepared for the weekend, many knew they were suddenly less wealthy by . . . 5 percent? 10 percent? More?
>
> —Tom Walker, *Journal-Constitution*[7]

Why did that story from afar merit front-page display? Because the stock market was headed down, and that certainly had "local" interest to thousands of investors among *Journal-Constitution* readers.

Note, incidentally, that writers of both *Journal-Constitution* stories were Atlanta-based staff writers. Coveted ***front-page*** bylines are yours if you can report stories like those, find the local angle and structure your writing to translate complicated issues into understandable language.

A couple months later, AirTran is back in the news—but way back in the paper, on page B-1. Here are the first two grafs:

> AirTran plans to furlough workers in Atlanta and other cities as it reduces its fleet by two aircraft.
>
> The company, which last week reported a $10.9 million third-quarter loss, said the cutback also reflects less optimism in its ability to further expand service this year. It did not say how much it had hoped to expand its schedule.
>
> —Christopher Seward, *Journal-Constitution*[8]

Now, why is this story on page B-1, not out front on A-1, like the strike story? Because this time editors deem the news of interest principally to those relatively few Atlantans who ***invest*** in the airline, not the many thousands who ***ride*** it.

On this later date, incidentally, the Wall Street story is way back in the paper, too, on B-8, not A-1, as in the first example. Why? Because the market had recovered somewhat from its shaky summer, and *Journal-Constitution* editors thus accorded it lower news priority.

Shuffling news priorities in just that manner, business journalists at newspapers of all sizes tune content to geographic markets.

If you're reporting for a small daily or weekly, your geographic market may be Main Street—and not much beyond. Many small papers use only The Associated Press wire copy for distant stories or concede the rest of the world to regional dailies, such as the *Journal-Constitution,* or national papers, *The New York Times, The Wall Street Journal, USA Today.*

Some magazines have tightly drawn geographic markets: city magazines *(New York),* for example, or state magazines (*Texas*) or regional publications *(Southern Living).* Most magazines, however, search anywhere for reader audiences defined by (1) common news interests a magazine can serve and (2) attractiveness to advertisers.

Broadcast offers you mixed opportunities. For aspiring business journalists, radio is principally a local medium and carries very little original news coverage and even less business news. Television, both local and national, frequently accords only superficial treatment to all but the most important economic news.

Cable television, however, offers growing career options. Channels devoted primarily or, increasingly, exclusively to business news are expanding as advertisers use that niche medium to reach affluent audiences drawn to such specialized coverage.

Private subscriber services delivered electronically offer splendid careers for business journalists who, with authority and accuracy, can cover specialized news for expert readers—bankers, brokers, business executives. Dow Jones, Bloomberg, Reuters, The Associated Press all deliver business news to computer screens and news tickers throughout the world.[9]

Know Your Demographic Market

Business journalists write, broadly, for two types of ***audience markets:***

Non-Expert Readers, Viewers and Listeners

Although their lives are affected every day by business, economic and financial news, these audiences may be unsophisticated in its complexities. For these audiences, you must serve principally as a ***translator,*** sorting through business and financial esoterica, then analyzing and interpreting meaningful developments in terms non-experts understand.

Newspaper reporters, for example, write "newspage" stories for page A-1, explaining in basic language for general-interest readers what's happening on Wall Street or in high finance. For these readers, you must explain "prime rate" as in other types of reporting you would explain neighborhood zoning regulations or a linebacker blitz.[10]

Here, for example, are the first two grafs of a *newspage* story written for *non-experts* about a highly complicated business development:

> The Microsoft court battle that begins Monday pits the world's most influential software company against federal antitrust regulators in a struggle to affect the course of the computer age.
> One of the most important business trials of the century, the outcome of the case could dramatically change how people buy and use software, including programs, called browsers, used to seek out information on the World Wide Web.
>
> —Ted Bridis, The Associated Press[11]

Note the story above, published on *front* pages across the country, contains background detail needed by non-expert readers but not required by computer experts, information service executives or lawyers.

Expert Audiences

These audiences don't need explanations quite so basic as you must write for casual front-page readers (although real pros among business writers assume all readers need a little translation now and then). For expert audiences, your reporting and writing must exude authority, precision, accuracy, meaningfulness. No business news writer ever can forget that a single news story can move millions of dollars!

| Box 1-1 | ## Now, That's Influence! |

A *Wall Street Journal* story on April 27 nearly caused a stock market panic by reporting the Federal Reserve was leaning toward an increase in interest rates. Wall Street pundits were certain the Fed had leaked the story to the newspaper.

Not so, *Journal* reporter David Wessel tells *Kiplinger's Personal Finance Magazine* (July). The story was based on public speeches and interviews with Fed officials.

Wessel said he was surprised by the story's impact. The Dow Jones industrial average fell 224 points before it rallied to close with a loss of 147 points.

The market was calmed the next day by *Washington Post* reporter John Berry, who reported that while the Fed was primed to raise rates, that didn't mean it would do so. . . .

—Tom Walker, *Atlanta Constitution*,
"Business Press," June 11, 1998, p. C-8

☞

Dow Jones & Co. shares jumped as much as 11.9 percent Monday in an apparent reaction to a magazine article reporting that the company's controlling shareholders may be agitating to boost its stock price.

Fortune magazine, in an issue available Monday, reports that some members of the family that controls Dow Jones are pushing management to focus more closely on the stock price, which has underperformed the broad market and its peer group in recent years. . . .

Dow Jones News Service,
dispatch for morning papers, Jan. 14, 1997

❧

Washington—While calling the economy's current performance "outstanding," Federal Reserve Chairman Alan Greenspan expressed worries today that the high-flying stock market could be headed for a tumble that could spell serious trouble down the road. . . .

The Dow Jones average fell 55 points as he read his statement. . . .

The Associated Press (which, with other news services,
covered Greenspan's speech minute by minute),
dispatch for morning papers, Jan. 21, 1999

Billions (not millions!) of dollars were at stake in the Microsoft antitrust suit, so coverage for ***expert*** readers quickly turned to highly technical detail essential to stakeholders—investors, lawyers, Microsoft competitors and Microsoft itself. For example, *The New York Times* published this detail in its ***business*** pages (not on its ***front*** page):

> . . . The Government contends that Microsoft's Windows operating system and its Internet Explorer browser are in fact two products bundled together for the purpose of forcing customers who want its industry-standard operating system to also take its browser.
>
> Microsoft says the browser is a feature of Windows, and thus that browser and operating system are a single product.

The New York Times [12]

Whichever your audience or medium, if you're in business news you'll be writing for people with generally upscale demographics—high income and educational levels. That must guide your evaluation of what is news and what isn't, and how you report and write it.

Newspapers, for example, especially attract upscale readers that advertisers love.

The Newspaper Association of America reports 67 percent of college graduates read newspapers daily, 77 percent on Sundays. Of Americans with less than a high school education, 43 percent read daily, 47 percent on Sundays.

Among Americans with annual household incomes of $75,000 or more, readership soars—69 percent daily, 78 percent on Sundays. In households with incomes under $40,000, readership drops to 53 percent daily, 60 percent on Sundays. [13]

The *Journal-Constitution* boast research showing their readers include 71.8 percent of all adults in the Atlanta market with household incomes of $100,000 or more; on Sundays, it's a whopping 83.4 percent.

Similar upscale characteristics emerge from research into the occupations of readers: In the "professional/manager" category, 75.9 percent read the Sunday *Journal-Constitution*. For "technical/sales," it's 71.5 percent, "administrative/clerical," 69.7 percent. Among "blue-collar/service" workers the percentages drop to 40.8 percent daily, 55.2 percent on Sundays.[14]

Gender and race are lesser predictors of who your readers will be. Black, white or Hispanic, male or female, Americans read news—particularly business news—when their education and income increase ***and they become stakeholders in the economy.***

The Newspaper Association finds nationally that 59 percent of women and 58 percent of men read newspapers. Readership includes 60 percent of whites, 53 percent of blacks and 48 percent of Hispanics—percentages that generally reflect the levels of education and income of the three groups. [15]

For national newspapers, reader demographics are extremely high. *Wall Street Journal* readers are the business world's movers and shakers with average household incomes exceeding $193,000 annually. A sister publication, *Barron's,* claims "one in every two *Barron's* readers is a millionaire."[16]

High-profile readers are attracted by thousands of specialized or "niche" industry and trade magazines. If writing for them, remember that your readers are discerning experts who will know instantly if ***you*** don't know your subject thoroughly.

Many special-interest magazines attract readers without reference to geography: Top people in brewing everywhere read *Beverage Journal;* food industry giants coast to coast read *Food Product Design.*

Well-defined geographic markets characterize some specialty magazines: In Cleveland, local residents with money—and those who want it—read *Crain's Cleveland Business.* In Atlanta, they read *Atlanta Business Chronicle.*

General business magazines—*Fortune* and *Money,* as well as *Forbes* and others—boast millionaires for readers. [17]

In broadcast, audiences have different demographics—and, thus, different news needs—and that drives business news writers in different directions.

Watch broadcast television news closely, for example, and you'll see heavy emphasis on general consumerism or "pocketbook" news directed at wider, more general audiences. Television's huge audiences of heavy viewers generally are downscale, demographically, from print media readers. TV writers, therefore, jump on consumer news—the cost of gasoline, food, housing—and write in terms easily digested by non-expert viewers.

You can draw guidance on what is news for magazine readers—and what ***isn't*** news for TV viewers—by studying a financial profile of heavy readers versus heavy TV viewers. This is from Magazine Publishers of America[18] research:

Table 1.1. Financial profiles of magazine readers and TV viewers

	MAGAZINE READERS	TV VIEWERS
	(U.S. AVERAGE = 100)	
Own $50,000+ life insurance	134	65
Own stocks	134	74
Own U.S. Savings Bonds	132	67
Have individual retirement account	121	76
Own $100,000+ homeowners insurance	126	73
Hold interest-bearing checking account	113	90

Know Your Audience's Psychographics

Your audience's psychographics—beliefs, interests, attitudes—must influence heavily your news values and judgments.

Think about it:

- A probing story on the financial structure of organized religion will have many readers among believers in the South's Bible Belt.
- The business of professional ice hockey will interest more people in New England and the Midwest than in New Mexico and Arizona.
- Union and labor news will be big news in Detroit, Flint, Cleveland, Buffalo, where many workers hold pro-union attitudes. In other cities, union news may be big news primarily when it affects the general public—as in Atlanta during a threatened airline strike.

Now, can we truly understand, from this complex mixture of geography, demography and psychographics, what readers, listeners and viewers want in their business, economic and financial news?

Yes. Read on.

So, What's News?

Americans demand many things from their media—news about Afghanistan and Washington, comics and crossword puzzles. But in business news we can isolate two themes central to what they want and need:

1. Readers tell us very clearly through our research that they ***want*** highly personalized information on how to improve their own economic well-being. Call it "road map" information on getting ahead in careers and business or "how-to" guidance on saving and spending more wisely, investing, financing a better home, buying a new car—simply, how to live better.
2. Readers ***need*** your early warnings on events they often don't even know about. These may be distant and complex events that sooner or later will

come home with impact on your readers' first interest, their own economic well-being. Regard yourself as a sort of distant early warning radar system, detecting incoming economic missile strikes—a bank failure in Japan, a move in Washington by the Federal Reserve Board—that will land on and affect, negatively or positively, your readers' everyday lives.

We can define all that broadly (and this book does so) in three news categories: economics, business, and finance.

Economics

This covers systems of production, distribution and consumption of wealth. For economists, economics is a science; for journalists it carries less perfection and predictability than we and our readers would like. Nevertheless, there is fertile journalistic ground in this wide-ranging subject and its attendant news areas such as labor relations, taxation, transportation.

Business

Interpret this essentially as the manufacturing, buying and selling of commodities and services. Initially, you'll probably concentrate on Main Street business activity with two approaches: writing (a) about business for ***business executives*** among your readers ("company news"), and (b) about business for a wider, more general audience of ***readers served by business*** ("consumer news").

Finance

This sector covers the supply, regulation and management of money, credit and capital. Again, you'll have, broadly, two audiences—those engaged in finance and those whose personal lives are affected by it.

Within those three categories, of course, you'll range widely (as will this book). Flip through *The Wall Street Journal,* the business section of *The New York Times* or your hometown paper to see just how widely business journalists range each day.

Covering economics includes writing for page one, for example, a story out of Detroit on U.S. vehicle sales, and what that means about consumer confidence and the vigor of the nation's economy. Or, it can be a Washington report, written for inside pages, on new factory orders for durable goods (electronic equipment, household appliances, industrial machinery) and what ***that*** means about the overall economy. In community journalism, your job is to relate those distant events to your local economy. How are ***local*** sales of cars, water heaters and appliances holding up? Is the ***local***

economy doing better than the national economy? Worse? The same? ***Whichever, you have a fine local story*** meaningful to local business executives and general readers alike.

Business coverage takes you into such stories as the resignation of the chairman of CBS, of compelling interest to investors in and advertisers on one of the country's biggest broadcast networks. Or, it can take you to plans for a new shopping center on the outskirts of your town or, even more narrowly, to plans for a new "lead" store (meaning, the principal or dominant store) in that shopping center. Big News, indeed, in small-town America!

Financial coverage involves stories as diverse as personnel shifts at the top in BankAmerica, the nation's second-largest bank, and mortgage interest levels offered by your Main Street banks.

Your Goals

Whether writing about economics, business or finance, you should strive toward four principal goals:

1. Localize Distant Events

Global markets are in upheaval, economists say.

"So what?" your readers say.

Your job is to ***answer the "so what?" factor*** and bring home to your readers the impact that distant event has on their lives.

Here's how Peter Behr did that on the front page of *The Washington Post*'s business section:

> The upheaval in global markets is starting to erode consumer confidence in the Washington area, though the region's economic performance has not been noticeably hurt, analysts said yesterday.
>
> A more cautious consumer outlook showed up in a survey of 1,000 area residents conducted for *The Washington Post* by the Grier Partnership and released this week, in which 46 percent of those surveyed in September said they expect to be better off economically a year from now. In March that figure exceeded 55 percent.

Post writer Behr now turns to the local meaning of all that, and he does it through comment from local analysts:

> "Now, there's an increased caution, not necessarily gloom and doom," said Sheryl Grier, vice president of the Bethesda survey firm.
>
> Ann Battle, regional economist for Crestar Bank, added, "I think people are getting nervous, but the current situation is still good."
>
> —Peter Behr, *The Washington Post* [19]

It's especially in localizing distant events that you must go beyond what readers know they **want** and tell them what they **need** to know.

Learning what they want is simple: Even small papers often do painstaking (and costly) research into reader wants. And, good reporters always move among their readers, seeking hints on what they want.

But determining what readers need, even if they don't know it—Ah! That's more difficult! We'll discuss this later in the book, but essentially you must look for those distant events that eventually will have local impact.

Does a new policy quietly announced by the Agriculture Department in Washington mean local dairy farmers will face a milk price crisis a year hence? Does collapse of the Indonesian economy signal tough times for a local company that exports to that country? Your job is to find out—and be first to tell your readers.

2. Report With Precision

You often encounter this in other journalism: A TV sportscaster reports a running back gained "about" three yards. A newspaper reports "an estimated" 200 persons demonstrated.

Such imprecision may be acceptable, even called for in some journalism (do we **really** need to know if precisely 200 or 210 demonstrated?). But such imprecision is **un**acceptable in the journalism we're studying.

Markets, money and, therefore, lives are moved by the news we report, and painstaking precision is required.

Thus, a financial news service doesn't report that Mobil Corporation's earnings fell "about half" or that profits were off "an estimated" $500 million. Rather, the precise picture is reported:

> The Mobil Corporation said today that its third-quarter earnings fell 45 percent because of low crude-oil prices, decreased production and less profit from making and selling fuel, especially in Asia.
>
> Profit before gains and charges fell to $497 million, or 61 cents a diluted share, from $907 million, or $1.11 a share in the quarter a year earlier. Mobil, second only to the Exxon Corporation as the largest United States oil company, was expected to earn 60 cents a share, the average estimate of analysts polled by the First Call Corporation. Revenue fell 17 percent, to $13.6 billion from $16.4 billion. . . .

> Bloomberg News[20]

3. Write to Translate

Experts in business—your sources—speak their own language, as do chemists, football coaches, nuclear scientists. And though other insiders understand, your readers often don't.

Your job is to translate for your readers the insider language of business, economics and finance, just as you would break down the insider lingo spoken by scientists, coaches or other expert sources.

Sometimes, your translator duties include providing basic definitions of what a story is all about. Note how a Dow Jones Newswire writer does that in his second graf (emphasis added):

> History may judge these recent months in the options market as the most difficult trading environment since the Chicago Board Exchange introduced exchange-traded options 25 years ago.
>
> ***Options give investors the right, but not the obligation to buy or sell stock at a specific price.*** But option prices are currently so volatile and stock prices so erratic that this generation of market makers and specialists is finding it difficult to hedge their risk after they sell defensive put options to scared investors trying to hedge their own stock portfolios.
>
> —Steven M. Sears, Senior Dow Jones Writer[21]

Often the more complex—or distant—a story, the more detailed your translation must be. For example, *The Dallas Morning News* knits together an elaborate story on devaluation of the Russian ruble and what that means ***in Moscow:***

> After spending billions of dollars during the last three months to prop up Russia's weak currency, the government gave up Monday and let the ruble's value drop by up to 34 percent.
>
> The move allows the ruble, previously at about 6.3 to the U.S. dollar, to drift to as high as 9.5 to the dollar and raised fears that soaring inflation and social instability could follow.
>
> Long-suffering Russians probably will be hit hard, as the price of imported items increases. Many of the goods on Russian store shelves, including groceries, clothing and household products, come from abroad.
>
> More pain also may be in store for Russia's 1,500 banks, which are overdependent on ruble assets. As many as half are expected to go belly-up in the next few weeks.

Deeper in the story the devaluation is translated into terms ***American*** readers need:

> Although instability in any world power is a concern, the effect of the devaluation on the United States economy will be negligible.
>
> The United States and Russia are not big trading partners. U.S. businesses don't buy a lot of goods from Russia and don't sell a lot to them, either.
>
> *Dallas Morning News*[22]

Quickly and smoothly, ***with minimum language or interruption of reading flow,*** two Associated Press writers insert translation (emphasis added):

The Senate overwhelmingly passed legislation Wednesday to overhaul bankruptcy laws **and make it harder for people to erase their debts.**

The Associated Press [23]

∽

A New Jersey phone company has agreed to pay $1 million to 20 states for phone "slamming"—**changing a customer's long-distance phone carrier without permission.**

The Associated Press [24]

4. Write to Engage Readers

It's true in all journalism: Write in lively, colorful, clear and engaging language or you won't get read.

And, if you're not read, your message and its important information won't be communicated. **Your readers (or nonreaders, rather) will be the losers.**

But, in any journalism—especially business news—you must not write so cleverly that you drive your story beyond its true importance. And that's easy to do.

Any experienced journalist knows how to "hypo" a story—inject it with false drama or exaggerated importance and thus make the story into something it really isn't.

It's a journalistic felony to do that with our specialty, news that moves markets, money and lives.

Now, having raised that warning, I urge you to develop a writing style that is open, truly engaging and inviting to readers who must be attracted to reading and comprehending your message. Note how these writing pros do that:

A *San Francisco Chronicle* writer is assigned a story on perks given executives when one company takes over another. Dullsville, right? Wrong.

> When ships sink, sea captains are the last to bail out. But when companies submerge following a takeover, captains of industry are often the first overboard.
>
> Their lifeboats are the equivalent of corporate yachts, equipped with a growing array of payments and perks.
>
> When one company takes over another, the top five executives of both firms generally get employment contracts that guarantee certain benefits whether they stay aboard or jump ship.
>
> —Peter Sinton, *San Francisco Chronicle* [25]

And note these gems:

> Chewing gum can actually make you smarter?
>
> So contends a company called GumTech International, which is marketing something called Brain Gum. As you chew, the gum releases the nutri-

ent phosphatidylserine, or PS, which is believed to improve intercellular activity in the brain, thereby making you more mentally alert.

—Ben Pappas, *Forbes*[26]

☞

The casualties are mounting in Battle Creek.

Kellogg Co., its growth and stock price as stale as a day-old bowl of cereal, said Monday that the president of its flagship North America division, Thomas Knowlton, resigned effective immediately—its second top executive to leave in the last week.

The shake-up at Battle Creek, Mich.-based Kellogg—the head of its European operations quit Sept 15—is the latest fallout from the company's struggle to reignite its sales and earnings and to halt a decade-old slide in its share of the U.S. cereal market.

—James F. Peltz, *Los Angeles Times*[27]

Bottom line of Chapter 1: Know your market, know your audience—***write to pull it in.*** More—much more—in chapters ahead.

Summary

- Writers must understand that the ***business goal*** of newspapers, magazines, radio and broadcast television is gaining audiences who can be "sold" to advertisers.
- Advertisers, who pay most of the media's bills, seek readers, viewers and listeners who are upscale, affluent spenders.
- All media base news judgments on the different markets they serve and the differing characteristics and needs of their audiences.
- How you define news and how you write it must be based in part on how your editors delineate their coverage area's ***geography.***
- News that breaks in your coverage area—be that a couple counties, a state, the entire nation—must be examined carefully for its value to readers, but news from afar is important, too, if it affects your local readers.
- Audiences also are defined by their ***demographics*** (incomes, education, occupations), and business news writers must learn to report for non-experts in those audiences and, as well, for experts, such as investors and business executives.
- Readers become interested in business news when they become ***stakeholders*** in the economy, and gender and race are lesser predictors of who your readers will be.
- Newspaper and magazine readers generally are upscale demographically and eager for news of investments, finance, corporate developments; heavy television viewers generally have lower incomes and education levels, so TV writers often emphasize everyday consumer news, such as cost of food or gasoline.

- Audience *psychographics*—beliefs, interests, attitudes—also must influence your news judgments; the business of professional ice hockey is bigger news to readers in Minnesota than in Arizona!
- "News," then, is highly personalized information that helps readers improve their economic well-being but also covers distant events that eventually will affect their everyday lives.
- Broadly, you'll hunt news in *economics,* which covers systems of production, distribution and consumption or wealth; in *business,* the manufacturing, buying and selling of commodities and services; and in *finance,* the supply, regulation and management of money, credit and capital.
- In covering those news sectors, you must *localize distant events,* then *report with precision, translate* the meaning of events and *write to engage readers*—to pull them into your story and help them comprehend its meaning.

Recommended Reading

The Wall Street Journal (http://wsj.com) will open for you a wonderful world of excellent news judgment, fine writing and expert editing. Read it for content, style and overall grasp of business, finance and economics. Also see the *Journal's* "Educational Edition," which is a "user's manual" on how to read and interpret the *Journal.*

Excellent business news sections are published by *The New York Times, Chicago Tribune, Atlanta Journal-Constitution, The Dallas Morning News, Los Angeles Times, The Washington Post* and other leading regional papers. Daily, disciplined reading of one or more of them is an education in itself.

Magazine's offering excellent overviews include *Forbes, Fortune,* and *Business Week.* Note *Forbes* particularly on how to report and write concise personality and corporate profiles with impact.

Two books will be helpful: Louis M. Kohlmeier Jr., Jon G. Udell and Laird B. Anderson, *Reporting on Business and the Economy* (Englewood Cliff, N.J.: Prentice-Hall, 1981), and Donald Kirsch, *Financial and Economic Journalism* (New York: New York University Press, 1978).

Notes

1. I discuss media business strategies in Conrad Fink, *Strategic Newspaper Management* (Neeham Heights, Mass.: Allyn and Bacon, 1996).
2. "CCE Tops Forecasts, Buys Bottler," Oct. 22, 1998, p. F-1.
3. Dispatch in "Company News," *The New York Times,* Oct. 22, 1998, p. C-4.
4. Front page of the "Business Day" section, *The New York Times,* Oct. 22, 1998.
5. This story was on the front pages of both papers on Oct. 22, 1998.
6. "AirTran Agreement Ends Threat of Walkout," Sept. 6, 1998, p. A-1.
7. "Signposts Hint at Direction of Stock Market," Sept. 6, 1998, p. A-1.
8. "AirTran Cutbacks Hitting Atlanta," Oct. 23, 1998, p. B-1.
9. I discuss media careers in Conrad Fink, *Inside the Media* (White Plains, N.Y.: Longman, 1990).

10. The "prime rate" is the interest rate commercial banks charge borrowers with the best credit ratings. It tends to set other interest rates and thus control flow of credit. Zoning regulates types of construction—homes or commercial, for example—permitted in neighborhoods. In a linebacker blitz, defensive players try to rush an opposing quarterback and strip him of his ball and senses.

11. Dispatch for Sunday papers, Oct. 19, 1998.

12. "Microsoft Describes Practices as Common," National Edition, Oct. 21, 1998, p. C-10.

13. Newspaper Association of America, "Facts About Newspapers 1998," quoting Simmons Market Research Bureau, p. 7-9.

14. "How Do AJC Readers Compare With the Atlanta Market?," marketing research quoting Atlanta Consumer Market Study, 1992, and issued by *The Atlanta Journal-Constitution.*

15. Newspaper Association of America, op cit, p. 7.

16. Author's telephone interview on Oct. 27, 1998, with Ms. Jeanie Cable, marketing research, *The Wall Street Journal; Barron's* claim is made in its advertisement, "Now With Every Aspiring Millionaire You Buy, You Get an Actual One Thrown in Free," published in *Advertising Age,* Oct. 21, 1998, p. 11.

17. Magazine writing and the impact on it of market characteristics are discussed in Conrad Fink and Donald E. Fink, *Introduction to Magazine Writing* (New York: Macmillan, 1994).

18. *The Magazine HandBook, 1992–1993,* issued by Magazine Publishers of America, quoting 1992 Spring MRI, p. 47.

19. "Consumer Confidence Begins to Fall in Area," Oct. 3, 1998, p. E-1.

20. Dispatch for morning papers, Oct. 29. Incidentally, we'll discuss this in detail later in the book, but "earnings" in this example is synonymous with "profit." "Diluted shares" is a total of all common stock owned by individuals and institutional investors *plus* the number of shares that would result if the company's convertible bonds and other instruments were converted to common stock.

21. "Risk and Uncertainty Wreak Havoc on Stocks," Oct. 14, 1998, p. C-1.

22. "Russia Gives Up Currency Fight, Devalues Ruble," *Dallas Morning News,* Aug. 18, 1998, p. A-1.

23. Dispatch for morning papers, Sept. 24, 1998.

24. Dispatch for morning papers, Oct. 24, 1998.

25. "Lifeboats Lined With Gold," Sept. 8, 1998, p. B-1.

26. "Transparent Eyeball," Oct. 5, 1998, p. 45.

27. "Kellogg Battling to Regain Its Place at the Breakfast Table," Sept. 22, 1998, p. D-1.

Exercises

1. Interview your local newspaper's business editor (perhaps your instructor will invite the editor to your class) and describe, in 300–350 words, how that editor defines the newspaper's geographic, demographic and psychographic markets. What news values and judgments does the editor apply to the newspaper's coverage area? ***Do you agree with them?***

2. Study front pages of today's business news sections in your local newspaper and *The New York Times* national edition (or another paper your instructor designates). In about 400 words, describe how each handled the day's news. Were some stories handled the same way? Some differently? Why do you think the newspapers' editors handled the news as they did?

3. Study the front page of today's business news section of *The New York Times* and, in about 300 words, describe the readers at whom you think the page was aimed. What occupations and levels of affluence and education were *Times* editors courting? Complete this analysis for each story on the page.

4. Study each story on A-1 of today's *The New York Times* national edition that has a business, economic or financial angle and each story on the front page of the *Times'* business section. In about 300 words, describe **local** news stories you could develop from ideas you encountered in the *Times'* stories.

5. Study today's *The Wall Street Journal* and, in about 350–400 words, describe how it translates technical economic and financial terms for readers. Cite examples of good and bad translation. Is the *Journal* written at a level most newspaper readers would understand? Or, is it written only for business executives and other experts?

PART TWO

Reporting and Numbers

Keys to Success

HERE'S AN INSIDER tip: You'll need a long time, ***perhaps years,*** to develop your own unique and highly creative writing style—and your editors will accept that.

However, from your first day on the job those same editors will demand top-flight ***reporting skills.*** That's because the first mission of all editors is protecting their business sections' credibility and authoritative tone, which flow ***only*** from strong, accurate reporting.

Proof is in the business news pages of leading newspapers and magazines. In them is wonderful writing—some truly ***great.*** But overall emphasis clearly is on accurate reporting and precise, fair presentation of information that moves markets, money and lives. "Color" writing, so important in other journalism sectors, is secondary to accuracy in business news.

Don't misunderstand: A great writing style will take you far. And even in the beginning you'll need, at minimum, a writing style that's open, readable, engaging.

But you first must turn, as a student and professional, to developing your reporting strengths. We take a step toward that in Chapter 2, Reporting: Sources Are Your Gold. Finding authoritative sources, human and electronic, is crucial.

Then, of course, comes your challenge of collating, evaluating and plugging into your stories the massive amounts of information developed in your reporting. Numbers, dollars and cents, percentages, facts of all kinds and shapes—all will build muscle on your business news writing.

And building such muscular factual strength in smooth, readable form is the writer's challenge we discuss in Chapter 3, Making Facts and Numbers Sing.

2

Reporting:
Sources Are Your Gold

You're a reporter in *The Miami Herald* newsroom, where fax machines receive up to *7,000 pages daily* from outside news sources. News services, syndicates and the U.S. Postal Service dump *millions* more of words atop all that.[1]

Or, you're an Associated Press reporter covering a big tobacco lawsuit, and one (just *one*) of the cigarette companies publishes *seven million* documents on the case.[2]

Help! What now?

Well, being a product of the electronic era, you may seek help on the Internet. But there you'll face a bewildering array of sources—by one estimate, *8,000 web sites* for stock market investors alone![3]

So, let's get to the point in our discussion of reporting economic, business and financial news:

FIRST, you'll receive such huge quantities of facts, figures, information of all kind, delivered electronically and on paper, that you'll be overwhelmed *unless . . .*

SECOND, you develop *human* sources who will point you in the right direction, lead you through the information maze and along the paper (and electronic) trail until you find, amid all the debris, noise, irrelevancies and clutter, *the news.*

You'll Begin With Disadvantages

You'll likely start in business news reporting with disadvantages to overcome.

FIRST, business executives, government officials and other expert sources crucial to your success probably will deal cautiously with you—if at all.

Many will assume you don't know enough to be trusted to write about—and quote them on—the hugely complex and important matters they handle daily.

SECOND, they'll probably be partially correct—if you're like typical beginning reporters. Many **don't** know much about business, economics, finance.

The business world's suspicion of journalists is deep-seated, long-standing. Attitudinal research reveals many executives suspect we journalists don't have the expertise in business routinely required of reporters, in, say, Washington politics or sports. And, even worse, many executives suspect we're anti-business, disdainful of people in the commercial marketplace.

Indeed, one researcher found business executives and journalists regard each other like "two scorpions in a bottle" or "lions and Christians." One business news journalist said that after she became vice president of Greyhound Corp., she learned business executives approach interviews with reporters "with all the enthusiasm of a missionary asked to dine with cannibals."[4]

How can you overcome such business world thinking?

Slowly, says Mickey H. Gramig, *The Atlanta Journal-Constitution* reporter whose Coca-Cola coverage we discussed in Chapter 1.

In reporting business news, Gramig says, you must understand it will take "much more time" to develop sources than in general assignment ("GA") reporting. In GA, you're developing sources among public officials, police officers and others who not only are familiar with reporters but who may be obligated to talk with them.

Many executives rise in major corporations without ever meeting reporters and, in fact, being shielded from them by over-eager public relations departments. And, business executives have no obligation to grant interviews. Many see only threat and no reward in meeting the press.

Winning the confidence of such executives is a long-haul process, Gramig says, accomplished by "really reading up"—doing a reporter's homework by studying the executive's industry, the company, the executive's own background **before** even requesting an interview. [5] (*See* Box 2-1 for more guidance from Gramig.)

| Box 2-1 | A Professional's Viewpoint |

Mickey H. Gramig switched from general assignment reporting and now covers major business stories for *The Atlanta Journal-Constitution,* papers with well over one million readers. Gramig presents below a "Care and Feeding Guide" for developing sources in business news.

By Mickey H. Gramig

Trust is key in developing and maintaining sources, particularly when it comes to high-level corporate types such as company presidents, chief executives or chief financial officers.

Think about it: Why should these folks squeeze you into their jam-packed schedules for one-on-one interviews, when they can have their press handlers issue carefully crafted comments that address the news-making events? Why risk losing control of conditions to answer your questions, much less grant extended interviews where whatever they say could be misunderstood or taken out of context?

Sources may have been burned in the past by careless or unethical reporters, or they know colleagues who were. Even if you're the most honest, careful, award-winning reporter around, they may be leery of the media or your publication in particular.

So you have to earn their trust—and respect. It all boils down to knowing your stuff, which you can do by:

Studying. Read everything you can get your hands on about the source, the company, the industry. Scour the annual report, quarterly earnings statement, analyst reports and company histories. Don't forget articles by your predecessors—and your competitors. Check the web. Research as if your job depended on it. It does.

Networking. Behind the scenes players can be invaluable. Take the company's PR folks to lunch. Pick the brains of analysts who follow the company or industry. Do the same with "industry experts," consultants and journalists in the trade press, who know the inside-baseball type of things that can broaden your knowledge. Go to trade shows, where you'll learn more than you could possibly imagine.

Planning. Walk in prepared when you get the big interview—or even the little interview. Find out how much time you'll be allotted, and think through what you want to learn. Be armed with questions that zero-in on the issue. Write out the questions, even practice them aloud if that helps. Keep tabs on the time, so no one gets off on a tangent that eats up the clock.

Sources can tell when journalists have done their homework, and this helps build the trust and respect that's so vital in developing good relationships. The rest—being fair and accurate, and simple things like showing up on time and being polite and professional—also plays a role.

One last thing. Trust and respect can't be earned overnight, but they can be lost that quickly. Remember that.

Interpret "reading up" very broadly. It means starting now, in college, preparing perhaps to follow Gramig one day in covering multibillion dollar Coca-Cola

Co. Or covering the broader story of global economics, the intricacies of Wall Street high finance—or the business beat on your local Main Street.

Journalism courses plus a minor in business, topped by **hands-on experience** at your college newspaper, would be an excellent start. Of course, throughout your career you must maintain disciplined reading in newspapers, magazines and books on your speciality.

Let's walk through an on-the-job reporting experience.

First Comes the Story Idea

Ah, yes, The Idea!

Much news "breaks" spontaneously and is recognized immediately as news when it does.

For example: A company announcement clearly is important news in California and deserves front-page display (which it gets) in *The Los Angeles Times* business section:

> In another example of a U.S. brokerage firm taking advantage of Asia's economic crisis, a subsidiary of San Francisco–based investment bank Hambrecht & Quist said Friday that it will acquire a controlling stake in one of South Korea's largest brokerages.
>
> —Debora Vrana, *The Los Angeles Times*[6]

Cable News Network's financial channel, CNNfn, transmits urgently via the Internet news that's recognized throughout business journalism as an obvious bell-ringer:

> The Federal Reserve Thursday said it cut two key interest rates by one-quarter of a percentage point each, citing growing caution among lending institutions and unsettled financial markets.
>
> The highly unusual move shocked investors and sent U.S. stock and bond markets soaring in late-day trading.
>
> CNNfn[7]

You'll handle much such **breaking news.** However, editors pride themselves in offering readers an extra dimension—call it **added value** or **enterprise** reporting—far beyond simply reacting to spontaneous news breaks.

And, that's where The Idea comes in.

Learn to survey your immediate news beat and **distant news horizons beyond** and suggest to your editor The Idea for an enterprise story. Newsrooms are crowded with reporters asking, "What do you want me to do now?" Harried editors **love** self-starters who arrive each morning with The Idea. For example, you might suggest:

"I note a San Francisco investment bank is acquiring a South Korean brokerage. How about me doing a survey of such international connections being established by local companies?"

Or:

"The Federal Reserve just cut interest rates. Why not let me do a big Sunday piece on the impact on local banks, and home mortgage interest rates?"

A smart business editor, relieved to have at least one reporter who can come up with The Idea, might reply with something like this:

"Bingo! Two great suggestions. Those interest rate cuts by the Fed are *timely.* They're likely to affect big business immediately throughout our market and Main Street shops, as well as most homeowners and consumers. Get on that story right away. But put aside that survey of international connections. You can get to that anytime over the next few weeks."

Now what do you do?

Reporting on the Business Beat

Remember Mickey Gramig: Read up!

The Wall Street Journal will be all over that interest rate story, as will *The New York Times, USA Today* and metropolitan papers.

The Associated Press, Reuters, Bloomberg and Dow Jones news services will report it quickly and fully.

All will provide initial explanations of what took place and its likely meaning—***which you need to head your local reporting in the right general direction.***

Even in its swift first report, CNNfn provided valuable definitions of the two rates cut: the discount rate ("which is charged on emergency loans to commercial banks") and the federal funds rate ("an overnight bank lending rate that is a benchmark for other short-term interest rates").

Computer-assisted reporting—using Internet resources and web sites— is invaluable at this stage of your reporting process. But two warnings:

- The Internet carries accurate, factual and useful information but also lies, intentional distortions and inaccurate data that can lead you astray. Beware! Always check out the source of Internet information ***and the motives behind its release***—just as you would check the credentials or authoritativeness of any source you encounter in any form of journalism.
- Remember those 8,000 web sites mentioned earlier? So much information is on the Internet that you could spend days, even weeks sifting through it for that Sunday piece on interest rates (and it's Thursday already)!

So, forget that vision sketched by some Internet enthusiasts, that a reporter need only sit at a computer and sift piles of data. You need human sources to point you in the right direction.

By the way, before charging out of the newsroom saunter over to a couple of old-timers. Every newsroom has them—veteran reporters who know most of the important news sources in town and who have seen interest rates come and go. Don't be afraid to ask *their* guidance.

| Box 2-2 | Tips From Three Pros |

On interviewing business executives:

. . . Most business people never have received a call from a reporter and have no conception of our deadlines, our demands or our way of thinking. Don't expect them to throw out quotes or information the way a politician or police chief does. They don't have to talk to us. And if they're approached for the first time by an ill-prepared reporter or editor, don't expect much of a response.

—Joseph Lewandowski, *Fort Collins (Colo.)*
Coloradoan quoted in *Gannetter,* March/April 1991, p. 3

On avoiding manipulation by sources:

. . . Part of what financial journalists owe readers is an effort to make sure that the sources they use are speaking the truth and to be concerned about the possibility of being used. That means not printing every rumor that comes along and it means trying to make clear the interests of those sources that are used, whether quoted by name or anonymously.
—Floyd Norris, "Media," *The New York Times,* national edition,
Jan. 8, 1996, p. C-9

On "translating" business esoterica for reader understanding:

Economics stories can be made readable and informative without sugar-coating or writing down to readers. The key is to look for the story behind the numbers. Make it real.

—Mark Rohner, Gannett News Services, quoted in *Gannetter,*
March/April 1991, p. 7

Sources: The Human Kind

Sources are to reporters what footballs are to quarterbacks, bats to baseball players: You can't play in the Big Leagues (Little Leagues, even) without them. That's why great reporters spend much time locating, developing, stroking, interviewing and, yes, I'll say it—*exploiting*—sources.

Great reporters attend more meetings, conferences and seminars than is healthy; great reporters never see hands they don't want to shake, never pass a chance to chat with people—average Joes and Janes in the supermarket as well as titans of industry and finance.

Great reporters read, clip stories and stow away the names, corporate affiliations, telephone numbers and business specialties of potential sources.

Thus, when The Idea arrives, great reporters can turn quickly to their personal source books—be they computerized files or tattered notebooks—and extract names of sources who can be hunted down to turn The Idea into important front-page copy.

C'mon! Let's go source hunting!

The Approach

Just getting through a source's front door to establish initial contact often is your biggest challenge in business news.

A few hints:

- Remember, many business world sources think talking to you promises only danger and no reward. You must determine how the **source** can benefit from an interview, personally or corporately, and stress that self-interest in your interview request.
- It's the reputation of your newspaper or magazine—and its readers—that are most important in wooing potential sources for interviews. People don't reach the top in American corporations without understanding the power of the press. But your **personal** integrity and professionalism are crucial. Start now, **today,** building your byline as the symbol of accurate, fair, balanced reporting. **Byline integrity is key to your success.** Let nothing—and no one—impugn it.
- **Always** apply directly to the source for an interview. Public relations practitioners (secretaries, too) can help you; they also can spin you away from the Great One, sometimes, they think, legitimately ("He's too busy.") but also out of naked self-interest—to maintain personal control of the process, a pure power grab, or perhaps to strengthen the PR department's role as sole source of information and thus ensure departmental (and personal) importance in corporate affairs.

Let's say you're doing that Sunday piece on interest rates for *The Atlanta Journal-Constitution.* Your story angle is the impact on home mortgage interest rates, of compelling importance to many (most?) of the one million or so readers of the Sunday paper. [8]

You want to interview the chairman of Atlanta's biggest mortgage bank, which is difficult to arrange—except that your newspaper's prestige and those one million or so potential readers give you, my friend, **real clout.** Learn to use your clout—wisely, judiciously but never maliciously. It's part of what great reporters do.

Still, you've got to reach and convince the Great One that an interview will be **mutually** rewarding.

You can't reasonably expect to walk into a huge bank without notice and be ushered into the inner chamber. Big Business doesn't operate that way.

Telephone, and the Great One's secretary will add your "call back" message to, what, 30, 40 or more already pending? Mail your request, and it will be delivered after your deadline.

Should you call the PR department? Do so and you've forfeited direct access, **and** the PR department may not have enough corporate influence to get you in. (**Never** invite PR spin artists into your reporting process unless it's absolutely necessary; but **always** be courteous and professional with them because you'll need their help before your story is finished.)

How about . . . yes! **Fax** a request. A faxed letter carries an aura of immediacy and importance, certainly more than do those pink "call back" telephone messages. A fax is more likely to get past the secretary (and the PR department) and directly to the Great One.

- *Play your clout.* Use your newspaper's letterhead stationery. Carefully craft your message, something like this:

  Dear Mr. _____:

  Noting the Fed's rate cuts earlier today, the *Journal-Constitution* will publish on Sunday an in-depth look at the impact on Atlanta banks and, particularly, home owners and prospective home owners.

  Since your bank is the city's largest mortgage lender and you personally are a respected leader in the mortgage lending, I would like to interview you as soon as possible. I could be at your office on short notice, day or night.

  I am seeking the views of leading bankers on how the Fed's move will affect our one million readers in Atlanta and the Southeast. Will your bank change its rates? Do you foresee an impact on your bank's lending? Will you be more competitive in making funds available for home mortgages?

  Of course, our chat would range more widely, particularly into areas you deem important to our reader-homeowners.

  I am an experienced reporter on the *Journal-Constitution* business desk, and I guarantee you careful, professional handling of your views. Because my deadline is near, I would appreciate a response by telephone or fax to these numbers: _____.

  Sincerely,

Now, let's look back through that faxed message for language and ideas you can use in approaching business executives for an interview:

FIRST GRAF: You're a professional, witness your use of slang shorthand ("Fed") that bankers use. You're alert, having noted the rate cuts and quickly seen their importance. "In-depth look" signals you're doing a major, reflective and important piece, not a quick hit-or-miss spot news story. You briefly but precisely state what your (powerful) newspaper is doing, which includes looking at the impact on banks (including, obviously, the Great One's).

SECOND GRAF: This may seem blatant flattery but the Great One likely will see it as fact: The bank and Great One are big players in town so, obviously, their corporate and personal views are important. What you want—an interview—is stated explicitly. A request for "information" might be forwarded to the PR department for answer. And, this graf makes clear that you will fit your working day (or night) around the Great One's schedule.

THIRD GRAF: *Other* bankers' views are being sought and, of course, the Great One will want to be represented in your story. Banking, after all, *is* a competitive business. How do mortgage banks make money? By borrowing money at low interest rates and lending it out at higher rates—and look, Great One, at the many potential borrowers who must be among our million readers! Note the outright reference to competition: "Will you be more competitive . . . ?"

FOURTH GRAF: You don't promise to limit the interview to questions listed in the third graf. And, importantly, the Great One can take the interview into areas advantageous to *the bank.* You're very clear: This interview isn't *threatening;* you're proposing to *chat,* just like two friends.

FIFTH GRAF: You're experienced, and on the *business desk;* you're not a cops reporter or sports writer unexpectedly assigned, without training in finance, to a banking story. Note the pledge of "careful, professional handling of your views." Titans of industry and banking fear they'll be misquoted or misunderstood, and that they and their corporations will suffer.

SIXTH GRAF: You need a quick response, not because you're impatient or don't recognize that the Great One has a busy schedule. Rather, you are under *deadline pressure.*

In sum, on a sports story, you can yell, "Hey, Coach! Got a minute?" On a cops story, a quick call to the desk sergeant can yield what you need. But to a business executive you might be a lion coming after a Christian, a scorpion about to leave the bottle. Careful, methodical planning is needed to get interviews in the world of business, finance and industry.

And when you get one, what then?

The Interview

Here's a recipe for *disaster* in your interview: Walk into that banker's office and open by asking, "Like, what is the discount rate, anyway?"

It's true: Success in interviewing is determined largely by your preparation—your "reading up"—even before you walk into that office.

Great reporters head into interviews with strategies carefully plotted. They would arrive at your banker's office with strong background on interest rates, the home mortgage business, the bank they're visiting, the executive they're interviewing.

With such preparation you'll be able to walk into that office in an aura of professionalism—and self-confidence. And that's crucial.

Men and women who rise in banking or any other industry are skilled at quickly assessing people they meet. They'll know immediately if you exude amateurism and lack of self-confidence. To them, you'll signal danger—and, remember, they *already* have doubts about you and the press in general.

But note this distinction: You can't project a know-it-all attitude, either. Even experienced reporters don't know it all, obviously, and you shouldn't be reluctant to admit you have much to learn. You must feel free to ask, "What does that mean?" or "Please explain what you just said."

That is, carefully plot the *tone* of your interview.

Try to sense quickly the interviewee's mood and time frame. If the Great One looks repeatedly at the wall clock, you must get directly to the point. If, however, the mood is relaxed (perhaps coffee is ordered in) you can ease into the interview, and that's best.

Whatever you do, don't walk in and whip out your notebook with a manner that says, in effect, this is a stickup: give me your facts.

Indeed, it's best to keep your reporter's notebook out of view until you can pull it out in a natural, nonthreatening way. One technique is to open with chatty informality until you hear a fact or figure, then pull out the notebook and say, "That's very interesting. Let me take a note so I quote you accurately."

That demonstrates you're a careful professional determined to ensure accuracy *and* this interview is on the record.

| Box 2-3 | The Anonymous Source |

Editors throughout journalism are campaigning against use of anonymous sources. Readers don't like unnamed sources and, unfortunately, some reporters have misused anonymity by attaching "sources said" to their own views.

Nowhere are anonymous sources more suspect than in business news, where people sometimes can benefit hugely by leaking information to you, while ducking responsibility for it.

Consider: An executive leaks word, anonymously, that his company is near a breakthrough in, say, genetic engineering—and watches happily as your story drives the price of the company's stock (much of which the executive owns) to new highs.

Consider: A land developer whispers, anonymously, that a huge shopping center is planned outside town—and chuckles as your story triples the value of land the developer owns out there.

MAKE IT A RULE: Press your sources to go *on the record* and immediately suspect the motives of any who decline.

Some stories vital to readers are available only on condition we grant anonymity. Even so, some editors will tell you to walk away from your shy source and try to develop the story elsewhere (and with the anonymous tip you probably can).

Some editors, though, will agree to anonymity and instruct you to proceed along these lines:

1. Ask the source to reconsider. You often can gain name identification if you press hard.
2. If not, negotiate language that will signal readers **what** the source is if not **who** it is. "A source" is not as strong as "a source at XYZ Chemical" and neither is as strong as "a high-ranking executive at XYZ Chemical." Readers deserve at least to know whether your sources are well-placed and authoritative.

Granting anonymity is serious business. Principled journalists have gone to jail to protect a source. If word gets around that you've betrayed a source, your reputation as a reliable reporter is gravely wounded.

It's important to ensure you and your source are on the same wavelength when discussing anonymity. Both of you should understand these widely accepted definitions:

- **Not for attribution** means you can use information with general attribution ("a source at XYZ Chemical said").
- **On background** generally is accepted to mean you can use the information but without attribution of any kind.
- **Off the record** mostly is interpreted to mean you cannot use the information (but, of course, you can use the tip to develop the same information from other sources).

WARNING: If you agree to grant anonymity, discuss with your source precisely how the information and attribution are to be used. A reputation for being precise—and trustworthy—in such matters will enhance your stature as a professional.

One way or another, immediately set ground rules. Establish that the interview is on the record; the Great One will be quoted and identified. Don't get trapped half way through by, "Say, this is off the record, isn't it?"

Try to judge how the interviewee will react to a tape recorder. Public officials and other "media sophisticates" might pull out their own, freeing you to do so, also. Other people less familiar with being interviewed freeze at mere sight of a recorder.

In note taking, **listen** to what's being said. Don't duck your head and try, like a stenographer, to catch every word. Learn to take selective notes.

CAUTION: If you don't catch a quote you need, ask that it be repeated. Later, in writing, pull full quotes only from your notebook—not your memory. Don't try to reconstruct, days or even hours later, a direct quote. If you doubt your notebook and memory, paraphrase. Better yet, call back to ask for a repeat.

Early in the interview, ask a couple general, **open-ended** questions: "What's your reaction to those rate cuts?" or "What impact do you think this will have on home mortgage lending?"

Open-ended question show you're not trying to dominate the process, that you're open to the ***banker's*** viewpoint. And, of course, the banker might take you in unexpected—yet rewarding—directions.

A problem: With open-ended questions you can lose control. They invite the interviewee to ramble, to steer you away from the news and into what the banker might regard as safe (and non-news) territory. This is dangerous particularly in business journalism, where you encounter powerful people used to having silent, respectful audiences sit still to hear "the line."

So, when your Great One takes unrewarding directions you must jump in with a specific, ***closed-ended*** question: "Excuse me, but that's a very interesting point. In suggesting your bank's lending will increase, ***precisely*** what percentage increase do you envisage?"

That requires a precise answer—and enables you to butt back in with more closed-ended questions and steer the interview in directions rewarding to you (and your readers).

Go into interviews with questions listed in your notebook. In your beginner years, particularly if you're unfamiliar with business news, you can get caught suddenly with nothing to ask. That wastes an interview possibility (and is very embarrassing).

Develop the ability to listen and simultaneously assign priorities to what's being said.

"Ah," you may think, "***that's*** my lead," only to hear something even more important a few minutes later. When news nuggets are dropped, circle back around them and pick up additional information and quotes.

Throughout, be alert for "spin" being put on information. Your keyboard is powerful; your story can move markets, money and lives, and for the interviewee to move you in favorable directions is only natural.

Just as naturally, it's your instinct to resist. Yet, your reporter's responsibility is to understand the interviewee's viewpoint, then reflect that in your writing (balanced, of course, with other views).

GOOD RULE: Assume everybody has a spin, a viewpoint, a personal motive in talking to you. (Brokers call it "talking your portfolio"—talking affirmatively about stocks they own in hopes news stories will drive up their prices). Understand the motives of spinners, then compensate for it.

| Box 2-4 | Manners in Interviewing |

Should a business news reporter ever act, well, a little ***impolite*** to get a story? Dyan Machan of *Forbes* describes his luncheon interview with the new chief executive officer of a major company on the first day he succeeded a legendary predecessor:

Sticking it to [the new CEO] a bit, I asked if he's to be a caretaker. That was a mean question to put to a guy who hates to lose, but I figured getting him riled up would help reveal his character.

He almost knocked over his soup.

"Absolutely not!" he roared. "[His predecessor] put [the company's] footprints across the world. My job is to bring all that together, link it and really make it a united company—not a group of affiliates."

In that one sentence, without my even having asked for it, this new chief executive clearly articulated his vision.

—Dayan Machan, "Tony Who?" *Forbes,* June 19, 1998, p. 98

And, think about this:

- *Persistence pays.* Aggressive reporters get crucial interviews by refusing "no" as an answer. And during interviews, they press for the information they need. Don't let your banker turn you away by answering your question with a question: "What do *you* think of the interest rate cuts?" the banker asks the reporter. "I'm not a mortgage banker; you are," says the reporter, declining to be rebuffed.
- *Professionalism pays, too.* Building your reputation as a pro means no secret taping of conversations, no "vigilante journalism" ("I'm out to reform the mortgage industry."), and no threats ("Give me what I need or you'll look stupid in my story").
- *Don't forget who you are.* You're a reporter and your job is to get the news. Cross the line from professionalism into friendship and you'll lose your journalistic independence. Don't kid yourself; the source knows why you're there: to get the news. So, call it exploitation of a source, if you wish, but get on with it. *However,* stroke that source a bit; maintain your relationship. You'll need to come that way again some day.
- *Never end an interview without saying something like this:* "Is there anything else important you would like to tell me about this story? Can you direct me to other sources?"

  Though expert in the corporate game of forcing their views forward, many business executives wait in press interviews to be asked. If you've overlooked an important point, your open-ended invitation to talk about "anything else important" may reveal unexpected and valuable information.

  And, increasingly these days, sources of the human kind will direct you to sources of another kind—electronic.

Sources: The Electronic Kind

The Internet is not a slave, or a hired brain or a crystal ball. It is a toolbox. It gets you access to information—resources that only professional traders and other insiders could get in years past. But what you do with the information is up to you.

—Hank Ezell, business news writer[9]

Enormous strength is added to business journalism (indeed, **all** journalism) by reporters who unlock the Internet "toolbox." In there, reporters today reach mountains of valuable data that in yesteryear were beyond reach of even the richest libraries or corporations.

Precisely **how** to unlock the toolbox or search it is beyond the scope of this book. But we must discuss **what** to look for. Let's relate that to the interview on home mortgage interest rates:

Seek Statistical Substance

To be meaningful, your story must be built on a strong framework of facts, figures, dollars and cents, with an overlay of analysis and interpretation.

Interpretation—the **meaning** of the rate cuts—comes from your interviews with human sources, your banker contact. However, even an interview of 30 or 60 minutes (a long time to a busy executive) cannot yield all the facts and figures you'll need.

Enter the Internet.

Banks, federal agencies, mortgage associations all offer electronic databases. Via the Internet you can find data (and analysis) developed by prestigious publications—*The Wall Street Journal, The New York Times, Forbes, Business Week, Money.*

Quickly, you can place the banker's comments in a wider factual context.

Identify Historical Trends

A weakness in business news reporting is a tendency to apply stand-alone meaning or significance to things or events without relating them to their impact on people over the long range.

That is, stock market reporters sometimes write of "Wall Street" or "the market" as if they are living, breathing things to be covered today for their own sake, when actually their only significance is their impact on people—investors and all other Americans whose fortunes are linked to how "the market" performed yesterday and how it may perform tomorrow.

Corporate "downsizing" (a delicate word for layoffs) has no stand-alone significance. Its meaning is in impact on people—those thrown out of work or investors in companies whose stocks may increase in value as downsizing cuts costs which, in turn, can increase profits. It's the reporter's job to find those linkages to the future and compare them to the past.

So, keep your eye on the true meaning of interest rate cuts and the real goal of your story: Will your readers enjoy lower mortgage rates? If so, what's the likely **dollars and cents** impact on their lives?

No journalist should predict the future; even your banker expert would be foolish to try. **But** you can use Internet sources to trace what happened in the past to mortgage interest rates when, as in our scenario, the Federal Reserve Board cut the discount and federal fund rates.

Events, corporations, people (and interest rates) many times react to-day to happenings as they reacted in the past. ***But not every time.***

Ultimately, you must provide historical trends and other information that permit *your readers* to judge the likely course of future events.

Seek Current Context

You hear it often: "The market hit 8,900 today" or "the market is up." What does that mean? Well, it generally refers to the Dow Jones Industrial Averages, one indicator of trading on the New York Stock Exchange.

But all that has true meaning *only if expressed in context,* something like, ". . . hit 8,900 today, up 200 points from yesterday, the largest single gain in three weeks."

Make it a basic rule in your reporting: No stand-alone figure carries meaning unless compared to another figure.

In reporting our scenario's one-quarter percent cuts in the federal fund and discount rates, CNNfn quickly noted the former "now stands at 5 percent" and the latter "is set at 4.75 percent." CNNfn also reported the last time the rates were cut and by how much.

So, let's say your banker comments the bank will cut mortgage rates by one-quarter percent. Go to the Internet and other sources to determine what other banks are doing in your town and state and nationally.

In other words, use the Internet to extend your story beyond financial abstractions; write a *shopper's guide* filled with comparative information your readers can use to improve their lives.

Seek Deviations From the Norm

Think of news horizons stretching monotonously into the distance. Suddenly, a mountain or valley breaks the sameness. In a reporting sense, that's where news is—atop the mountain, in the valley.

That is, in business reporting you must determine how things normally work, then pounce on deviations from the norm.

A quick trip on the Internet will reveal the norm among mortgage bankers elsewhere reacting to the Fed's cuts. If they cut rates and your banker doesn't, that's news. If they don't cut rates and your banker does, that's news, too.

(Not to suggest that you practice "crisis journalism"—a belief that news is *only* departures from the norm. Report also when things are proceeding as expected and, for sure, report when there is good news in the business world—just as a cops reporter should write the good news when not everyone in town is shooting or robbing somebody.)

Seek Distant Authority

It's a modern marvel: The Internet extends your reporter's reach far beyond the city limits and into distant human and electronic repositories of authoritative information.

You can join a global fraternity of bankers, government officials, corporate executives, academics, think tank experts of all kinds.

You can passively view their web sites; you can pursue them aggressively, via e-mail, to their inner sanctums.

Clearly, your source notebook must be global in reach and the Internet your avenue to distant authority.

Shout "Help!"

All reporters, sooner or later, face The Moment—the instant when they realize they're stumped, that they don't know where to turn next.

When that happens to you (as it will), shout for help on the Internet. Go to conversation groups or "chat rooms" of people with similar interests. A request for guidance can draw wonderful assistance.

| Box 2-5 | Beware! |

. . .Web sites proliferate exponentially, uncontrolled by any standard of excellence, or even morality.

—Ben Bradlee, former executive editor, *The Washington Post*,
in "It All Starts With Newspapers," *The New York Times*,
an insert, Sept. 14, 1998

Other Important Sources

In addition to the interview and Internet, you can develop multiple sources elsewhere. Let's look at three of the most important ones:

Public Relations Sources

You've heard, of course, that reporters dislike "PR types," and some do—and vice versa. Truth is, however, **both sides need each other.**

Public relations practitioners need the press to disseminate information about the personality, institution, cause or idea they represent. Your banker's PR department realizes the bank won't be known widely unless the public is reached through the media, not to say **your keyboard.**

And believe it: Many are the reporters alerted to a major story by PR sources, then guided through its complexities by background from PR departments.

Remember, of course, that PR people are paid to put the best light—the best **spin**—on your story. They represent the **bank,** not the public or, certainly, the interests of your readers.

News Service Sources

Daily newspapers and news magazines receive a constant flow of business news from news services and syndicates.

Dow Jones, Bloomberg, Reuters and others specialize in fast delivery, computer-to-computer, of all types of business, economic and financial news. Watch them closely for breaking news. You can read CNNfn and others via the Internet.

Editors sort through those services for items to be published as received, or they might throw you Dow Jones and Reuters versions and ask you to weave pertinent material into your story.

One service, The Associated Press, has an additional "interactive" characteristic. Whereas your newspaper is a ***subscriber*** of Reuters, Dow Jones or the others, it is a ***member*** of The AP, a newsgathering cooperative. That membership gives you the right to call on AP bureaus throughout the world for special help—say, comments from state legislators about home mortgage rates or the views of banking regulators in Washington.

In most newsrooms, AP is a vastly under-utilized resource. Strengthen your reporting by using it.

Surveys and Polls

Polls and surveys can strengthen your writing. But remember two things:

1. A poll might ***look*** scientific but, in fact, be based on faulty methodology and, thus, yield unreliable results.
2. A survey might ***appear*** to be objective but, in fact, be born of ulterior motives and be aimed at distorting public opinion (by, first, distorting your reporting).

When weaving poll results into your reporting, ask yourself:

- Do I know who sponsored the poll and with what motives? Are those sponsors truly after dispassionate, objective findings?
- How many people were polled? Experts generally say, for example, that nationwide polls cannot deliver accurate results on fewer than 1,000–1,500 returns.
- How were questions asked? "Do you want a cut in the discount rate?" will yield answers quite different from replies to, "Do you want lower home mortgage interest rates?"
- When was the poll taken? Questions asked the day after the rate cut might yield results dramatically different than those of a month later.
- What was the margin of error? Statisticians can calculate margin of error, and reputable pollsters will publish it.

Finally, sit back and ask yourself:

- Does this poll, simply put, make sense? Does the math work out? Do the results truly strengthen my story or just clutter it up?

And, when you write your story, answer for your readers the questions you just asked yourself. Readers deserve to know the authority, credibility and reliability of the poll results you're giving them.

Summary

- Your writing style will take years to develop properly but you must build strong reporting skills immediately.
- You'll need human sources to guide you through the maze of data and information of all kinds received by newspapers and magazines from print and electronic sources.
- Business executives often distrust reporters on grounds they know little about the subject and hold anti-business attitudes.
- Overcoming such thinking takes a long time and requires becoming expert in how business operates.
- You'll strengthen your appeal to editors if you develop the ability to suggest how distant news events can be localized for readers.
- Computer-assisted reporting strengthens your writing enormously but remember that much information cannot be trusted or is disseminated by sources with ulterior motives.
- Careful planning is key to obtaining and being successful in interviews with business executives.
- When interviewing experts display professionalism and concern for accuracy while striving for the nonthreatening atmosphere of a friendly "chat."
- Immediately suspect the motives of anyone who offers you information only if you grant anonymity; they may be "spinning" you for their own gain.
- The Internet can give you access to distant authoritative sources and add **statistical substance** to your reporting.
- Identify **historical trends** that put your story in wider context, and seek **current comparatives** that lend meaning to figures obtained in your reporting.
- Look for **deviations from the norm** but don't lapse into "crisis journalism," a belief that **only** departures from the usual are news; report good news, too.
- Other key sources include **public relations practitioners, news services** and **surveys and polls.**

Recommended Reading

Don't miss these two books: Christopher Callahan, *A Journalist's Guide to the Internet* (Boston: Allyn and Bacon, 1999), and John Ullmann, *Investigative Reporting* New York: St. Martin's Press, 1995). *Also see* Lauren Kessler and Duncan McDonald, *The Search* (Belmont, Calif.: Wadsworth, 1992), Tom Koch, *Journalism for the 21st Century* (New York: Praeger, 1991).

For help in surfing the Internet, see Andrew Harnack and Eugene Kleppinger, *Online!* (New York: St. Martin's Press, 1997).

Check *The Business Journalist,* published by the Society of American Business Editors and Writers, Inc. (www.sabew.org).

Read *Business Week* (bwreader@mgh.com) and *Forbes* (5096930@mcimail.com). See *The Wall Street Journal*'s Web site (http://wsj.com). Other leading business sections are available via the Internet, too.

Discussion groups for journalists are available through the Society of Professional Journalists (listserv@netcom.com) and Investigative Reporters and Editors (listserv@mizzou1.missouri.edu). When you need help finding electronic data go to Computer-Assisted Reporting and Research (listserv@ulkyvm.louisville.edu).

MediaNet is a free research service that will help you find sources and information (71344.2761@compuserve.com).

PR Newswire, an international public relations organization, offers valuable information, including archives on nearly 1,000 companies (www.prnewswire.com) and breaking news (briefs@profnet.com).

I discuss reporting techniques in Conrad Fink, *Introduction to Professional Newswriting,* 2nd ed. (New York: Longman, 1998) and Conrad Fink and Donald E. Fink, *Introduction to Magazine Writing* (New York: Macmillan, 1993).

Notes

1. Dawn Kopecki, "Fax Overload," *The Business Journalist,* June/July 1998, p. 1.
2. Todd Lewan, Associated Press dispatch for Sunday newspapers, Sept. 13, 1998.
3. Hank Ezell, "Money & More, Information on The Internet," *The Atlanta Journal-Constitution,* Sept. 20, 1998, p. U-1.
4. This research, principally by Dr. Joseph R. Dominick, is discussed in Conrad Fink, *Media Ethics* (New York: McGraw-Hill, 1988) on pages 225–226. The business reporter who joined Greyhound was Dorothy Lorant. Her quote is on p. 226 of that book.
5. Mickey H. Gramig, telephone interview, Nov. 5, 1998.
6. "Expanding East," Sept. 19, 1998, p. D-1.
7. "Fed Cuts Key Interest Rates," a CNNfn dispatch at 3:45 p.m., Oct. 15, 1998.
8. Audit Bureau of Circulations reported *The Atlanta Journal-Constitution*'s Sunday circulation was 677,019 as of Sept. 30, 1998. On average, U.S. newspapers get 2.2 readers per copy sold.
9. Hank Ezell, *The Atlanta Journal-Constitution,* op cit.

Exercises

1. Read today's *Wall Street Journal* (or another newspaper your instructor designates) and describe, in about 350 words, four **localized** stories you could report and write of stories you sighted in the *Journal.* Describe briefly the local sources you would contact.

2. In about 200 words, list campus sources you would contact for a story on tuition fees. For each source, describe two questions you would ask.

3. Map the strategy you would follow to gain an interview with a local banker for a story on student loans. Your story would need details on availability of credit, interest levels and how students can qualify for loans. In about 300 words, describe how you would convince the banker to grant the interview, then list 10 specific questions you would ask.

4. Your assignment is to describe, in about 300 words, the contents and types of stories in a single issue of *Business Week* magazine. Note particularly coverage in three broad areas—economics, business, personal finance. You may visit the magazine at bwreader@mgh.com.

5. Seek the advice of at least three professional business journalists on how students should prepare for a career in business news. If possible, conduct live interviews with local professionals. But you also may shout "Help!" on MediaNet, at 71344.2761@compuserve.com, or contact the Society of American Business Editors and Writers, Inc., at www.sabew.org. Describe your findings in about 350 words.

3

Making Facts and Numbers Sing

Reporting techniques discussed in Chapter 2 will fill your notebook to overflowing with facts and numbers.

That's good, of course. It's also a problem.

On the good side, facts and numbers drive business, economics and finance—and, obviously, they must drive your writing. Without strong factual substance and, especially, numbers, a business news story is meaningless.

Your problem arises in how to handle the huge volume of facts and numbers uncovered in business news reporting. Inexperienced reporters sometimes panic over this. No need.

In Chapter 3, we'll discuss three steps you can take to ensure the mountain of data you've collected doesn't topple over on you—or your readers.

FIRST, *ruthlessly evaluate* your reporting results, putting aside all secondary material and focusing on information truly key to your story's central thrust. It's tough to throw away material you've collected with great effort. But the unacceptable alternative is a story cluttered with irrelevant facts and numbers.

SECOND, *write* facts and numbers in language and context that explain their importance and characterize their meaning for your readers. Informing readers that "home mortgage rates are rising" is one thing; it's quite another to report they "are rising by one-half percent, meaning house owners will pay $500 more annually on mortgages of $100,000."

THIRD, *pace* your writing carefully, feeding facts and numbers to readers quickly enough to maintain their interest, yet not too fast or in big bunches that choke them.

Evaluating Your Reporting Results

Like a poker player studying cards just dealt, a business reporter must sort through facts and numbers to decide when to hold 'em and when not to.

Let's say, for example, you interview several bankers and collect fascinating insights into a day in the life of a banker.

You also gather hard dollars-and-cents information indicating home mortgage interest rates will be increased soon.

Your mind and notebooks are jammed with anecdotes, color background and feature-like material on how bankers live and work. Your notebooks also overflow with facts on the historic levels of mortgage rates, numbers on current levels and figures on predicted levels.

If you now sit staring at your keyboard, uncertain which direction to take, turn off your computer. You've got serious thinking to do.

You obviously have not decided precisely what your story is to be, and until you do you cannot evaluate information you collected. *You can't decide which writing direction to take or which facts to use until you decide where you want to go.*

In Chapters 1 and 2 we discussed *external* considerations—the target audience, for example—that help us determine the general direction a story must take. Now it's time to set up a checklist for determining what the *internal* components of the story must be, and how to handle them.

The "What's News?" Fact Check

As you evaluate each fact and number you collected, consider these influences:

Audience

Audience again comes first. All media (and smart reporters) strive for large audiences. *It's our business.*

You'll sometimes intentionally focus on facts and numbers important to only small audiences—say, decision-makers in finance with influence beyond their limited circle. But mostly you'll pick internal story components meaningful to the largest audience. Hard-news facts and numbers on home mortgage rates will pull a larger audience than soft, feature-like insights into how bankers live.

So, here at the first stop on your "what's news?" fact check, you've got to opt for numbers-filled writing on interest levels.

As you plow through your notebooks, assign lower priority to numbers and facts that detract from your story's principal thrust. Put aside for another day anecdotal information on how bankers live.

IMPORTANT: Hold only those facts and numbers that **non-expert** home owners will understand; toss aside numbers and quotes on the arcane art of high finance comprehensible only to Big Banking Insiders.

It will help if you visualize a single target reader—your neighbor Charlie perhaps or your Aunt Betty. Is this fact or that number crucial to them? Would they understand? If yes, hold it; if not, put it aside or think deeply how to explain it to them.

This trick of visualizing a real-life person helps enormously as you reduce the huge amounts of data collected to manageable dimensions.

Impact

In business news, an implied contract exists: Pay 50 cents for our newspaper, dear reader, and we'll give you a "heads up" on hard-news developments that will have impact on your life.

So, at the second stop on the "what's news?" fact check you again must opt for hard news, fact-filled writing on interest rates.

Your reporting might have uncovered the fascinating fact that the town's leading mortgage banker rises at 5 a.m. for an hour of yoga and 100 push-ups. Does that fact, do those numbers have **impact** on interest rates your readers will pay? No. So put aside those "soft" facts and numbers.

Timeliness

We call them **news**papers and **news**casts for a reason: They deliver new news, not old news, not non-news.

That means you must assign high priority to facts which, if you publish them immediately, will help your readers protect their financial interests.

In our scenario, facts right now on how bankers live are not urgent. You can use them weeks from now. But substantive reporting right now that higher interest rates are ahead gives readers time to act before mortgages become more costly.

Not to say everything you write must be hard, timely news with huge impact. There is room—need—for softer, more entertaining dimensions. So keep watch for stories on the humorous, novel, unusual. But not right now.

At **timeliness,** the third stop on your "what's news?" fact check, you again must opt for a hard-news approach. Winnow your notebook for timely facts and figures.

Competition

Count on it: If your newspaper—and you—consistently lag behind other media in covering important news, you both will be out of business.

There is a ***business purpose*** for your newspaper to be first (but always correct, of course) with important facts; there are real career reasons for you personally to be on the cutting edge, too.

So, at ***competition*** on the "what's news?" fact check, assign higher priorities to information you obtained exclusively. A banker tells you alone that rates are likely to rise by half a percent? ***Focus on that.***

Figures on increases over the past decade are history, available to any less-enterprising reporter. And remember: No reporter ever scored a beat by relying on press conferences or PR handouts.

Other Factors to Consider

The newsworthiness of facts and figures must be judged by other measurements commonly used in general news, sports and other news sectors. But judge carefully.

Proximity

In sports, the numbers on a local high school quarterback's touchdown pass are news; numbers on a winning pass in a game 1,000 miles away aren't. Take the same general approach to sifting facts and numbers in business news—the closer to home they occur, often the bigger their news value.

However, in business news distant events can be most important. For example, those local bankers you interviewed weren't working off only local numbers; indeed, it was a touchdown pass by the Federal Reserve Board in far-off Washington that signaled higher rates coming locally!

When sifting facts, view proximity carefully. Those from over distant horizons may be real news.

Conflict and Prominence

Conflict and prominence must be on your fact check. But, again, judge carefully their newsworthiness. If Acme Stump Removal Co., heretofore unknown to most, fires its president, loved principally only by family and a few friends, that's not news. But if the well-known chairman of your town's largest bank is tossed out, that ***is*** news—and so are figures on his salary, his severance bonus and the facts about the corporate conflict that led to his career demise.

Well, in just that manner you must run down the "what's news?" fact check to refine your story angle and determine which facts and numbers to include. If you start writing when uncertain about the essential point of your story, you'll wander aimlessly and your readers will be awash in point-less facts and statistics.[1]

Putting Facts and Numbers in Context

Do you know how much $1 billion is? How about $1 trillion?

When a drug company reports $55.1 million in second-quarter profits, is that good news? Great news? Or terrific?

Learning what numbers mean and putting them in context—translating—them for readers is a tough challenge. Your writing must weave in those many facts and figures that are essential to understanding business, economics and finance.

Yet you must write in an open, readable way, creating **news stories** un-derstandable by non-expert readers, not dry treasurer's reports or accountant's mumbo jumbo understandable only by experts.

For example, look at how three professional writers handled context in addressing the questions above.

Matthew Miller, a syndicated columnist, comments that President Clinton boasts of obtaining $1 billion to improve class size in schools. Miller's point: It's a **tiny** amount. And this is how Miller puts the figure in perspective:

> One billion dollars is roughly one-third of 1 percent of all K-12 spend-ing. It's less than a day's worth of Social Security checks, a rounding error in the $1.7 trillion federal budget. It's a sign of how stenographic the national press is—and how easily our eyes are averted from the bulk of federal activ-ity—that something so small can be puffed up rhetorically into something so consequential.
>
> — Matthew Miller[2]

Okay, so $1 billion is a tiny amount. How about $1 **trillion**? Well, a *New York Times* writer is more impressed with that figure in a story on a capital management firm entering into financial transactions valued at $1.25 trillion. The writer plunks into his story this paragraph:

> For perspective, it may be useful to note that if somebody wanted to dis-tribute $1 trillion equally among all 240 million Americans, he would have to dispense more than $4,000 to every man, woman and child.
>
> —Michael T. Kaufman, *The New York Times*[3]

Now, how about that drug company's profit (or **earnings)** report? Good news? Terrific news? Note below a writer leaves that interpretation to readers (who, after all, might buy or sell stock on this story). **But** the writer surrounds the profit figure in a **comparative context** that assists an investor in evaluating the news:

> McKesson, the biggest domestic drug wholesaler, reported fiscal second-quarter earnings rose 39 percent as acquisitions and increased sales to hospitals and pharmacies helped it beat earnings forecasts.
>
> Profit before charges was $55.1 million, or 52 cents a share, against net income of $39.6 million, or 41 cents, a year earlier. The results exceeded the 50-cent average estimate of analysts. . . .
>
> Bloomberg News[4]

Be heartened! As illustrated above, there **are** ways to make facts and numbers make sense. Check these, too:

Evaluate Your Audience

Your audience's ability to absorb technical data must guide how you present facts and numbers.

Obviously, fanatical readers of business pages will bring to your story on, say, the stock market a higher level of understanding than those who spend most of their reading time in *Organic Gardening*.

But even within the pages of the same newspaper we often write at different levels for readers of differing expertise.

For example, there is a big jump in Wall Street trading. On its ***front page,*** a stopping point for all readers, non-investors as well as investors, *The New York Times* presents this version:

> Glee shoved gloom aside yesterday in the nation's stock markets as two of the main gauges surpassed their summer peaks and reached new highs.
>
> Investors who stayed with stocks through the downturn in the fall now have outsized gains for the year, even by standards set in this bull market's last few years. The Dow Jones industrial average, which set a record yesterday, is up 18.54 percent for the year, while the Standard & Poor's 500-stock index, also a record-setter yesterday, has risen 22.44 percent. Although the technology-heavy Nasdaq composite index did not hit a record yesterday, it has beaten the other gauges for the year, up 25.92 percent.
>
> —Gretchen Morgenson, *The New York Times*[5]

The *Times* story above is a "newspage" stocks story—written in language non-expert readers can handle and run in general news, not business news pages. Note the emphasis on colorful descriptive writing, with ***very few numbers*** in those first two grafs.

The same day, the *Times* publishes on the front page of its ***business section*** this version:

> Glee shoved gloom aside in the nation's stock markets yesterday as main gauges surpassed summer peaks and reached new highs. Investors now have outsized gains for the year.

This performance represents a U-turn in investor sentiment. Stock euphoria is back, with the Dow rising 214.72 points, or 2.34 percent, to 9,374.27. The S.&P. 500 rose 24.66 points, or 2.12 percent, to 1,188.21, also a record. The Nasdaq index did not post a record but jumped 49.21 points, or 2.55 percent, to 1,977.42.

The New York Times[6]

Note above that the *Times* aims its business-section version at expert readers. It jams numbers (***and*** percentages) into the second graf. It makes no effort to explain the "Dow," which on the front page was fleshed out as, "The Dow Jones industrial average," or "The S&P" which was explained for front-page, non-expert readers as "the Standard & Poor's 500-stock index."

In this same edition, the *Times* produces a third version of the story, this one by Floyd Norris, a commentator normally found in the business section. On this day, Norris writes for the ***editorial page*** a commentary designed to answer, "What's going on?" Norris' piece has almost no numbers, few hard facts, but is long on interpretation. His opener:

Wall Street panicked this summer, but Main Street doubted the sky was really going to fall. So far, at least, those who kept their heads—or at least their stocks—have done better than those who sold.

Indexes of big American stocks including the Dow Jones industrials and the Standard & Poor's 500, set records yesterday. Smaller stocks and junk bonds are showing new life.

What's going on? Wall Street analysts list a number of causes. . . .

—Floyd Norris, *The New York Times*[7]

Clearly, your audience's level of comprehension (and likely ***interest***) must drive how you handle facts and numbers.

Compare and Characterize, Too

Quick! If Venezuelan government bonds trade 27 points above U.S. Treasury bonds, is that a wide margin? "Whopping," says *The Economist*.[8]

If McKesson Corporation's share prices ended the day down 14.3 percent, did they slide, fall, drop? "Tumbled," says Bloomberg News, putting a serious face on the number.[9]

That same day, J.P. Morgan & Company's third-quarter earnings "plunged" 60 percent, Bloomberg reports.[10]

Characterizing, as above, the magnitude and ***importance*** of a figure can help readers. But beware overdoing it. John Rothchild of *Time* magazine notes:

You have to feel sorry for the reporters who write these stories day in and day out. They get bored with words like up, down, gain and loss. In only a month's worth of papers, the Dow has galloped and soared; technology stocks have slumped, rallied and lifted; stocks in general have hobbled, languished, dipped, rebounded, treaded water, plummeted, jumped, slipped, surged, barreled, broken through milestones, defied gravity, come down to earth, shrugged off surprises, limped through fitful sessions, taken breathers, run out of gas and staged a wildly mixed performance.

—John Rothchild, *Time*[11]

Direct comparison of a number with another is essential to help readers understand.

For example, *Forbes* determines a company's revenue is equivalent to $188,000 per employee. That's a measure of managerial efficiency, all right, but the figure is meaningless if standing alone. So *Forbes* rushes to add that the $188,000 is "pathetic compared with IBM's $290,000 or Hewlett-Packard's $352,000."[12]

Ah, now I understand!

Note below how *The San Francisco Chronicle* presents comparatives:

Despite a volatile stock market, institutional investors continued to pour money into high-tech and other startups during the past quarter.

Venture capital firms invested $1.1 billion in 168 Bay Area companies in the three months ending June 30. That was up from $773 million invested in 119 local companies in the first quarter, according to VentureOne, a San Francisco research firm. The total also was higher than the $1 billion poured into 161 companies during the second quarter of last year.

—Peter Sinton, *The San Francisco Chronicle*[13]

Note below how an Associated Press writer characterizes a number ***before*** giving you the number:

Consumer confidence has fallen to its lowest level in nearly two years amid the economic turmoil spreading around the globe.

The Conference Board reported Tuesday that its index of consumer confidence fell 9.1 points to 117.3 in October. The last time it was lower was in December 1996.

The Associated Press[14]

Beware the urge to characterize ***motives*** behind numbers. Is *Forbes* drawing a judgmental, even pejorative characterization in describing a computer company's financing plan as a "gimmick?" Or do you prefer the ***factual*** characterization *Forbes* also offered:

But consumers may not be enticed. The average interest rate is about 17%, which is about 1½ percentage points above the average charge-card rate.

—Michelle Conlin, *Forbes*[15]

Highlight Impact

Remember that readers are searching the facts of your story for the meaning to their pocketbooks, their lives. A *USA Today* writer highlights impact (emphasis added):

> Crude oil prices tumbled to five-month lows Wednesday, ***and cheap gasoline prices await motorists during next week's Thanksgiving holiday.***
>
> With threat of a U.S. attack on Iraq lifted, the December contract for the benchmark light sweet crude fell as much as 80 cents a barrel, or 6.4%, to $11.65 before closing at $12.14 on the New York Mercantile Exchange. It was the lowest close since June 19.
>
> Oil prices have fallen 12% in the past four days and are approaching a 12-year low of $11.42 set on June 15.
>
> —Chris Woodyard, *USA Today*[16]

Forbes characterizes impact in reporting growth in the number of planes in the U.S. fleet of commercial airlines (emphasis added):

> . . . It is forecast to grow to nearly 4,700 by 2002—faster than the projected rate of passenger growth. ***Filling all those extra seats will inevitably lead to cheaper fares.***
>
> —Howard Banks, *Forbes*[17]

The San Francisco Chronicle uses a precise number to characterize the meaning of a huge corporate takeover (emphasis added):

> British Petroleum PLC ***plans to cut 6,000 jobs, mostly in the United States,*** as part of its $49 billion purchase of Amoco Corp.—the biggest foreign takeover of an American company.
>
> *The San Francisco Chronicle*[18]

A fact about numbers: Somewhere behind most numbers lurks meaning for the lives of real human beings. Search for the meaning. ***A number seldom will strengthen your writing unless you can show how it affects lives.***

Consult Experts

Quoting experts can lend authority to your story as well as meaning to individual figures you use. It doesn't take much:

• Dow Jones News Service reports a blizzard of numbers on stock prices for companies that operate on the Internet and quotes a brokerage firm expert as saying, "The bubble is starting to burst on a lot of Internet stocks."[19]

- *The Wall Street Journal* gives readers figures on a large buildup in company inventories and lets a bank economist characterize the meaning: "That could slow economic growth considerably."[20]
- *USA Today* reports the numbers on Japan's plan to energize its economy, then adds, "Economists say the plan largely mirrors one released in April that had little impact."[21]
- Knight Ridder Newspapers runs a wide-ranging story on the U.S. economy and turns for interpretation of the numbers to an authoritative researcher: "Favorable economic conditions and confidence about the health of the economy over the next six months have lifted consumer spirits. [22]

During your career you'll likely become an expert in many sectors of business news, but you'll still be a reporter. And even expert reporters take the facts and figures to the ***real*** experts for interpretation!

Compare Only True Comparables

Or, compare oranges only to oranges, apples only to apples.

For example, you're obviously leading readers astray with numbers designed to show a mom-and-pop ice cream shop on Main Street is managed inefficiently because its profits are lower than IBM's.

It's not smart, either, to compare, without elaboration, ice cream sales in January to those in July.

Seasonal fluctuations in business make it imperative that you compare *like periods,* as does an AP writer (emphasis added):

> The Dayton Hudson Corporation's third-quarter profits rose 14 percent *from the corresponding period a year ago*. . . .
>
> The Associated Press[23]

Bloomberg News reports new housing construction is up, in part due to "improved weather in the southern United States," which permits carpenters to work outside. Bloomberg adds (emphasis added):

> The Commerce Department said today that housing starts rose 7.3 percent in October, *to a seasonally adjusted annual rate* of 1.695 million units. They had declined 2.6 percent in September.
>
> Bloomberg News[24]

Sometimes, special business activity in one period invalidates direct comparison with the earlier like period. Alert your readers, as does this writer in reporting on Netscape Communication Corp. (emphasis added):

> Profit, *excluding special items* for the period ended Oct. 31, 1998, was $4.2 million, or 4 cents a share, compared with net income of $10.2 mil-

lion, or 10 cents, for the period ended Sept. 30, 1997. ***Netscape shifted to a fiscal year ending in October from a calendar year.***

Bloomberg News[25]

Check the Math

No one—nothing—is infallible in business news. That includes accountants, their computers, chief financial officers of major corporations.

So, bring your handy calculator into play:

* Check numbers you've been given. Are sales really down $256 million, as the man said, if they drop to $437 million from $693 million? Check. Your readers will.
* Find more meaningful ways of making the point. You aid reader comprehension by calculating that the $256 million drop is a ***36.9 percent*** downturn.

Note below how ***percentages*** are much more meaningful than would be raw dollar figures standing alone:

Shares of Campbell Soup Co. rose 93.75 cents, to $56.4375 on the New York Stock Exchange.

The company's chief executive, Dale F. Morrison, has been slashing purchasing and ingredients costs. Campbell's cost of goods sold fell 7 percent, lifting the gross profit margin to 54 percent from 51 percent a year ago.

Advertising and selling costs rose 7 percent, as the company spent more on ads, in-store promotions and new products. United States soup marketing expenses alone rose 30 percent.

The payoff, Campbell hopes, will come from more soup sales this winter.

Bloomberg News[26]

Be Consistent in Style

Which will it be: "three and a half," "3½" or "3.5"?

The writers' stylebook used by your newspaper or magazine will answer that question. Learn the stylebook's guidance on use of numbers and ***be consistent*** in your writing. Your readers will thank you. (Incidentally, the AP stylebook, standard for most print media, calls for "3½" in this instance. *The Wall Street Journal* agrees—in this case, but not always.)

Stay Cool With Facts and Numbers

Proponents of ideas and causes sometimes get, shall we say, overly enthusiastic about numbers and distort their meaning for partisan purposes.

That is, participants in controversies often try to manipulate you by manipulating the numbers. That should be no surprise to you; it happens every day in journalism.

Forbes found widely varying interpretations of numbers while doing a story on private businesses hiring prison inmates. Unions and some "social reformers" used their own numbers to show that prisoners might be exploited or would compete with workers on the outside. *Forbes* reported all that, then added perspective:

> Still, gainful employment among the striped-suit set is small: 2,539 of 1.8 million prisoners are working for private businesses, as authorized by a federal law. But that's up 31% in the last two years.
>
> —Michelle Conlin, *Forbes*[27]

A *Milwaukee Journal* writer stays cool amid fears that huge companies are buying up real estate in his city. The writer poses that fear, then squelches it:

> Will real estate investment trusts someday own the world?
>
> It might seem that way, given the explosive growth of publicly traded REITs over the past few years. In the Milwaukee area alone, REITs have purchased dozens of shopping centers, office buildings, industrial properties and other commercial real estate.
>
> But some real estate industry observers are now suggesting the REITs—while not a fad—are far from the dominating influence that some make them out to be.
>
> Adding to this debate is a new study written by a University of Wisconsin-Madison professor that challenges the notion that a few large real estate investments trusts will eventually dominate the apartment market . . .
>
> —Tom Daykin, *The Milwaukee Journal Sentinel*[28]

If Meaning Is Unclear, Say So Honestly

Don't get trapped into thinking a reporter must answer definitively every question raised by facts and numbers. Business news—like life—has its eternal mysteries.

Your obligation is to solve those mysteries you can and for the others provide readers with ***informed judgments from authoritative sources.***

Examples:

- AP reports International Paper is buying Union Camp Corp., raising many questions about the future cost of paper, the companies' stock prices and whether employees will be downsized. AP reports an International Paper spokesman says it is "too soon to talk" about the impact of all that.
- AP reports a plunge in corporate profits. Will stock prices rise or fall? Who knows? AP makes clear the question is unanswerable right away, quoting one expert as saying investors will be pessimistic; others say optimistic.

You cannot repeatedly throw before your readers numbers and facts you don't understand. It's a journalistic felony to simply pass your confusion on to your readers.

But when meaning is unclear, say so. It's the only honest thing to do.

Pace Your "Feeding" of Numbers

Read this once (and only once!):

> The U.S. economy grew at a healthy 3.9 percent annual rate in July-September, significantly stronger than last month's initial 3.3 percent estimate. Three cuts in interest rates helped strengthen investor confidence and the Dow Jones Industrial Average rose by almost 215 points yesterday. Also, Americans imported $6.2 billion less in foreign-made goods in the third quarter.

Did you catch all that on your first reading? Of course not. Who could? That single graf is jammed with so many numbers and facts that first-time reading comprehension is near zero (probably on the second and third readings, as well).

I'm the culprit in that example above of impenetrable writing. I sorted through a story by Robert A. Rankin of Knight Ridder Newspapers for all those facts and figures, then jammed them into that single graf. Rankin, a writing pro, paces his delivery much more sparingly:

> Washington—The U.S. economy is showing surprising strength, according to government data released Tuesday.
>
> The report suggests the likelihood of recession in 1999 is slim and recently soaring stock prices are rising from a foundation more solid than mere wishful thinking.
>
> The economy grew at a healthy 3.9 percent annual rate in the July-September quarter, according to revised data from the Commerce Department. That is significantly stronger than last month's initial 3.3 percent estimate.

Note above that Rankin gives readers *no* figures in his first two grafs. He paces his delivery carefully, easing readers into his story with a short, crisp lead that characterizes the numbers' meaning (. . . "the economy is showing surprising strength" . . .).

When he finally gets to numbers, in his third graf, Rankin gives his readers just two—the 3.9 percent growth rate, compared to a 3.3 percent estimate.

In his fourth through seventh grafs, Rankin is similarly sparing with numbers. ***Numbers, in fact, are used principally to support Rankin's characterization of what's happening:***

> Ironically, stock prices had plunged during those months, driven down by fear that spreading global financial panic might knock the U.S. economy into recession.

But three cuts in interest rates by the Federal Reserve since Sept. 29 have helped restore confidence to investors, who drove the Dow Jones average of blue-chip stock prices up almost 215 points to a record high Monday before trimming gains Tuesday.

Consumers are enjoying a similar surge of confidence, according to a widely tracked survey released Tuesday by the Conference Board, a business research center in New York. Consumer confidence snapped back in November after slipping the four previous months.

Because consumer spending powers about two-thirds of U.S. economic production, the survey suggests good news for next year. While the pace of growth is expected to slow, many observers agree that recession appears increasingly unlikely.

—Robert A. Rankin, Knight Ridder Newspapers[29]

LESSON: Just because you collect numbers doesn't mean you automatically deal all of them out to readers. Indeed, most aren't included in your story; instead, use them to help *you* understand what's happening so you, like Knight Ridder's Rankin, can compare, characterize and elaborate for your readers.

Think of it this way:

You learned in basic newswriting of the Five Ws (who, what, where, when, why) and How. In Rankin's story above, the "what" is a 3.9 percent growth rate for the U.S. economy.

In business news writing, you must use that 3.9 percent "what" factor to get at the *real what*—the deeper meaning of the figures. In Rankin's story, the *real what* is that the "U.S. economy is showing surprising strength" and (second graf) that there is slim likelihood of recession in 1999.

Sometimes, of course, a single number is so astonishing that it alone characterizes meaning—and deserves first-graf mention. Note:

In a deal that combines two mighty gateways to the World Wide Web, America Online Inc. agreed to acquire Internet pioneer Netscape Communications Corp. in a $4.28 billion stock swap.

—Thomas E. Weber, *The Wall Street Journal*[30]

Note below how a writer gives first-graf prominence to another single (and impressive!) number in an acquisition story, then carefully deals out two grafs of numbers showing consequences of the deal.

International Paper announced a $6.6 billion deal Tuesday to buy Union Camp, sending other paper stocks up in anticipation of better control over supply and prices in the industry.

Among the beneficiaries was Atlanta-based Georgia-Pacific, which jumped $5.68¾ to $59.62½.

Union Camp rose $16 to $64.93¾, while International Paper lost $1.81¼ to $44.

Now, the writer quickly adds background from analysts:

> Analysts have long viewed the paper and forest products industry as in need of some consolidation, making this latest deal—which comes just as Stone Container completed its merger with Jefferson Smurfit—a welcome piece of news.
>
> Dow Jones News Service[31]

The writer above used only those figures readers need to understand the deal and its immediate impact. Don't plunk numbers into your story just because you have them in your notebook.

A significant figure sometimes can be set off by a typographical device that draws readers' eyes. Note this use of dashes:

> Tokyo—For years, investors have nagged the Toyota Motor Corporation to put its huge pile of cash—some $20 billion at last count—to work.
>
> —Stephanie Strom, *The New York Times*[32]

For many readers, percentage figures aid comprehension more than raw dollar numbers. Two *USA Today* writers recognize that:

> The trade deficit unexpectedly shrank by 12% in September, the government reported Wednesday. But experts say that's only a temporary respite from the rising sea of red ink.
>
> The improvement in the deficit—to $14 billion from $15.9 billion in August—was because of a big jump in aircraft exports that experts do not expect to continue.
>
> —Rich Miller and Beth Belton, *USA Today*[33]

Below, a writer opens with a percentage figure, then quickly uses dollar figures and comparative percentages to put the central thrust—Buffett lost money—in perspective:

> Omaha—Berkshire Hathaway Inc., the investment and insurance company led by Warren E. Buffett, had a 15 percent drop in assets in the third quarter, when the value of some of its biggest holdings plunged.
>
> The value of Berkshire's stock portfolio fell 25 percent in the quarter, to $31.2 billion from $41.6 billion on June 30. That decline exceeded a 10 percent drop in the Standard & Poor's 500-stock index and a 12 percent drop in the Dow Jones industrial average. . . .
>
> Bloomberg News[34]

Even a single percentage figure needs to be compared and characterized, of course. Note how a writer does this three times, in the first graf and second, as well (emphasis added):

> Hong Kong—Hong Kong's unemployment rate rose to *a higher-than expected* 5.3 percent in the August–October period, as businesses continued to cut workers to adjust to a slowing economy.
>
> The August–October jobless rate, *the highest on record,* was *up 5 percent* in the July–September period.
>
> Bridge News[35]

Now, we've discussed how *minimal* use of numbers helps you achieve writing clarity. But we cannot leave this subject without noting that real professionals develop ability to cram into their writing a great many facts and figures but *still* achieve smooth, readable style. Here's how a *Wall Street Journal* pro does that:

> Chicago—Smurfit-Stone Container Corp., formed by the recent merger of two packaging-industry rivals, disclosed plans for restructuring that will cost as many as 3,600 workers their jobs and generate as much as a $350 million fourth-quarter charge.
>
> Smurfit-Stone said the restructuring will include a 17% reduction in its containerboard capacity, as well as a substantial cut in its market pulp capacity.
>
> The company said it expects to reduce employment, which stands at about 36,000 workers, by as much as 10%. The moves, including write-down of the value of idled mill capacity, closure and severance costs and other expenses, will require a charge in the current quarter in the range of $300 million to $350 million, the company said.
>
> —James P. Miller, *The Wall Street Journal*[36]

Summary

- To avoid overwhelming readers with numbers and facts, ruthlessly discard all secondary material your reporting uncovers.
- Write facts and numbers in language and context that explain their importance and characterize their meaning for non-expert readers.
- Pace your writing carefully and deal out facts and numbers quickly enough to maintain readers' interest but not so fast you overwhelm them.
- If you turn to your keyboard not knowing which writing direction to take or which numbers and facts to use, turn off your computer and decide precisely what your story is to be.
- Evaluate numbers and facts for their relevance to your audience, perhaps considering whether they're meaningful to—and understandable by—a neighbor or relative.
- Evaluate numbers also for their timeliness and whether you have them exclusively.
- Proximity, conflict and prominence of events or individuals in the news are other factors to consider in evaluating the newsworthiness of numbers.

- Strive to put facts and numbers in a context readers will understand by characterizing how large and important a number truly is.
- Always go behind the "what" of a story—what happened—and seek the "real what," the event's deeper meaning.
- Behind virtually every number in business news reporting there lurks impact on people—and that is where the news is.
- Even though you'll become expert in business news, you always should turn to authoritative experts in the field you're covering for interpretation and evaluation of facts and numbers.
- Double check the math when you're given numbers and **stay cool** to avoid being swayed by people trying to manipulate the numbers—and you.
- If the meaning of facts and figures is unclear, say so honestly and avoid the trap of thinking a reporter must have answers to all mysteries in the business world.
- Using percentage figures and carefully pacing your writing delivery will help readers sort through your story for its true meaning.

Recommended Reading

A college accounting course would provide valuable experience in handling numbers and understanding their meaning. Also see *How to Read a Financial Report,* an excellent how-to-do-it for non-accounting majors. It's available as Code 10006-0197 from Merrill Lynch Response Center, P.O. Box 20200, New Brunswick NJ 08968-0200.

For style questions, see *The Associated Press Stylebook and Libel Manual,* 6th ed., the standard followed by most newspapers. All major newspapers and magazines have their own stylebooks, of course.

Notes

1. Evaluating news is discussed more fully in Conrad Fink, *Introduction to Professional Newswriting,* 2nd ed. (New York: Longman, 1998) and Conrad Fink and Donald Fink, *Introduction to Magazine Writing* (New York: Macmillan, 1993).

2. "Clinton's Still in There, Fighting," *The Atlanta Constitution,* Oct. 21, 1998, p. A-15.

3. "A Billion, A Trillion, Whatever," national edition, Oct. 18, 1998, Section 4, p. 2.

4. Dispatch for morning papers, Oct. 28, 1998.

5. "Broad Rally Puts Wall Street Back in Record Terrain," national edition, Nov. 24, 1998, p. A-1.

6. "Business Digest," *The New York Times,* national edition, Nov. 24, 1998, p. C-1.

7. "Faith in Stocks: The Dow Hits a Record High," national edition, Nov. 24, 1998, p. A-30.

8. "The Bankers Take Cover," *The Economist,* Sept. 19, 1998, p. 87.

9. Bloomberg News dispatch for morning papers, Oct. 20, 1998.

10. Ibid.

11. "Does Anyone Have a Clue?" July 24, 1995, p. 52.

12. Bruce Upbin, "Too Little and Probably Too Late," *Forbes,* Oct. 5, 1998, p. 70.

13. "Venture Capitalizing," Aug. 12, 1998, p. B-2.

14. Dispatch for morning papers, Oct. 28, 1998.

15. "For Whom the Dell Tolls," Aug. 10, 1998, p. 46.

16. "Cheap Gas to Fuel Holiday Travel," Nov. 19, 1998, p. B-1.

17. "Airlines: The Party's Nearly Over," Aug. 24, 1998, p. 50.

18. "BP, Amoco to Create Oil Giant," Aug. 12, 1998, p. A-1.

19. Dow Jones News Service dispatch for morning papers, Nov. 20, 1998.

20. Lucinda Harper, "Economists Expect 3rd-Quarter Growth to Be More Sluggish Than Anticipated," Aug. 29, 1994, p. A-2.

21. Sara Nathan, "Analysts Doubt Japan's Latest Plan," Nov. 19, 1998, p. B-12.

22. Robert A. Rankin, Knight Ridder Newspapers dispatch for morning papers, Nov. 25, 1998.

23. Dispatch for morning papers, Nov. 18, 1998.

24. Dispatch for morning papers, Nov. 20, 1998.

25. Dispatch for morning papers, Nov. 25, 1998.

26. Dispatch for morning papers, Nov. 19, 1998.

27. "Up From License Plates," Sept. 21, 1998, p. 84.

28. "Land & Space," Nov. 27, 1998, p. D-1.

29. Robert A. Rankin, Knight Ridder Newspapers, op cit.

30. "AOL Sets Accord to Purchase Netscape in a Stock Transaction for $4.3 Billion," Nov. 25, 1998, p. A-3.

31. Dispatch for morning papers, Nov. 25, 1998, p. C-11.

32. "Shouldn't Toyota Stick to Cars?" national edition, Nov. 20, 1998, p. C-1.

33. "Trade Deficit Falls 12% in Sept." Nov. 19, 1998, p. B-3.

34. Dispatch for morning papers, Nov. 16, 1998.

35. Dispatch for morning papers, Nov. 17, 1998.

36. "Smurfit Set to Cut up to 3,600 Jobs, Take Big Charge," Nov. 25, 1998, p. B-13.

Exercises

1. Examine today's lead story on the front page of *The New York Times* business section (or another newspaper your instructor selects). In about 300 words, discuss how the story is structured. Did the writer focus on a central theme and carry through with that? Or did the writer swerve off into distracting side streets? Did the writer ruthlessly evaluate the newsworthiness of numbers and facts presented to the reader? Or, were there irrelevancies?

2. Examine all stories on the first business page of a nearby metropolitan daily (or another newspaper your instructor selects). Were facts and numbers presented

in language and context that explained their importance and characterized their meaning? Or were some facts and numbers left unexplained? Write your views in about 300 words. Give examples.

3. As you know, we evaluate news in terms of what our audience wants and needs. In about 250 words, describe what you think is the most important consumer news story you could write for your college audience. Which facts and numbers would you need for that story? Which sources would you pursue?

4. Consulting experts can establish the importance and magnitude of numbers uncovered in business news reporting. In about 250 words, describe campus experts you would consult for a story on student tuition and fees. List specific questions you would ask officials in interviews and numbers you would seek.

5. Study a nearby metropolitan newspaper (or another newspaper your instructor selects) and select five examples of writing that delivers numbers and facts in a context readers will understand. Are the numbers compared and characterized properly? Also collect five examples of writing that failed to explain the "real what" behind numbers. Analyze your findings in about 300 words.

PART THREE

Writing Forms and Structures

WELL, YOU'VE STUDIED how to evaluate what's news in the business world, how to report it and how to juggle facts and numbers.

Now all you have to do is slam the stuff into a column of newsprint and let the customers work their way through it.

Right? Wrong.

In business news, as in all journalism, you must write well or you'll lose readers *and* thus fail in your reporter's obligation to interpret important events. If you're not read, your message is lost.

In the two chapters of Part Three we'll examine tricks of the writing trade that will help you develop a writing style that's accurate and painstakingly precise, yet lively; that's complete and detailed, yet open and engaging.

Your first responsibility is to develop writing forms and structures that communicate *hard-news* information in a straightforward manner—the Five Ws and How, plus the *real what*. Your mission of communicating clearly through the hard-news story is the subject of Chapter 4, The Straight Stuff: Five Ws and How.

In Chapter 5, Capturing the Human Element, we'll look at writing that emphasizes the human element in business news—writing about people for people.

Throughout, remember that business news writing need not—indeed, *cannot*—be dull and stodgy.

4

The Straight Stuff:
Five Ws and How

IN BUSINESS news, your first mission is to get it right, get it fast and express it clearly.

For that enormous challenge, there is no better writing structure than the good old straight news story—the who, what, where, when and why (plus, of course, how), all sculpted carefully in inverted pyramid form.

This time-proven structure is valuable particularly to reporters inexperienced in the complexities of business news and still struggling to produce accuracy and clarity more than poetic writing. When you're under deadline pressure, find the facts and numbers, quote authoritative sources and write it straight. The poetry can come later.

Reporters for AP, Reuters, Dow Jones, Bloomberg and other news services especially are adept at this writing approach because they work under cruel minute-by-minute deadlines. But daily, weekly and monthly publications have deadlines, too, and at any of them you'll have to write under time pressure. Why? Managing Editor Paul Steiger of *The Wall Street Journal* explains:

> Being first is more important for a business publication than for any other kind of publication. You exist to help people manage and invest their money, and in this day and age, the cliche is true—time is money.[1]

However, in writing the straight stuff of business news you must modify the standard mixture of who said or did what, when, where and why by adding an ***explanatory dimension*** to help readers understand what's happening.

Arthur Levitt, chairman of the Securities and Exchange Commission, a federal regulatory body, illustrates readers' needs and your challenge: A "financial literacy crisis" exists in the United States, he says, and even though, for example, 35 million households (more than one in three of all households) invest *trillions* of dollars in mutual funds, "too many people don't know how to choose a financial investment."[2]

Let's look at how you can help readers make those dollars-and-cents decisions so important to their lives. Your tools include writing structures that answer the obvious Five W and How questions that *all* news stories must answer but also go beyond that and into business news specifics.

Stir New Chemistry From Old Elements

Look back just a few years at news writing and you'll see many writers actually reduced the traditional Five Ws and How to just four elements—who, what, where and when. The *why* and *how* went unexplained in many stories.

In business news, you must ensure the *why* and *how* are in your writing and, further, you must modify the traditional formula to include the *real what,* an extra dimension of explanation of what really happened and what it really means.

That, in turn, requires modifying the traditional inverted pyramid structure which, of course, involves stuffing (but gently!) the Five Ws and How into the lead graf, then adding detail in ever-descending order of priority.

Note below how a Bloomberg News writer does that in laying out details of a complex event, yet achieving near at-a-glance reading comprehension. The explanatory dimensions—*the real what*—are in italics:

> Bay City, Mich.—Dow Corning Corp. yesterday agreed to pay $3.2 billion to women who are suing over its silicone breast implants and $1.3 billion to commercial creditors *in its plan to emerge from three years in bankruptcy court.*
>
> The company filed its first joint plan with the women's attorneys four months after reaching an agreement in principle with the group.
>
> The plan, one of the largest public health settlements, *moves hundreds of thousands of women closer to getting money* to have implants removed or for the treatment of serious diseases, such as lupus, that they say were caused by the implants. The settlement *ends months of negotiations* between the company and plaintiffs' lawyers.
>
> *"Women could get payments by the end of 1999,"* said Dow Corning attorney Barbara Houser.

Let's examine the story above.

The inverted pyramid structure permits an editor to chop the Bloomberg News dispatch from the bottom and fit it into virtually any available space. On deadline, an editor even could plug that first graf alone into a column of business briefs and at least alert readers to the settlement and its magnitude.

That is, you don't write this type of story as a tightly crafted stand-alone piece of 600 poetic words that cannot be edited down. Rather, you stack compellingly important facts and numbers in ***descending order of priority*** —crucial facts come first, secondary facts follow.

Short, punchy sentences highlight the most important facts and numbers and thus aid reader comprehension. Bloomberg's writer holds the lead graf to 36 words. Subsequent sentences average 22.5.

Did Shakespeare write longer and more beautifully? Yes. Is he easier to understand quickly? No.

Stakeholders are served quickly in the Bloomberg story—investors in Dow Corning, investors in its competitors, women involved in the lawsuits, women concerned about implants.

Before touching your keyboard, consider who among your readers have stakes in the outcome. Quickly answer their obvious question: What impact does this event have on me?

Add important elaboration. In seven grafs that follow the four reproduced above, Bloomberg's writer elaborates on the size of the settlement ("second-largest public health settlement"), how and when details will be distributed among stakeholders (170,000 women want their implants removed) and how Dow Corning's creditors will be paid.

Always insert the numbers. As in all business news, readers of the Dow Corning story need specific numbers. Bloomberg's writer inserts them in four carefully crafted grafs reproduced below. Note how you can read and digest without being overwhelmed.

> Midland, Mich.–based Dow Corning is a joint venture of Corning Inc. and Dow Chemical Co. The shares of Midland-based Dow Chemical closed at 98⁹⁄₁₆, down 2¼, while Corning, N.Y.–based Corning dipped to 38¾, down ¾.
>
> The plan would give women with various ailments about 20 percent more than women got from manufacturers in other mass settlements. Other former implant makers, including Bristol-Myers Squibb Co. and Minnesota Mining & Manufacturing Co., settled in Alabama with about 88 percent of U.S. women with claims against them.
>
> The Dow Corning plan will be funded over 16 years, with $1 billion coming in the first year. The present value of the fund is $2.35 billion.
>
> Women would get as much as $250,000 for the most serious illnesses. They could get $2,000 with no claim, $5,000 for simple removal of the implants, and $20,000 for a rupture with no disease.
>
> Bloomberg News[3]

| Box 4-1 | Wordsmiths at Work |

Business news writers deal in dull subjects and write dully? No way. Look at these leads:

> The Dow Jones industrial average took center stage Friday, with much of Wall Street and millions of stock investors expecting to watch "The Dow 10,000 Show." But it just didn't play in Peoria.
> One of the old stalwarts of the Dow, Peoria, Ill.–based Caterpillar Inc. turned in a sorry earnings performance Friday, which took its stock down and the blue chip index with it. . . .
>
> —Bill Deener, "Dow Takes a Detour," *The Dallas Morning News,*
> March 13, 1999, p. F-1

☙

> Gothenburg, Sweden—Volvo car workers are nervous about what life will be like under their new owner, Ford Motor Co. After all, they might lose their badminton courts.
>
> —Almar Latour, "Workplace," *The Wall Street Journal,* March 3,
> 1999, p. B-1

☙

> The Dow Jones industrial average floats near 10,000. Jobs are plentiful. Wages are rising. Spending is everywhere. The economy booms, month after month. And nothing seems to shake the public sense of prosperity. So why are the oracles of the economy talking like Nervous Nellies?
>
> —Louis Uchitelle, "The Stronger It Gets, the Sweatier the Palms,"
> *The New York Times,* March 21, 1999, Section 4, p. 1

☙

> In 1946, Ulysses "Blackie" Auger Sr. opened the venerable Blackie's House of Beef in the heart of Washington's old West End. Today, next door to this enduring magnet for the carnivore, a family descendant is feeding on a fat new market in a fast new age.
> It's the market for high-speed Internet service, specifically for hotel guests and apartment dwellers. Pursuing it are Blackie's son Ulysses G. Auger II and the company he heads, CAIS Internet. . . .
>
> —Mark Leibovich, "Techway," *The Washington Post,* Washington
> Business section, p. 5

Strive for Leads That Grab

Yes, the straightforward hard-news story has the basic mission of informing. ***But to fulfill that mission it must be read.*** So you should strive to top any story, whatever its subject, with a nicely crafted lead that grabs readers.

That may overstate the lead's importance. But not by much. Consider: Your readers, on average, spend under 30 minutes in the ***entire newspaper,*** so you're in fierce competition for their attention. Your lead must grab those roving eyes or they'll move elsewhere.

In the hard-news story form, your best "grabber" often is the ***single-element lead*** because it is so easily and quickly understood.

Note how a *Boston Globe* writer focuses a 29-word lead on a single element (emphasis added):

> A large New Orleans ***utility has emerged as the leading candidate*** to purchase the Pilgrim nuclear power plant from BEC Energy, according to sources familiar with the ongoing talks.
>
> —Ross Kerber, *The Boston Globe*[4]

But, that single-element lead is so one dimensional that it's almost flat, without substance. With care, you can create a ***double-element*** lead, expanding your wordage a bit and offering readers more substance. Reuters does that in 40 words(emphasis added):

> New York—ABC technical workers ***filed an unfair labor practice charge*** against the TV and radio network yesterday for locking them out of their jobs, ***and they said prominent politicians and at least one Hollywood celebrity were honoring their picket lines.***
>
> Reuters[5]

Expanding to a ***three-element*** lead requires great writing care ***and*** holding wordage to a minimum nevertheless. AP does that in just 35 words (emphasis added):

> New York—***Stocks rose yesterday*** as a ***strong election showing*** by Democrats ***raised expectations*** that impeachment efforts will run out of steam and enable President Clinton to focus on the U.S. economy and the global financial crisis.
>
> The Associated Press[6]

Be certain to read your writing aloud, particularly if you expand beyond single-element leads. If you run out of breath half way through the first graf, you'll know your writing is starting to sprawl. The solution often is simple: plunk in a period and create a ***two-sentence lead.*** Here is a fine example:

> New York (AP)—For folks who shy away from complex analyses, one of the best barometers of the overall economy is the health of residential housing. Last week that industry registered a setback, however slight.
>
> The Associated Press[7]

Note in the example above that those two sentences number 23 and 9 words, respectively. Short, punchy sentences are a must in this type of hard-news writing. Look what happens in the following example, which bloats up to 45 words and certainly could use at least one more period.

Attorney General Scott Harshbarger's office said yesterday it was not swayed by Insurance Commissioner Linda Ruthardt's explanation of a private meeting with an auto insurance industry official, but the office postponed any formal action on its bid to oust her from the 1999 rate hearings.

The Boston Globe[8]

Timeliness Is Key

Fast delivery of operative information is a basic mission of the straightforward hard-news business story (and, indeed, of most journalism).

Note, for example, that all but two illustrations of leads cited in the previous section are written for morning newspapers and carry a "yesterday" time element. One exception is New Orleans utility "has emerged" and the other a Sunday sum-up (housing industry "last week"). All those leads were written immediately on spot-news developments and delivered quickly to readers.

Sometimes, however, even the most alert reporters stumble on news a little late. Note how two pros in that situation adroitly handle a ***nine-day-old*** time element in a story published on September 23 about a September 14 event:

Polaroid Corp., its stock price reeling from a disappointing first half, has shuffled its management team and merged its big consumer- and commercial-imaging divisions.

The reorganization, announced in a Sept. 14 internal Polaroid memo, removes Carole J. Uhrich, one of corporate America's highest-ranking women, from the job she has held since March 1997 as head of commercial imaging, a division with sales of just under $1 billion last year. Instead . . .

—Laura Johannes and Joann S. Lublin, *The Wall Street Journal*[9]

With the "has shuffled" neutral time element in their first graf, the two pros above make a point: old news is still new news if your readers don't yet know it!

But, no need to rub your readers' noses in an old time element in your lead. You're not cheating (although you may be ***fudging*** just a wee bit) if you strive for freshness in your lead by going to present tense and dropping the "old" time element to your second graf.

It is essential, however, that somewhere in your story you honestly lay out the chronology of events. Their timing can be of great significance to readers. Investors often move ***within seconds*** of learning important news. Disguising your lateness and enticing them to move ***now*** on old news can be for them an investment disaster and for you a journalistic felony.

Basic Decision: Precision or General Lead?

Hard-news leads fall broadly into two categories: general explanatory leads or fact-filled precision leads.

As in so much business news writing, which to write must depend on two factors: type of information you must communicate and your audience's capabilities to absorb it.

In the following, obviously aimed at a wide reading audience, a Reuters writer uses a **general explanatory lead** rich in **why** and **real-what** analysis. Imagine how impenetrable this lead would be to non-expert readers if jammed full of all those facts and figures from the second graf!

> Detroit—General Motors Corp. and Ford Motor Co. yesterday reported higher U.S. sales of light vehicles in October as consumers shrugged off economic uncertainty and pushed the industry's growth to one of its highest rates this year.
>
> Auto makers sold 1,371,981 cars and light trucks in October, a 9.8 percent gain from a year ago. The seasonally adjusted annual sales rate hit 16.6 million units—compared with 14.8 million in October 1997 and 15.6 million in September.
>
> Reuters[10]

For hard-core investors (who read numbers as smoothly as you eat ice cream), *The Wall Street Journal* uses a fact-filled **precision lead** that moves without pause into a second graf jammed with figures:

> Fort Lauderdale, Fla.—Sports Authority Inc., hammered by weak same-store sales and pressure on margins, reported a net loss of $64.9 million, or $2.04 a share, for the fiscal third quarter.
>
> The company said the results included a charge of $54.6 million, or $1.72 a diluted share, related to the closing of 18 stores, asset impairments, write-downs, and other charges. Excluding the charge, the company had a loss of $10.2 million, or 32 cents a share.
>
> *The Wall Street Journal*[11]

(Incidentally, skip over those references in the example above to "diluted share" and excluded charges. We'll get to them in a later chapter.)

If you're unsure on precision versus general, write a compromise approach. A *Columbus (Ga.) Ledger-Enquirer* writer does that by using a single number for a semi-general lead graf and reserving others for a jam-packed precision second graf:

> Aflac Inc.'s third-quarter profits rose 12 percent, beating Wall Street estimates, as the Columbus-based supplemental insurer continued to fight off the effects of a sputtering Japanese economy.
>
> Profits rose to $107.6 million, or 39 cents a share, from $96.1 million, or 34 cents, a year ago. Wall Street analysts had predicted that Aflac would report earnings of 37 cents in the third quarter, according to a survey by First Call, a Boston-based investment research firm.
>
> —Greg Groelier, *The Columbus Ledger-Enquirer*[12]

Readability is a primary goal in leads, and your decision on which form to use must take that into account. Write a lead, read it aloud, edit or rewrite—and don't let it go until you're satisfied readers can grasp it easily.

Find the Look-Ahead Angle

Want to be the best-read reporter on your newspaper? Want readers to flock to your byline?

If so, build a reputation for reporting the *look-ahead angle*—reporting *today* the news that *tomorrow* will move money, markets and lives. The business world moves on news, and enormous audiences are yours if you deliver it first.

WARNING: Getting it *right but late* is more important than getting it *first but wrong.* So, don't let this discussion turn you from reporter into crystal-ball gazer. Journalism's junkyards are filled with bylines of reporters who tried to predict events, tried to get too far ahead of the facts.

Below is a hard-news lead by two *Wall Street Journal* reporters who *stuck with facts* but were first in putting them together in a meaningful look-ahead way for readers. (As background, "insiders" are people working in industries and thus equipped with intimate knowledge of how profitable their industries likely will be. When "insiders" buy shares in their own companies that signals strength and "outside" investors often plunge in, too.)

Industry insiders in aerospace and defense have been snapping up the beleaguered shares of their own companies.

The buying picked up about six weeks ago and accelerated in August, according to Bob Babele, president of insider-data tracker CDA/Investnet, Rockville, MD. A year ago, he notes, defense industry executives and directors ranked third in selling their companies shares. Now, their selling has all but dried up.

Insiders at companies as diverse as aerospace leader Boeing to diversified-electrical-equipment conglomerate Rockwell International have been buying their own shares. There have also been purchases at United Technologies, Howmet International, Loral Space & Communications and Moog, which makes precision-control components and systems for commercial and military aircraft.

Note two factors in the above:

1. The lead is superbly crafted—short (just 17 words!) and tightly focused on the central point (insiders are buying).
2. The authors quickly cite an *authoritative source.* Readers, who may plunge into the market on the story, deserve to know the source of a look-ahead angle.

Now, the authors expand on what their source says **and cite other balancing sources:**

> "I think this collective action reflects an attitude that they sense the worst may be over for defense-budget cuts in the U.S.," says Mr. Gabele. "When we see this kind of consensus," he adds, "we get the feeling that something is going to improve in the industry involved."
>
> But industry analysts say there are other reasons for the recent buying surge. "There is some increased [defense] spending that may occur," says Goldman Sachs aerospace/defense-industry analyst Howard Rubel, but "not so much that it's likely to lift revenue beyond a few percentage points."
>
> —Laura Sanders Egodigwe and Frederic M. Biddle,
> *The Wall Street Journal*[13]

In the look-ahead example below, a writer positions his readers to **decide for themselves** the likely outcome of a forthcoming event. Note the effort to provide background until the fourth graf where the writer mentions—very carefully— what the outcome might be (emphasis added):

> As Federal Reserve officials meet today to decide whether another cut in short-term interest rates is needed, they will be confronted with unusual crosscurrents of strength and weakness swirling through the U.S. economy.
>
> On the side of strength, the Commerce Department reported Friday that retail sales rose strongly last month as consumers snapped up new cars and light trucks. Sales were so strong that forecasters said the economy may grow faster than previously expected—at a healthy pace of 3 percent to 4 percent—in the final three months of the year, with consumers egged on by high and rising stock prices.
>
> But Fed Chairman Alan Greenspan remains concerned that other forces at work could sap the economy's strength months from now. On the side of weakness, the forces include turmoil in parts of the world's financial markets, a slump in manufacturing, smaller monthly gains in payroll employment, rising trade deficits and lingering consumer uncertainty about the outlook. A few economists even predict a recession will hit the United States next year.
>
> The risk of a downturn is why **many, but by no means all, financial analysts expect Greenspan and his colleagues will decide today to essentially buy an insurance policy and reduce short-term interest rates by another quarter-percentage point.**
>
> —John M. Berry, *The Washington Post*[14]

Note below how the writer ups the ante on the look-ahead angle with an "is expected" lead that virtually predicts an outcome.

> The Securities and Exchange Commission is expected to vote today to clarify its professional-misconduct rules for accountants who audit corporate financial statements.
>
> —Elizabeth MacDonald, *The Wall Street Journal*[15]

In hundreds of words that follow, writer MacDonald cites sources within the SEC—including the chairman—to back up her lead. But the bottom line is inescapable: It is the ***reporter*** who makes the "is expected" prediction. That's dangerous stuff, particularly for business news beginners.

Remember that ***billions*** of dollars can move on the news you report. You're better off quoting authoritative sources—by name—on what ***they*** expect.

Remember the "Housekeeping" or "Nut" Graf

An effective device for communicating the ***real what***—the real meaning—of an event is a single, tightly written graf of explanation plunked into your story.

Call it the "housekeeping" or "nut" graf, its mission is to cut through the often confusing details of a hard-news story and present, quickly and precisely, its meaning.

For example, there's a shake-up at Universal Studios, and two *Washington Post* reporters lead their story this way:

> The top executive of ailing Universal Studios resigned yesterday in a shake-up of the creator of such recent movie flops as "Primary Colors" and "Fear and Loathing in Las Vegas."
>
> Universal's Chairman and Chief Executive, Frank Biondi Jr., quit under pressure from his boss, Edgar Bronfman Jr., who heads Universal's parent company, Seagram Co. Bronfman has been reshaping Seagram, the Montreal-based liquor company founded by his grandfather, into a movie, music and theme park giant over the past three years.

Now, what does all that mean for Universal? The *Post* writers explain in this "housekeeping" graf (emphasis added):

> The departure of Biondi ***gives Bronfman, 43, more direct control of Universal's entertainment operations.*** Biondi, one of the most experienced executives in the entertainment industry, joined Universal just two years ago after being forced out of the No. 2 job at another entertainment giant, Viacom Inc.
>
> —Paul Farhi and Sharon Waxman, *The Washington Post*[16]

Judging the complexity of material you're covering and your audience's ability to absorb it, you must decide where in your story to insert the "nut" graf. In the story above, the *Post* writers held it to third graf position. In the story below, the "nut" graf is inserted in ***second-graf*** position. Guess why.

> Frankfurt—In the most coordinated action yet toward European monetary union, 11 nations simultaneously cut their interest rates today to a nearly uniform low level.
>
> The move came a month before the nations adopt the euro as a single currency and marked a drastic shift in policy. As recently as two months ago, European central bankers had adamantly resisted demands from polit-

ical leaders to lower rates because they were intent on establishing the credibility of the euro and the fledgling European Central Bank in world markets.

—Edmund L. Andrews, *The New York Times*[17]

In the story above, the writer obviously considered several factors when deciding to insert the ***real what*** in such a high position: The monetary union's move was "drastic," and that required immediate explanation. Furthermore, for American readers, a single currency in Europe was a relatively new concept. And, frankly, the whole matter was mighty complicated stuff. Thus the second-graf position for "nut" information.

Incidentally, deeper in the story, in fifth-graf position, the writer inserts ***comparatives:*** "When the dust settled," he wrote, all 11 European nations but Italy had reduced their key interest rate to 3 percent, and the comparable U.S. rate "is now 4.75 percent."

Ah, now I understand!

Insert high any housekeeping detail that will alert readers that you are quoting sources with vested interests in the news and that the information thus might be skewed. This is important especially when you're quoting from reports or surveys.

For example, *The Washington Post* reports consumer commerce on the Internet is growing rapidly. Great news for Internet retailers, right? Yes, and the *Post* writer points out, ***in the first graf,*** that the good news comes from the retailers themselves (emphasis added):

> Consumer commerce on the Internet is growing by more than 200 percent annually, even though most people online still are not making purchases, ***according to a report released yesterday by an Internet retailer's association.***
>
> —Leslie Walker, *The Washington Post*[18]

A noncontroversial report gets second-graf attribution in the story below (emphasis added):

> Washington—Manufacturing weakened in the United States in September for a fourth consecutive month, as exports slumped, while prices paid by industrial companies fell to the lowest level in almost half a century.
> ***The National Association of Purchasing Management said today that . . .***
>
> Bloomberg News[19]

Now, read the following two grafs carefully. When you're finished I'm going to ask you two questions.

> For years, most women have assumed that once they smashed through the glass ceiling, they would obtain the ultimate prize: parity in pay. They were wrong.

A study released yesterday by Catalyst, a New York women's research group, reported that even when women reach the top of the corporate hierarchy, they earn less than male colleagues with the same responsibilities and skills.

—Diana E. Lewis, *The Boston Globe*[20]

Questions:

- Should the *Globe* story above have contained a "nut" graf on what the Catalyst agenda is and who runs it? (The story didn't contain that essential housekeeping detail.)
- Did the writer err in stating she knows what "most" women assumed and in flatly stating, "They were wrong"?

Strengthen Your Writing With Quotes

Search for quotes. Find them, hold them, cherish them.

Quotes from the right people on the right subject do two things for a hard-news story:

1. They lend precision, authority, **believability.**
2. They add flavor, color and interest to stories that, frankly, can be dry and colorless.

For example, would a *Forbes* writer add authority and believability to a story on McDonald's Corp., by simply stating that founder Ray A. Kroc was competitive? Yes, but not much.

Now look at what Dyan Machan adds with a quote:

Referring to competition, Kroc once said, "If I saw a competitor drowning I'd put a live fire hose in his mouth."

—Dyan Machan, *Forbes*[21]

Note the color (and authoritative explanation) added by a third-graf quote in an otherwise standard Wall Street story:

"We saw major carnage in the market Monday," said Alfred Goldman, director of market analysis at A.G. Edwards & Sons Inc. in St. Louis. "But we wore out the sellers, and now the buyers are coming back."

San Francisco Chronicle[22]

Even a partial quote can do the job. For example, there is speculation for weeks that a privately owned investment bank will go public (sell shares on the public markets) and that the firm's partners are divided over whether to do it. The bank announces its decision, and Dow Jones News Service uses a partial quote for precision:

New York—Partners at Goldman & Sachs & Co. "overwhelmingly approved" a plan to take the company public, the investment bank said yesterday.

The partnership vote follows a decision in June by the firm's six-member executive committee to pursue an initial public offering, after an informal vote by its 190 partners.

Dow Jones News Service[23]

Write to Be Read

Want to be read? Write well.

Write to entice readers, to lure them in, to enliven the hard-news material you are communicating.

Can you *not* want to read stories with leads like these:

The U.S. Patent and Trademark Office's search for a huge new Northern Virginia headquarters has gotten tangled up in a shower curtain.

—Maryann Haggerty, *The Washington Post*[24]

Nearly all consumer electronics products in U.S. homes will go on ticking without taking a licking from the millennium bug, an industry leader assured a congressional panel Thursday.

—Andrew J. Glass, Cox Newspapers[25]

On July 15, large stocks started to fall. On Oct. 15, small stocks started to rise. Is it a sucker's rally? Bear trap? Dead-cat bounce?

Or long overdue?

—Joseph N. DiStefano, *The Philadelphia Inquirer*[26]

Boeing blues

U.S. markets lost altitude early Wednesday as investors digested the implications of Boeing's layoff announcement. Shortly after the opening bell the Dow Jones industrial average sank more than 100 points.

CNNfn[27]

Summary

- Your basic mission in business news is to get the story right, get it fast, express it clearly.
- For that, no writing structure is better than the inverted pyramid with its who, what, where, when, why and how.
- However you owe readers an extra explanatory dimension to help them understand the complex news you're laying before them.

- Go beneath the standard ***what*** to write clearly the ***real what***—what an event really means.
- Short, punchy sentences aid reader comprehension.
- Ensure your stories enlighten and serve ***stakeholders,*** those whose lives will feel the impact of events.
- Single-element leads are effective because your readers can understand easily and quickly your principal thrust.
- Double-element leads, focusing on two related developments, offer readers more substance than single-element intros.
- Expanding to three-element leads requires great writing care and holding wordage to a minimum nevertheless.
- Timeliness—getting it now, writing it now—is crucial in business news because readers make decisions within seconds of learning important news.
- One basic decision you must make is whether to write general or explanatory leads or fact-filled precision leads.
- Find the look-ahead angle, today's news that will move markets tomorrow, and readers will flock to your byline.
- Always include a "housekeeping" or "nut" graf that explains the meaning of a hard-news story.
- Search for strong, colorful quotes that lend precision, authority, believability to your writing.
- Want to be read? Write well. Write to entice readers, to lure them in, to enliven hard-news material.

Recommended Reading

For examples of straightforward and clear hard-news writing see Dow Jones, AP, Reuters and Bloomberg News dispatches in the business sections of major metropolitan newspapers. Disciplined reading and analysis of those dispatches can push forward your writing skill.

If you're rusty on the elements of strong hard-news writing, see Rene J. Cappon, *The Word,* 2nd ed. (New York: The Associated Press, 1991); William Strunk, Jr., and E.B. White, *The Elements of Style,* 3rd ed. (New York: Macmillan Publishing Co., Inc., 1979); James J. Kilpatrick, *The Writer's Art* (Kansas City, Mo: Andrews, McMeel & Parker, 1984); and one of my old and all-time favorites, Brier and Heyn, *Writing for Newspapers and News Services* (New York: Funk & Wagnalls, 1969).

Notes

1. David Shaw, "The Pride and Perils of Fast Reporting," *The Los Angeles Times,* Aug. 5, 1998, p. A-1.
2. Dow Jones News Service, dispatch for morning papers, Dec. 4, 1998.
3. Dispatch for morning papers, Nov. 10, 1998.

4. "Pilgrim Plant Sale Seen Near," Nov. 5, 1998, p. C-1.

5. Dispatch for morning papers, Nov. 6, 1998.

6. Dispatch for morning papers, Nov. 5, 1998.

7. Dispatch for Sunday, Oct. 25, 1998.

8. Bruce Mohl, "Harshbarger Delays Action Against Ruthardt Over Rate Hearings," Nov. 10, 1998, p. D-5.

9. "Polaroid Revamps Management Team, Shifting Roles of Two Top Executives," Sept. 23, 1998, p. B-9.

10. Dispatch for morning papers, Nov. 5, 1998.

11. "Sports Authority Posts a Loss of $64.9 Million on Soft Sales, Margins," Nov. 25, 1998, p. B-17.

12. "Aflac Reports 12 Percent Gain in Profits," Oct. 27, 1998, p. C-8.

13. "Defending Their Own Shares, Aerospace Insiders Are Buying," Sept. 23, 1998, p. C-1.

14. "Fed Must Digest Mixed Signals," Sept. 17, 1998, p. C-9.

15. "SEC to Clarify Misconduct by Accountants," Sept. 23, 1998, p. A-8.

16. "Universal Studios Chief Resigns," Nov. 17, 1998, p. C-11.

17. "European Banks, Acting in Unison, Cut Interest Rate," Sept. 4, 1998, p. A-1.

18. "Internet Retail Sales Rising Sharply," Nov. 18, 1998, p. C-11.

19. Dispatch for morning papers, Oct. 2, 1998.

20. "Even at Top, Women Seen Earning Less Than Men," Nov. 10, 1998, p. D-1.

21. "Polishing the Golden Arches," June 15, 1998, p. 42.

22. AP dispatch for morning papers, Sept. 2, 1998.

23. Dispatch for morning papers, Aug. 11, 1998.

24. "Battle Heating Up for Patent Office Space," Sept. 25, 1998, p. F-1.

25. Dispatch for morning papers, Sept. 25, 1998.

26. "Making the Case for Small Caps," Nov. 3, 1998, p. E-1.

27. Dispatch for Dec. 2, 1998.

Exercises

1. Study three examples of news service copy (from AP, Reuters, Dow Jones or Bloomberg) published in today's *New York Times* (or another newspaper your instructor designates). In about 300 words, discuss weaknesses and strengths of the writing styles displayed in that copy. Is the copy clear and easily digested? Why?

2. Study the lead story in today's *Wall Street Journal* (or another newspaper your instructor designates) and discuss, in about 300 words, whether the writer serves all **stakeholders** whose lives will be affected by events reported in the story. Does the story explain **how** they will be affected?

3. Find two examples of double-element or three-element leads in the business section of your local newspaper (or another newspaper your instructor designates). Are the leads clear, concise and easily understood? Rewrite them to meet **your** standard of good journalism.

4. Study a general explanatory lead in today's *Wall Street Journal* (or another newspaper your instructor designates). Rewrite it into a fact-filled precision lead that is clear, understandable and concise.

5. Study a look-ahead angle in a story in today's *Wall Street Journal* and, in about 200 words, discuss (a) whether the story gives readers news they can make business decisions on immediately, (b) whether the look-ahead angle is attributed to authoritative sources and (c) whether you think the writer exceeded the standards of cautious journalism in predicting an "is expected" outcome.

5

Capturing the
Human Element

THE ***human element*** was nearly invisible in Chapter 4's focus on accurately reporting hard-news facts and numbers clearly and objectively.

Of course, such straightforward, if dehumanized, writing is what readers need when, for example, you report a spot-news break affecting General Motors, and they wonder whether to buy or sell GM stock. As they dial their brokers it matters little whether GM's chairman is short, tall, usually smiling or usually gruff.

After you interview a banker, your readers wonder mostly whether their mortgage interest rates will rise or fall, not whether the banker is a dapper dresser or grows tulips on weekends.

Now, however, we turn to reporting and writing that type of human detail, and for good reason:

FIRST, banks and corporations don't make business decisions or set policies that will affect our lives. People managing those institutions do. So, who those people are is of compelling interest to your readers. And, yes, readers need to know how those decision-makers dress, walk and talk—***if those details signal how our lives will be affected.***

SECOND, and simply put, people are interested in other people. Report the human element in business, economic and financial news and you'll increase tremendously your chances of attracting readers and thus fulfilling your mission of communicating important news.

In Chapter 5, we'll discuss reporting techniques and story structures you can use to find and tell the human element.

Note: Although we of course sometimes write about people just because they're interesting we're not discussing here peeping-Tom journalistic voyeurism. Rather, we're after ways to highlight the human factor as it affects business institutions, economic and financial policies and, thus, our readers' lives.

Why People Are News

One reporter calls it the "Greenspan effect"—the power of one man to move **billions** of dollars with a single remark or, even, by saying nothing.

Greenspan, of course, is Alan Greenspan, chairman of the U.S. Federal Reserve throughout the 1990s and, as such, one of the most powerful persons in the world of business, economics and finance.

Gretchen Morgenson of *The New York Times* coined "Greenspan effect" in writing one day about what Greenspan **didn't** say:

> When Alan Greenspan talks, the market listens. And most of the time it doesn't like what it hears.
>
> In the last two years, on 31 occasions, the Federal Reserve chairman has testified before Congress on a variety of matters. On 21 of those dates, almost 70 percent of the time, the market fell immediately after his testimony.
>
> Make that 22. Yesterday, the Dow Jones industrial average dropped by 216.01 points, a loss of 2.67 percent. It was the first full day of trading after Mr. Greenspan's testimony on Wednesday, in which he told the House Banking Committee that there was no coordinated effort among the world's central banks to cut interest rates.
>
> Investors were clearly disappointed that Mr. Greenspan presented no solutions to the economic problems that have terrified many of the world's markets. . . .

In the story above, writer Morgenson adds that tracking what happens to stocks after the Fed chairman's testimony—"what might be called the Greenspan effect"—is virtually a cottage industry. She quotes one investment advisor as saying:

> "It seems to be his personality that he has been able to talk down the market with words rather than action. But it is funny how the market and investors hear what they want to hear in the words that cross his lips."
>
> —Gretchen Morgenson, *The New York Times*[1]

Is Alan Greenspan, **fiscal policy-maker,** the mover of billions of dollars, news? You bet.

Does that make Alan Greenspan, **the man,** news? Yes, again, and it's news also how he walks, talks, smiles or scowls, and what he does on weekends.

By any legal measurement, Greenspan is a public official and figure, wide open to press scrutiny. By any journalistic measurement, he—and powerful individuals like him—are *hot* news.

Whether you write for a campus paper, a small-town daily or *The New York Times,* you'll encounter powerful individuals whose words and actions make things go, make dollars move. And your readers will have a right and need to know about those individuals.

Frequently, the human element will explode on your news scene with dramatic impact and you will write about it with hard-news urgency and economy of wordage:

> Shares of Electronic Data Systems rose $2.87½ to $43.62½ Friday on expectations its new boss will shake up the sleepy computer services company and restore shareholder value.
>
> Electronic Data Systems announced Thursday after the market closed that Richard Brown, the chief executive of Cable & Wireless, will be its new chairman and chief executive. . . .
>
> On Friday, four of the 22 analysts covering the company upgraded the stock. . . . Three of the analysts raised their rating to a "buy" from a "hold" and the fourth to a "strong buy" from "hold."
>
> Dow Jones News Service[2]

Sometimes, you'll be able to take an in-depth look at the human element. Luckily, you have fascinating writing vehicles for that.

The Profile

Successful profiles are written about many things—a town, a cat, a hurricane. Such profiles can be entertaining and, in their own way, informative.

But we'll stick here to profiles of *individuals* that illuminate for readers of business news how *institutions* work and who makes them work.

Below, a writer uses the human factor to pull you into what really is a profile of . . . well, read on, then *you* decide what is being profiled:

> Washington—Just before 9 on Tuesday morning, if tradition holds, Alan Greenspan will stride through a doorway behind the desk in his private office and into the Federal Reserve's ornate board room. He will take his seat at the head of the 27-foot-long mahogany and granite table and then, for the 91st time in his 11 years as chairman of the central bank, call to order a meeting of the Federal Open Market Committee, the group that sets interest rate policy.
>
> The process is almost ritualistic. But with much of the world reeling from the financial shocks set off last year in Asia, and with the markets and the economy at home in flux, the situation confronting Mr. Greenspan and his colleagues these days is anything but predictable.
>
> Mr. Greenspan ascended to icon status through his success at the monumental, but well-defined, task of extinguishing inflation. The question now is

whether he can guide policy as successfully through a period in which both the economy and the threats to it are changing with blinding speed. . . .

The profile's direction now is clear:

- Seize reader attention by sketching briefly a man (Greenspan striding) and positioning him where momentous decisions are made, at *a 27-foot-long mahogany and granite table!*
- But quickly relate that to how an institution works (the Fed's "almost ritualistic" process).
- Zero in on how the man's thinking is important, then *tie the profile to a timely event* (next Tuesday's decision on interest rates).

For hundreds of words, the writer moves ahead on Greenspan's policies, the markets, his critics, the Fed, but aside from noting that Greenspan is 72, the author gives us no details on the man himself. Then this:

He is the ultimate economic wonk, immersing himself in official statistics, raw data, Wall Street numbers and anecdotal information passed along to him directly or indirectly by business executives. His briefcase is often full of trade publications like Aviation Week.

He rarely gets out to factory floors or fast-food kitchens, and other than occasional visits with labor leaders, rarely seems to interact much with anyone but the elites in government, economics, business and finance.

But he can draw on the 30 years he spent as a consultant advising a wide range of industries for a sense of what all those arcane facts and statistics mean in the real world.

For another hundred words or so, the writer expands on what is at stake (continued U.S. business expansion), and then this:

Just what is Mr. Greenspan thinking amid the swirl? He rarely answers questions directly, as anyone who tries to parse his public comments soon discovers. So economists, investors and politicians have been trying to read his mind since he was appointed to replace Paul A. Volcker as the Fed chairman in 1987. They have learned to pick up any major shifts in policy and, often, to anticipate the next interest rate move. Despite signs of continued economic strength, the guessing now is that Mr. Greenspan will trim rates by a quarter-point on Tuesday, following two cuts earlier this fall, to make sure that a gradual slowdown does not become a recession.

That illuminates Greenspan's work habits and the life experience his thinking presumably draws upon—and that essentially is the thrust of this major profile, which runs to thousands of words.

Virtually the only concession to traditional descriptive profile writing is this:

A guest at a party a few months ago on the South Lawn of the White House remembers seeing Mr. Greenspan and his wife, Andrea Mitchell, the

NBC News correspondent, standing not far from President Clinton. Mr. Clinton happily posed for pictures; Ms. Mitchell chatted with friends. Mr. Greenspan stood awkwardly, as if dreading the possibility that someone would approach to ask if it was a good time to refinance.

Yet Mr. Greenspan's dour public face is to some degree a mask. Born in New York in 1926, he was a baseball fan and a talented musician; after attending the Juilliard School, he signed on with a swing band and toured the country playing saxophone before receiving an economics degree at New York University. . . .

—Richard W. Stevenson, *The New York Times*[3]

In business news, that is, a profile can succeed even if you insert only minimal "color" detail normally associated with writing about an individual.

Or, your profile can focus intently on the individual, as does *The Wall Street Journal:*

> Seated in the dining room of the Ritz-Carlton Hotel in Cleveland, wearing a custom-made suit and a diamond ring the size of a nickel, T.D. Jakes looks every inch the celebrity. And he is as impressed with himself as anyone. "If I go to Hollywood or to Beverly Hills," he says proudly, "billion-dollar actresses will know me."
>
> Mr. Jakes is not a rock star or a politician, but a country preacher from West Virginia who, at 41 years old, is running a multimillion-dollar religious-media empire. His message has struck a vein so rich that mainstream companies are courting him with big deals. Last year, he signed a $1.8 million, two-book contract with Penguin Putnam Inc., and now he is crisscrossing the country in charter planes and limousines to hawk the first book, "The Lady, Her Lover and Her Lord," a self-help guide peppered with Scripture. This fall, PolyGram's Island Black Music label is releasing a sexy gospel-pop album by the same name, which Mr. Jakes calls "sacred music for married couples."
>
> Blending his characteristic charm and grandiosity, Mr. Jakes beholds all this with satisfaction. In these ventures, "I am the power and the kingdom and the glory," he says, "and I think I kind of like it that way." . . .

But, you may ask, what's the deeper meaning, ***the purpose*** of this *Journal* profile? It is to illuminate the economics and management styles of some African-American churches. The *Journal* writer moves to that with a transition graf:

> Since the zenith of the civil-rights movement, African-American churches have struggled with how to inspire constituents who have been moving into the middle class and away from social-justice issues. The past decade has seen the rise of black "megachurches," huge, middle-class congregations whose pastors preach a "prosperity gospel"—an optimistic message that glorifies personal and economic success while shunning the role of victim.

Quickly, however, the *Journal* writer returns to the minister as the principal vehicle for carrying readers through thousands of words that follow.

Color detail on his personality is intertwined with broader financial and church marketing information. The next graf:

> Mr. Jakes is one of the best and most successful of these new prophets; certainly, he is the most visible. His emotional exhortations bring the members of his congregation at the Potter's House, his 16,000-member Dallas church, to tears every week. He is also a shrewd entrepreneur who nurtures, protects and markets his product—himself—with meticulous care.
>
> —Lisa Miller, *The Wall Street Journal*[4]

What you read above is a classic example of a story structure I call the ***neck of the vase.*** It looks like this:

Figure 5.1.   Example of the neck-of-vase story structure.

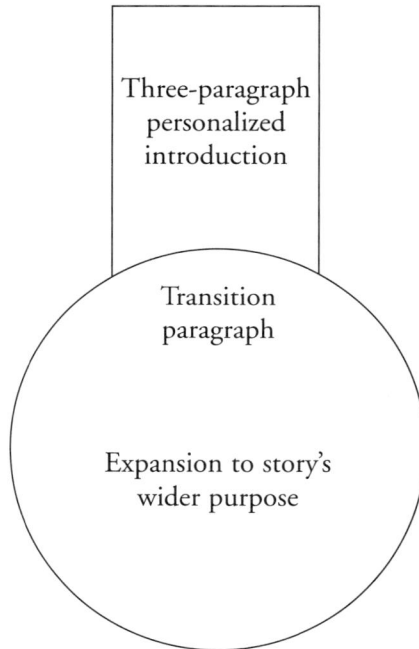

Three-paragraph
personalized
introduction

Transition
paragraph

Expansion to story's
wider purpose

Sometimes, the personalized intro—the "neck"—can be much shorter. Below, a writer jams color detail into the lead graf, then moves quickly to the broader story—a company's performance:

> Larry Ellison slides from the couch to the floor, where he looks crumpled, his long legs awkwardly folded under the low-slung coffee table. His tan is faded, there are dark circles under his eyes and, at this moment, he looks every minute of his 53 years. Ellison's Japanese-style garden is in riotous mid-

summer bloom and on full display through large plate-glass windows. But the tranquilizing view seems lost on him now.

His apparent fatigue is the result of months of 12- and 14-hour days spent getting Oracle Corp., the company he cofounded in 1977, back on track. Oracle, hyperactive in the late 1980s, had grown almost lethargic. "We used to need Ritalin," he says, with a shake of the head. "Now we need caffeine."

It's not good enough that Oracle's revenues grew 26% in the fiscal year just ended, to $7.1 billion, and earnings (before a writeoff) grew 7.7%, to $955 million. That kind of growth is dangerously close to a standstill in Silicon Valley. . . .

—Julie Pitta, *Forbes*[5]

Box 5-1

Don't Write Too Many Poodle Leads

Newspapers, in an attempt to keep pace with television, have also featurized their stories. I'm so tired of finding almost every story in my paper starting out with "Mary Jones was walking her poodle, Jaundice, down Main Street yesterday when. . ." You have to read 27 paragraphs of an O. Henry story to get to the finish. That's a misuse of newsprint.

—Walter Cronkite, quoted in Nancy Lloyd, "And That's The Way It Was," *Modern Maturity*, September–October 1998, p. 37

Box 5-2

The Forbes View

Our writers learn to look beneath the surface of things, to find what others are missing. Our stories have conclusions, none of this on-the-one hand—on-the-other-hand-wringing. Each article, ideally, should be something of a morality tale from which the reader comes away thinking there is a useful lesson.

—Steve Forbes, "Ideal Editor," *Forbes*, Jan. 11, 1999, p. 32

However you use personality color, ***it should lead readers to deeper meaning of a broader point.***

Above, you saw writers use color intros to pull you into broader understanding of a new trend in the economics of some African-American churches and how a corporation is being managed through tough times.

Below, a writer describes changes in management style that followed David Arledge's replacement of Oscar Wyatt (who "lives in a baronial estate") as chairman of Coastal Corp. This color detail, wonderfully illustrative of those changes, is used not in the intro but, rather, deeper in the story:

David Arledge, 53, is short and stocky. He wears his thinning black hair combed tightly to the side. A lawyer by training, Arledge cut his teeth at the accounting firm now known as Deloitte & Touche. He joined Coastal's tax department 18 years ago. For a good night out, Arledge and his wife chow down at a Mexican restaurant near their modest suburban Houston home.

Whether consciously or not, Arledge is signaling to the troops that he is not Oscar Wyatt. Although he has been chairman of Coastal for more than a year, Arledge refuses to park in Wyatt's old parking place, which remains empty.

—Christopher Palmeri, *Forbes*[6]

That is, color detail has greater impact—and more forcefully illustrates your point—if packaged in a couple tight grafs and inserted in your story. Don't dribble out such detail—age in second graf, height in fourth, weight in ninth.

Well, then, what should you watch for when interviewing people ***and studying them*** for a profile?

What They Look Like

Draw a "picture" of the individual—height, weight, hair color, type of dress. Note that "diamond ring the size of a nickel," the "dark circles under his eyes." Don't tell us; let us "see."

What They Sound Like

That *Wall Street Journal* writer we looked at above wrote that the minister sang to his congregation "and 'whooped,' a rhythmic, keening exhortation." Another writer describes an auto executive "cheerfully acknowledging" a point. A *Washington Post* writer quotes an executive as recalling an earlier business decision and "now laughing at the idea." For one writer, an executive has "the stoic demeanor of an oversize Buddha," and this executive doesn't ***speak,*** he "intones."

How They Move

How they walk, wave their hands, nod their heads—all add to the ***word picture*** you must draw.

Remember in the example above how that executive "slides from the couch to the floor"? What a picture that draws!

A writer watches his profile subject playing doubles tennis. The subject's partner takes a painful fall and the writer notes his subject "scored the point before ***ambling*** over to help his friend to his feet." How's that for letting readers ***see*** competitive executives at play!

Where They Work and Live

A magazine writer profiles an executive in his office:

With its worn carpet stacked high with management books, and with photos of his children on every available surface, his space looks more like a den than the office of the chairman of an almost 200-person company that has more than doubled in sales. . . . Appreciation plaques cover the walls. A baseball-cap collection circles the upper shelf.

—Stephanie Gruner, *Inc.*[7]

Can you **see** it? And does it add to your understanding of the man who works there?

A reporter recalls visiting Rose Blumkin, "the legendary Omaha furniture queen":

She was 96 and still scooting around her carpet warehouse on a three-wheeled electric cart, schmoozing the customers and terrorizing salesmen.

—Andrew Cassel, *The Philadelphia Inquirer*[8]

See?

Writing Traps to Avoid

They're marvelous devices for grabbing readers, but personality profiles can take you in wrong directions.

Beware of Subjective Language

Did that executive "***walk confidently*** into the boardroom" or "***stride in cockily***"?

Did the official "smile" or "smirk"?

Was it "a laugh" or "a giggle"? A "chuckle," maybe?

It takes only a word or two, a phrase slipped in here or there—and you skew reader perception of your subject. Pick descriptive words carefully.

Avoid Irrelevant Detail

You lead readers astray if, in a 1,000-word story on a company, you devote 500 words to describing the chairman's woodworking hobby.

Is your fulsome description of how the broker dressed the day the market crashed truly pertinent to your story's main thrust—that the market crashed?

Use personality color detail to strengthen and flesh out your story, ***not*** to detract from your story's central thrust.

Don't Extrapolate Too Much

Personal conduct, dress, mannerisms, speech habits—all ***can*** illuminate deeper meaning. But don't get carried away.

Two *Forbes* reporters corral a reluctant executive and open their account:

Lanky John Jones, 63, tips his leather chair backward when he speaks, crossing one long leg over the other knee. He doesn't much like talking with the media, but he's willing to talk with a *Forbes* reporter about his ideas.

—Bruce Upbin and Brandon Copple, *Forbes*[9]

That's meaningful color detail, fair to subject and readers alike.

Another writer focuses on a wall painting in an executive's office. The painting shows a ferocious hawk swooping in ruthlessly for a kill. Extrapolation: The executive is a killer in business negotiations. Fair? Nope. Truly meaningful detail? Nope, again.

Now, *you* decide about this one (emphasis added):

Face flushed and sandy *hair askew,* [John Jones] *bursts* through the revolving doors into a Park Avenue office building, *barks* into a cell phone, extends a hand and *flashes a smile* to a visitor, and scans the lobby directory to locate his 9:30 appointment. His pace reflects his obsession with time. A minute spent on only one task is a minute squandered, and wasted time *infuriates* [Jones]. He *shouts* at a taxi driver for taking the wrong route, *slams down* the receiver *in disgust* when a vendor puts him on hold, *rips up* an employee's work because she didn't follow his exact instructions. And to his family, fiancée, and friends, he issues a *stern warning*: "If you are not producing revenue, do not call me during the day." [Jones'] mantra is speed, and heaven help you if you get in his way. So what's the rush?

—Donna Fenn, *Inc.*[10]

Stay Out of Their Heads

Lunch with executives, follow them through their work schedule, spend days—weeks—with them *and you still won't know what they think.*

Make it a rule: Quote what individuals *say;* don't presume you know what they *think.*

| Box 5-3 | Eating on the Job |

I've found that you can often discover more about a person over a plate of food than when he or she is sitting behind a desk. I've had lunch at some of the best restaurants in Manhattan and in a soup kitchen. As long as the guest is fascinating, I'll go anywhere.

—Dyan Machan, "Lunch With Dyan," *Forbes,* June 15, 1998, p. 14

Don't Forget the Little People

We profile important people who make important policies. How about the little people *affected by those policies?*

For Anne Marie Borrego of *The Dallas Morning News,* the story is ***not*** high-paid executives who planned AT&T's rate hike; rather it's Mr. Average Guy who must pay the bill:

> [John Jones] was infuriated when he got his latest long-distance bill.
>
> After switching to AT&T Corp.'s One Rate plan earlier this year, he had expected to see big savings on his monthly statement. What he got was an unexpected rate hike to the tune of 5 extra cents a minute for calls made inside Texas—adding at least $10 more to his bill.
>
> And [Mr. Jones] wasn't the only one. AT&T customers across Texas were hit with similar rate increases, and the resulting ruckus persuaded the phone company to postpone the higher rates for three months.
>
> —Anne Marie Borrego, *The Dallas Morning News*[11]

Note above that writer Borrego uses the human element in abbreviated form, in just the first two grafs of her story. In the third graf, she transits from [Mr. Jones] into other AT&T customers and the central thrust of her story—the statewide "ruckus" over telephone rates.

Compare the lead above with this:

> AT&T customers across Texas are complaining about the company's rate increases.

No contest, right?

You can employ the human element to good advantage in another way: Open with a general lead, then transit into examples of impact on people. Note this *USA Today* lead:

> Financial statements for August are landing in the nation's mailboxes, and that sound you hear is investors screaming.

Now, *USA Today*'s writer discusses what experts say about a drop in stock prices that caused the screaming. Then, starting in the sixth graf, this:

> "Even though I expected it, the news was pretty awful," says [John Jones], 67, a retired engineer living near Gulf Shores, Ala. His net worth dived 7% in August. "I never thought it would come down so far, so fast."
>
> But [Jones] is undaunted. He and his wife plan to do some rebalancing and shift some cash to stocks. "We see it as an opportunity," he says.
>
> "I really had no idea how much I was going to lose" says [Martha Smith], 38, of Pittsburgh, whose accounts fell about 20%. "But I don't use that money for my living expenses, so I can wait for it to recover."
>
> [Betty Ann Black], 67, of . . .
>
> —Kerry Hannon, *USA Today*[12]

What is a drop in stock prices? A significant event.

What is a drop in an elderly person's net worth? ***A human tragedy.***
See the difference?

Write People-Oriented Sidebars

Many stories break nationally with huge impact on your local readers.
Something like this out of Washington:

> Despite a fresh wave of corporate downsizing announcements, the
> government reported Friday that more Americans are working than ever
> and that the overall economy continued to create jobs at a robust clip.
>
> While corporate giants from Boeing to Johnson & Johnson are planning
> to lay off tens of thousands of employees because of various business diffi-
> culties, American employers expanded their payrolls by an estimated 267,000
> workers in November alone, the Labor Department reported. Unemployment
> fell from 4.6 percent to 4.4 percent, coming close to the lowest jobless rate in
> the past three decades.

The story above led page A-1 of *The Atlanta Journal-Constitution*. An alert
staff writer got on that same front page with a localized and humanized
sidebar—a related story—run alongside the Washington story:

> [Alice Smith] is working the equivalent of two full-time jobs because
> the Captain D's she manages in Mableton has become a revolving door for
> workers.
>
> "I lost five people in about two days about two weeks ago," [Smith]
> lamented on Friday. With metro Atlanta's unemployment rate hovering around
> 3.2 percent, [Smith's] 75-hour workweeks are likely to continue. The Floyd
> Road store relies mostly on teenage workers, and a sign outside promises $100
> signing bonuses to workers who stay a month on the job.
>
> "It's very difficult to get people in here to work. We had to put the
> sign up to get them motivated to work," said [Smith].
>
> —Tammy Joyner, *The Atlanta Journal-Constitution*[13]

Remember: Virtually every significant national business or financial story
has a ***local human angle.*** Find it, write it. You'll aid reader understanding
(and, ahem, get some of those cherished front-page bylines)!

Ask Readers to "Come Along"

You can make a strong connection with the human element by leading
your readers into an office, by letting them listen to an interview, letting them
watch you at work.

Come along with a *Time* writer:

"I know we're not normal," Jerry Yang says with a boyish grin, making a halfhearted effort to straighten up his cubicle for his visitor. It's not much of an office by mogul standards: just a nondescript desk, a couple of cheap plastic milk crates bulging with papers, an old futon. Magazines are piled in a corner, and a window offers a distinctly declasse view of the parking lot.

Of course, by the standards of David Filo, 32, Yahoo's other co-founder, 29-year-old Jerry's digs are West Coast Donald Trump. Filo's office is truly a Goodwill collection truck of a workspace, with dirty socks and T shirts jumbled in with books, software and other debris. Even more startling is his office computer: a poky clone running an outdated Pentium 120 chip. Why wouldn't the chief technologist of the Internet's No. 1 website use the top of the line? Filo just shrugs. "Upgrading is a pain."

Could this be the face of 21st century capitalism? You'd better believe it.

—Michael Krantz, *Time*[14]

A *Wall Street Journal* reporter rides with an executive and let's us come along:

Tucson, Ariz.—George Kalil pulls into the parking lot of a Just for Feet shoe store. He immediately sees red.

A massive sign for Coca-Cola's latest summer promotion beams from the store window. Inside sits a brightly lit Coke vending machine. Mr. Kalil knows he has a difficult mission. For 50 years, the Kalil family has owned and run an independent bottling firm, which now distributes 7 UP, RC Cola, Crush orange soda and a panoply of other drinks not owned by Coca-Cola Co. or PepsiCo Inc. "The Good Guys at Kalil," the slogan plastered on Kalil Bottling Co.'s delivery trucks, is a common sight in this desert city.

A silver-haired bear of a man with an impish grin, the 60-year-old Mr. Kalil introduces himself to the manager and asks if the store would consider putting in a Kalil vending machine. . . .

—Nikhil Deogun, *The Wall Street Journal*[15]

As always in business news writing, you should use the "come-along" structure to communicate a serious message. In the example above, the message is a lengthy *Journal* examination of family-owned bottling companies, such as Kalil's, struggling against giants in the soft drink industry.

One excellent tactic is to undertake personally a business or financial experience meaningful to readers, and report the outcome. Apply for car insurance, and report where the bargains are found; interview stock brokers, then write how to get started in investing; shop for computers, then write a price-comparison story.

One reporter underwent a test by a company's new lie detector machine and reported, "The system did nab me when I recited the names of eight fictitious ex-wives. But it believed me when I insisted I was a world-renowned geophysicist and a giant duck."[16]

And, although you may have been told *not* do it, do it anyway: Insert the perpendicular pronoun "I" on occasion. I do, and so does this writer who really warms up things for readers:

> It is 98 sweltering degrees in Bay Town, Tex. when I meet Henry Schimberg, chief executive of Atlanta-based Coca-Cola Enterprises. He is standing in the middle of a Kroger's parking lot with ten men in black. Mostly Texas CCE managers, the ten look like cartoon characters with the heat making wavy, radiating lines off their wool suits.
>
> Schimberg, I've heard everywhere, is Coke's other secret formula. This was a guy I had to meet. He said okay, but at a price: I had to accompany him on one of the 5,000 store visits he makes each year.
>
> —Dyan Machan, *Forbes*[17]

How can readers *not* want to "come along" on that one?

Talk One-On-One With Readers

Ruthlessly strip stuffiness from your writing and whenever possible, write to "you," the single reader, not to "them," those faceless masses.

Jane Bryant Quinn, a markets writer read by hundreds of thousands, gets her dialogue down to across-the-kitchen-table levels:

> Think of this year's markets as a practice run. Are you really in stocks for the long term, or did night sweats almost chase you out? You've heard ad nauseam that you need to know your "tolerance for risk." Price drops show you pretty quickly where your tolerance lies. Now is a good time to reassess the logic of your investment plan, before the day that stocks stumble into something worse.
>
> —Jane Bryant Quinn, *Newsweek*[18]

How about this lead:

> Private investors now can buy the stock of a brokerage firm or bank. Why not an exchange itself?

I wrote that one myself, and it's okay, but just, right? Now the real version:

> You can buy the stock of a brokerage firm or bank now. Why not an exchange itself?
>
> The Chicago Mercantile Exchange, taking a step toward the alteration of its nonprofit ownership structure, said it will hire an investment-banking firm to help it evaluate conversion to a for-profit corporation.
>
> —Terzah Ewing, *The Wall Street Journal*[19]

Which lead above is warm, chatty, inviting? The *you* lead!

Sometimes, of course, the "you" isn't meant literally but even then it can make readers feel welcome:

> Where do you go to find a visionary in the television business? One place to look, according to Wall Street analysts, is a spare cubicle in a bunker-like building in a neighborhood of aging, weather-beaten, frame row houses in Baltimore.
>
> From that unlikely nexus of power and prestige, David D. Smith, chief executive of the Sinclair Broadcast Group, runs a collection of TV stations that has grown so fast he is unsure exactly how many he now controls.
>
> —Bill Carter, *The New York Times*[20]

Write to "you," the reader, in terms *all* readers will understand. How many of your neighbors and school chums will connect immediately if you write (as one writer did) a "you" lead asking them to understand that "Scott Fitzgerald was wrong when he said there are no second acts in American lives." Somehow, I don't think that communicates well with a general audience of business news readers who may or may not know who Scott Fitzgerald was!

Here is one usage of "you" that works but note the writer's second-graf concern that he's reaching only some of his potential audience (emphasis added):

> You remember how startled you were the first time you saw someone on the street talking into a wireless phone.
>
> ***Unless you are fairly young,*** the commercial introduction of cellular technology in the mid-1980s probably appeared to be a dramatic shift from the tethered communications of the past. Maybe you looked at the person holding that wireless phone and thought he or she looked pretentious or silly. Or maybe futuristic, or just plain rich.
>
> One thing for sure, he or she looked unusual.
>
> Now wireless phones have morphed from novelty to necessity for many people.
>
> —Michael E. Kanell, *The Atlanta Journal-Constitution*[21]

Clearly, a danger in reaching for the human element is that you can limit too severely your audience, as does this lead:

> San Francisco—Anyone wondering what was on the minds of money managers attending the Nationsbanc Montgomery Securities investment conference last week got their answer Monday afternoon at a presentation by Judith Estrin, chief technology officer at Cisco Systems.
>
> —Edward Wyatt, *The New York Times*[22]

I don't know about you, but that lead above eliminates me from the audience. I really wasn't wondering what was on those managers' minds!

And beware asking the reader to relate to distant times and events. Do you, my dear reader, relate well to what happened in the *1950s,* half a century ago? This writer asks you to do so:

> Back in the days of what's reputed to be the great productivity boom of the 'Fifties and 'Sixties, consumer durables weren't so durable; you counted yourself lucky if you managed to finish paying for your car before it rusted out. Today, in the midst of what is supposedly the era of the great productivity slowdown, the curse of tinworm has long since been conquered, and cars last well past 100,000 miles. What makes this landmark achievement possible? The wonders of information technology (IT).
>
> —Gene Epstein, *Barron's*[23]

Sometimes, you can forge a warm human link to readers by writing in a tone of we're-all-in-this-together. Note:

> As much as we may enjoy bragging about our most successful investments, few things in life are as paralyzing as making investment decisions.
> Let's face it: None of us knows enough to be 100 percent confident about picking stocks. On the other hand, many of us know ourselves well enough to be 100 percent terrified about do-it-yourself investing.
>
> —Hank Ezell, syndicated columnist[24]

Now, you make the call: Does the following writer stretch too far in trying to tie writer and reader together with the chummy "us" factor? Can *you* really picture yourself as President Clinton or Monica Lewinsky?

> Most of us will never have to endure the high-profile humiliation President Clinton and ex-White House intern Monica Lewinsky are facing. But the ongoing soap opera at 1600 Pennsylvania Ave. brings up a timely question: How do you recoup after making a mess of your career?
>
> — Tammy Joyner, *The Atlanta Journal-Constitution*[25]

Below is nice use of the *tie-in factor* by *Folio,* an industry trade journal covering the magazine business. Note the "peg"—a baseball player—is a very human link to what many Americans were buzzing about at the time.

> Mark McGwire and *Sports Illustrated* both entered the record book last month. The St. Louis Cardinals' slugger broke baseball's single-season home run mark and, for the first time in its 44-year history, the Time Inc. title published twice within one week in order to capture the event.
> A total of 530,000 copies of the *SI* newsstand-only special were on the street at the usual cover price of $2.95 on the Thursday following McGwire's Tuesday night blast. A day earlier, the magazine's regular edition for the week of September 14 had hit the newsstands.
>
> —Mary Harvey, *Folio*[26]

Write to Entertain—Within Limits

Nothing captures the human element like a cute twist on words, a sly phrase—something to lighten your reader's day. Note:

> Washington—Has the urge to merge in the phone business cut off the fuel to duel? That's the view of some key legislators and government regulators who see the ghost of old Ma Bell rising anew.
>
> —Andrew J. Glass, Cox Newspapers[27]

☞

> It's no secret that a new breed of customer-oriented megachurch is using the tactics of business to win what might be called market share for Jesus.
>
> —Daniel Akst, financial consultant[28]

But don't lapse into a cliche, as did a *Baltimore Sun* writer: "As Wall Street ***gnashes its teeth*** over the latest swing in the stock market . . ." [29]

And, believe it: Shakespeare was first, and by the time a *Chicago Tribune* writer got around to using it, this cliche had become, well, ***revolting:***

> To convert or not to convert?
> That is the question bearing down on owners of individual retirement accounts as the deadline approaches on a tax break for conversion of traditional IRAs to Roth IRAs.
>
> —Kathy Bergen, *The Chicago Tribune*[30]

And, speaking of being revolted, check your stomach after this one:

> If the market is these days a stormy sea, buffeted by Asian typhoons and icy winds off the Russian steppes, mutual funds can be likened to small but doughty sailing ships. As the Dow and other indexes soar and plunge, the crews manning those bobbing bits of flotsam rush from port to starboard and prow to stern, tightening lines, furling sails, turning into the wind and adjusting ballast in a desperate bid to keep afloat.
>
> —Andy Zipser, *Barron's*[31]

Feel a little ***seasick?***

Summary

- By writing the ***human element*** in business news you inform readers about who is making decisions that affect their lives.
- The human element frequently explodes on the news scene with dramatic impact, and you'll write it with hard-news urgency and economy of wordage.

- However, sometimes you can take an in-depth look at the human element, and for that, the ***profile*** is a fascinating writing vehicle.
- Profiles are written on many things—towns, cats, hurricanes—but for readers of business news you should concentrate on profiles of individuals that illuminate how business institutions work and who makes them work.
- Some profiles work well with only minimal "color" detail normally associated with writing about individuals.
- Many profiles, however, focus intently on individuals, and the "picture" thus drawn reveals to readers a larger meaning, a bigger story.
- In writing profiles, inform readers what the subjects look like, how they sound and move and where they live and work.
- Traps in writing profiles include using subjective language, including irrelevant detail, extrapolating from limited information and guessing what people think, rather than quoting what they say.
- Don't forget to profile the "little" people—those affected by policies laid down by important people you normally profile.
- You can humanize copy by writing "come-along" stories that invite readers to follow you into an executive's office, to listen as you conduct an interview, to let them watch you work.
- Ruthlessly strip stuffiness out of your writing and "talk" to readers in an across-the-kitchen-table tone.
- You can warm up a story by writing a "you" lead that speaks to individual readers, not the great mass of readership.
- Write to entertain with a cute twist of words or a sly phrase or two, but discipline yourself to avoid cliches or overstretching to ridiculous lengths.

Recommended Reading

Aspiring business news writers have splendid models for learning how to get the human element into their copy:

Forbes magazine's writers are (I think) unbeatable in profiling individuals and companies, in minimum language for maximum reading punch. That magazine's one-page profiles are outstanding instructional models.

The Wall Street Journal is unsurpassed in long take-outs, sometimes running to thousands of words, that move brightly and swiftly ***because its writers find and stress the human element.*** Note particularly how *Journal* writers use "neck-of-the-vase" story structures to strong advantage.

I discuss profiles and other writing structures in three books: *Introduction to Professional Newswriting* (New York: Longman, 1998); *Writing Opinion for Impact* (Ames, Iowa: Iowa State University Press, 1999), and *Introduction to Magazine Writing*, with Donald E. Fink (New York: Macmillan, 1993).

Notes

1. "The Man Who Moves, and Scares, Markets," national edition, Sept. 18, 1998, p. C-1.

2. Dispatch for morning papers, Dec. 12, 1998.

3. "Inside the Head of the Fed," national edition, Nov. 15, 1998, Section 3, p. 1.

4. "Prophet Motives," Aug. 21, 1998, p. A-1.

5. "Cool Chair, Hot Seat," Aug. 10, 1998, p. 42.

6. "Deconstructing Oscar," Oct. 19, 1998, p. 136.

7. "Irreconcilable Differences," September, 1998, p. 74.

8. "A Foreign Entrepreneur Found Prosperity in U.S.," Aug. 14, 1998, p. C-1.

9. "Creative Destruction 101," Dec. 14, 1998, p. 92.

10. "Built for Speed," September, 1998, p. 61.

11. "Complaints Put AT&T Rate Hike on Hold," Aug. 10, 1998, p. D-1.

12. "Financial Statements Too Graphic for Some," Sept. 16, 1998, p. B-3.

13. The Washington story was by Sylvia Nasar and transmitted by New York Times News Service for morning papers of Dec. 5, 1998; Joyner's sidebar was "Good Workers Are Hard to Keep, Bosses Lament," on the same page.

14. "Click Till You Drop," July 20, 1998, p. 34.

15. "Bottled Up," Sept. 16, 1998, p. A-1.

16. Stephen Manes, "Lie Detector," Oct. 5, 1998, p. 179.

17. "There's Something About Henry," Oct. 5, 1998, p. 82.

18. "Should You Be Worried?" Aug. 17, 1998, p. 40.

19. "Chicago Merc Could Convert to 'For Profit'," Aug. 21, 1998, p. C-1.

20. "From Baltimore, Dave Smith Stares Down the Networks," national edition, Oct. 4, 1998, Section 3, p. 1.

21. "Companies Eager for Piece of Growing Wireless Market," Sept. 27, 1998, p. R-5.

22. "Investing," national edition, Sept. 20, 1998, Section 3, p. 7.

23. "Economic Beat," Oct. 12, 1998, p. 42.

24. Published in *The Atlanta Journal-Constitution,* special supplement, as "Money & More," Sept. 20, 1998, p. U-34.

25. "Money & More," Oct. 11, 1998, p. R-3.

26. "Chasing McGwire, *SI* Hits for Extra Bases," October 1998, p. 27.

27. Dispatch for morning papers, Sept. 27, 1998.

28. Published in *The New York Times,* "The Culture of Money," national edition, Oct. 4, 1998, Section 3, p.5.

29. Jean Marbella, dispatch for Sunday papers, Sept. 6, 1998.

30. Dispatch for Sunday papers, Nov. 8, 1998.

31. "Mutual Choice," Oct. 12, 1998, p. 45.

Exercises

1. Identify three local individuals who fit the "Greenspan effect" definition of Chapter 5—individuals in business who, by word or deed, have impact on money

and lives in your community. Describe in about 300 words the types of profiles you think appropriate to show your readers the power those individuals possess. A local banker might be one.

2. Search today's *The Wall Street Journal* (or another newspaper your instructor designates) for ***spot-news stories*** involving business world personalities. In about 300 words, discuss how the writers described the individuals and defined how and why they are in the news. Are they news because of business decisions they made; promotions they received; policies they laid down?

3. Examine a personality profile in *Forbes* magazine, *The Wall Street Journal* or in another newspaper your instructor designates. Discuss, in about 300 words, the story's structure, its "color" detail and, importantly, the underlying mission of the writer. Was it to explain how a company operates, why a certain policy was laid down? Did the writer succeed in ***humanizing*** what might otherwise have been a dull story?

4. Study, in *The Wall Street Journal* or another newspaper your instructor designates, a story structured with a "neck-of-the-vase" intro. Does the writer succeed in pulling you in, as a reader? Is use of color minimal, or does the story fully describe an individual? What's the writer's purpose in this story? Does the writer succeed?

5. With your instructor's approval, interview a local individual with power in banking, business, commerce or economics. In about 650 words, write a personality profile that (a) fully describes physical characteristics and mannerisms of the individual and (b) ties that color detail into the individual's job, business responsibilities and impact on local business life.

PART FOUR

Three Major News Sectors

YOU HAVE MANY uses for the reporting and writing techniques we've studied so far in this book.

In writing, as you've seen, the only limitation on story structure or your own wordsmithing is the limit of your imagination. You need not—indeed, *cannot*—write dully, woodenly just because you're in business news.

In reporting, you can turn your skills to many subjects. Readers are interested in virtually any relating to money—particularly their own.

In Part Four, however, we focus on writing in three major news sectors where professional business journalists spend much of their time. For beginners in business journalism, all three offer immediate starting points, in campus journalism or on your first professional job "out there."

In Chapter 6, Economics: Bringing the Big Picture Home, we discuss how you can get started covering the production, distribution and consumption of wealth, which generally is what economics is about. Message of this chapter: Learn how to read distant news horizons for important signals on what's to come, then how to translate them meaningfully for non-expert readers in your home audience.

In Chapter 7, Business: Walking the Main Street Beat, we leave those distant horizons and move closer to home, searching for clues on covering business for Hometown America. This takes you closer to your readers' everyday lives. It is one of the most fascinating news beats in business journalism.

In Chapter 8, Finance: It's Their Pocketbooks That Count, we move very close to your readers—as close as their pocketbooks. We study how to cover the management of money, credit and capital in terms meaningful to those local pocketbooks.

In the three chapters ahead make it your Writer's Mantra: You must translate the complex and esoteric into terms and language your readers understand, then write accurately and carefully and—always—with a light touch. ***Write to lure 'em in!***

6

Economics: Bringing the Big Picture Home

IF YOU'RE a typical beginner in business news it'll be some time before you're called on to draw the "big picture" in economics.

Normally, only senior, experienced journalists are assigned to cover the national—indeed, global—story of the production, distribution and consumption of wealth.

However, starting right now, you can play a major role by (dare I write it!) *taking snapshots* of the big picture to bring home to your readers the meaning distant events have for their everyday lives.

And believe it: Those distant events, in Washington, London, Tokyo and points beyond, *do* have local impact, on *your* Main Street, in *your* neighborhood.

But how can you sort through the astonishing amount of news and information zipping between those capitals and find what's important to your readers? *By watching economic indicators.*

Watch Distant Indicators

Broadly, we watch three types of economic indicators:

1. Current economic indicators

These measures of economic activity signal growth ahead or maybe recession or slowdown—in other words, turns in the business cycle. They are watched closely in all world capitals and on Main Streets everywhere.

Two of the most important current indicators are *gross domestic product* (GDP), which measures total output of all goods and services *within* the United States, and *gross national product* (GNP), which also measures output, except it includes all Americans, in or out of the country.

Other current indicators include total personal income, industrial production, employment and unemployment, wholesale or consumer prices, and retail sales.

2. *Leading economic indicators*

These indicators are watched for their signals ***in advance*** of changes in economic performance.

Early warnings often come from formation of new business enterprises, new orders for durable goods, construction contracts, hiring rates and hours of work performed.

3. *Lagging economic indicators*

These indicators ***follow*** economic performance and thus report on what happened in the past. However, the past may also signal what's ahead, so lagging indicators must be watched closely for clues on what's coming over the economic horizon.

Lagging indicators include such things as inventories of finished goods (products not yet sold), long-term unemployment, yield on mortgage loans.

Now, you may ask, can all that be sorted out to yield meaningful signals for your readers? Sure! Below, a *Wall Street Journal* pro shows how:

Washington—Signs of a global economic recovery are everywhere. So are signs of a global economic catastrophe.

American labor productivity is up, as is South Korea's stockpile of foreign currency. But auto sales in Brazil are plummeting, and U.S. banks are taking a beating on investments in Russia.

Should you spring for that new in-ground swimming pool? Or is it time to squirrel away canned food and ammunition in the basement? With reams of contradictory news landing on the doorstep each morning, it's tough to figure out whether things are getting worse or better. . . .

Note in the third graf above how the writer reduces global signs to something we all understand—swimming pool in the backyard, canned beans in the basement.

The writer now alerts readers (and aspiring business writers) on what to watch for ***ahead:***

The definitive evidence of a rebound, of course, will appear well after the fact, when government statistics prove that the economies of Asia and Latin America are growing again, and the U.S. has secured its own prosperity against foreign instability.

The trick is to spot early warning signs. . . .

The signs of recovery, like the global crisis itself, will arrive in two pieces. The first is financial: the markets for stocks, bonds and currencies. The second is economic: factories, jobs and wages. The two, of course, are closely linked. . . .

—Michael M. Phillips, *The Wall Street Journal* [1]

Below, Louis Uchitelle, who covers economics for *The New York Times,* reduces global events to their impact on a narrow sector of American households—those with incomes of $50,000 or more (a ***prime*** demographic tar-get for *Times* circulation executives, incidentally):

> The global financial crisis and the plunging stock market are begin-ning to unnerve the nation's more affluent families and make them more cau-tious in their spending.
>
> Consumer spending, particularly among families with annual incomes above $50,000, is far and away the biggest source of economic growth in the United States. Through months of turmoil, this consumption has remained strong. . . . Now the first crack has appeared in the will to spend.
>
> The crack is most evident in recent consumer surveys that ask specifi-cally about a household's "financial situation"; that is, its savings, stock port-folios and real estate holdings—its wealth—as well as its income from wages. . . . Households with incomes above $50,000 were optimistic about their financial situation before the summer's sharp selloff in the stock market, but then in September their optimism fell significantly.
>
> "We are starting to see consumers who feel nervous about the stock mar-ket and are becoming more cautious in their spending behavior," said Richard Curtin, director of the University of Michigan's Consumer Surveys, whose monthly polls are widely followed by economists. . . .
>
> —Louis Uchitelle, *The New York Times*[2]

Note above that the *Times*' Uchitelle demonstrates two characteristics of strong business writing:

- He focuses on the meaning that global events have for ***readers of his newspaper.*** You'll recall Chapter 1's advice that you must know—and write for—the geographic and demographic audiences of your newspaper.
- Uchitelle, though in his own right a recognized commentator on eco-nomics, cuts quickly, in his fourth graf, to ***quoting an authoritative source.*** Find—and quote—the experts!

Now, a *San Francisco Chronicle* writer who ***really*** translates global events into local meaning:

> The global financial crisis has opened the door a bit for Bay Area homebuyers.
>
> The increase in home prices has slowed as the financial crisis has caused mortgage rates to plunge to their lowest levels in more than 30 years.
>
> More houses are being put on the market, as owners try to sell while they can. As a result, the severe inventory shortage that produced a lopsided seller's market over the past two years has all but evaporated. . . .

Well, you say, that's nice ***general*** reporting. But where are the ***specifics?*** They're here:

With investor capital pouring out of the world's stock markets and into relatively safe fixed-income investments, the interest on fixed-rate, 30-year jumbo mortgages—those totaling $227,150 or more—now averages 6.7 percent.

That's down from 7.4 percent a year ago and 8.3 percent two years ago.

With a $250,000 loan, every 1 percent decline in the mortgage rate slashes about $150 off the monthly payment. Current mortgage rates may offer buyers a once-in-a-lifetime opportunity.

If you look for a house now, you should find plenty to choose from, and should have enough time to consider them rationally.

—Arthur M. Louis, *The San Francisco Chronicle* [3]

Note several factors in the story above (which, incidentally, **led** the *Chronicle*'s business section):

- The writer **opens** with local impact. No need to junk up early grafs of this story by describing indicators of the "global financial crisis." They've been on front pages for weeks; details are well known.
- Quickly, the story moves from general intro to dollars and cents specifics on what mortgages cost. That's important how-to-do-it guidance.
- And, in the last graf reprinted above, writer Louis talks to "you"—his reader—about house-hunting tactics and thus personalizes his writing.

In sum, the three writers cited above address economics on three levels—Phillips of *The Wall Street Journal* on the global level; Uchitelle of *The New York Times* for affluent *Times* readers nationwide; Louis of the *Chronicle* at the neighborhood level.

Let's look at specific economic indicators you can handle for local readers.

Localize These Indicators

Gross Domestic Product

Because it measures total output of goods and services, the GDP probably is the most closely watched indicator of all. It signals whether the nation's business activity is increasing, holding steady or decreasing.

The GDP includes consumer spending, investment by businesses in their plant and equipment, housing activity, the balance of exports and imports, and federal, state and local government purchases.

Below, a *New York Times* writer, serving a **national** audience, handles new GDP figures:

The latest snapshot of the United States economy showed yesterday that the long-predicted slowdown is still more forecast than fact.

The economy performed better during the summer than had been originally reported and consumer confidence bounced back this fall, according to a fresh batch of data released yesterday. Along with other signs of buoy-ancy—in jobs, retail sales and housing—the new data suggest that growth re-mains surprisingly solid.

Despite financial turmoil abroad and tremblings at home, the nation's gross domestic product grew at an annual rate of 3.9 percent in the third quar-ter, revised upward from an initial estimate of 3.3 percent, the Commerce Department said yesterday. . . . Inflation, meanwhile, was less than 1 percent.

Note above the writer's **characterization** of the news, in the first and sec-ond grafs. The **numbers** are held to the third graf—and, when presented, are **compared** (actual 3.9 percent against estimated 3.3 percent).

The writer continues with a graf of elaboration, then a **look-ahead angle:**

Consumer confidence, as measured by an index by the Conference Board, a private research group in New York, has risen this month after four consecutive declines that brought it to an 18-month low in October.

Armed with the latest data, forecasters are saying that growth in the current quarter could run as high as 3 percent but cool sometime in the new year. "The slowdown turns out to be a 1999 story rather than a 1998 story," said John Jones, chief economist at Fleet Bank.

—Sylvia Nasar, *The New York Times*[4]

Look again at the final two grafs above. Note:

- An authoritative source (Conference Board) is cited and its sponsorship (private) is mentioned. Always include your source's credentials and who is funding those many boards, conferences, think tanks and associations you'll be quoting. Help readers decide what the **motives** of those groups might be.
- Reporting where the economy has been is important; where it's going is even more important. Always try for the look-ahead angle and, as in the last graf above, search for authoritative sources to give your readers their best bets.

Now, don't merely stand by and watch your newspaper grant major display to an outside writer, such as the *Time*'s Nasar, with a nationally an-gled story. **Get a local piece of that story!**

Just think: If your local economy **outperforms** the national economy, as reflected in the GDP, you have a story. If it **equals** or **underperforms** the national economy, you have a story, too.

But how to measure the local economy?

1. Don't try to match components of the national GDP with some sort of "local GDP." Measuring local consumer spending, business investment, housing activity and so forth is far beyond the resources of most newsrooms.
2. Nevertheless, you **can** establish a good "feel" for local economic activity

through interviews with business executives and other authoritative sources, such as business councils, research groups and, don't forget, local college professors who monitor business activity.

CAUTION: Many business executives believe that talking slowdown creates slowdown, that talking good business makes good business. So when a local executive tells you business is "great," *ask for figures that back up that assessment.* Your readers need hard numbers, not chamber of commerce hype.

Incidentally, GDP figures are released from Washington about two weeks after the end of each quarter. News services and national media will carry them immediately.

Consumer Price Index (CPI)

Value this economic indicator for it enables you to reach out and touch your readers by writing about the cost of where and how they live.

Each month, the U.S. Bureau of Labor Statistics issues the CPI for price changes in the previous month, including cost of housing, food, fuel, transportation and clothing.

Price changes are obtained in urban areas nationwide, where the Bureau prices a "market basket" of nearly 400 items. As a measurement of inflation the CPI is awaited eagerly in business and financial circles, so news services and other media urgently transmit each report. AP transmitted this in mid-December:

> Washington—Consumer prices barely budged last month as moderation in food and energy costs kept inflation under wraps. In good news for holiday shoppers, the prices of computers, video equipment and toys all declined.
>
> The Labor Department reported today that its Consumer Price Index edged up just 0.2 percent in November, matching the October increase.
>
> So far this year, inflation is rising at an annual rate of just 1.6 percent, even better than last year's 11-year low of 1.7 percent.

AP's writer rushed (as all AP writers must) this story to the wire. But note the story nevertheless is written carefully to include a seasonal "peg"—it ties the CPI report to "good news" for Christmas shoppers. That's a beautiful example of how a business news writer, even under pressure, must search distant events for meaningful ways to tie the news to readers' everyday lives.

Now, AP's writer explains the *why*—why did consumer prices barely budge?

> American consumers have reaped benefits from the global economic turmoil, which has sent the prices of a number of commodities, including oil, skidding to their lowest levels in a decade. The steep plunge in Asian currency values has meant lower-priced imports of key consumer goods from autos to toys.

While American manufacturers and farmers have been battered by the rising U.S. trade deficit, the absence of inflation has given the Federal Reserve maneuvering room to cut interest rates three times this fall to make sure that weakness in those sectors does not lead to a U.S. recession.

The Associated Press[5]

Note above the reference to why lower-priced toys are coming from Asia. That is a tie-back explanation of the lead's references to holiday shoppers and toys.

Make it a rule: After you've written three or four grafs, pause and ask yourself: Does my lead make promises (cheaper toys)? If so, fulfill your promise by answering the *why* (lower-priced imports).

AP's writer, in the next graf, provides a ***look-ahead angle:*** Federal Reserve policy-makers will meet next week to consider interest rates "but the expectation is they will leave rates unchanged." . . .

Note how AP's writer, so quickly and concisely, addresses three essential elements of strong business writing—the ***what*** (CPI barely budged), the ***real what*** (there's only minimal inflation) and the ***look-ahead*** angle (the Fed probably won't change rates).

Now, how can you localize the CPI story? Well, don't try your own market-basket survey of prices on nearly 400 items! But, you ***can*** select a representative sample, say 15-20 items, and price them as a sidebar to monthly CPI reports out of Washington. Be sure to crank in consumer costs peculiar to your locale, perhaps heating fuel costs in the North during the winter or cost of electricity for air conditioning in the South during hot months.

Unemployment Rate

Chicago Tribune readers awakened one Saturday morning to find this story, by Stephen Franklin, prominently displayed on the business section's front page:

Consider the growing mound of pink slips.

Boeing Co., the world's largest aerospace firm, is slashing 48,000 jobs. Another 9,000 positions will be lopped off when Exxon Corp. and Mobil Corp. merge.

Then there are the merging banks, the steel companies hammered by foreign products, the gasoline companies joining ranks, the stock brokerage firms pinched by Wall Street's convulsions and the farm machinery manufacturers hurt by farmers' own financial woes.

That doesn't read like writing inspired by a dry, statistics-laden report issued each month in far-off Washington. But that's what it is.

A day earlier, on Friday, the U.S. Labor Department, as it normally does on the first Friday of each month, reported on the size of the nation's civilian work force and number of people unemployed. That economic indicator, like all we're studying, was transmitted urgently by AP and other news services.

Tribune editors, however, didn't simply plug into their page a bunch of bare-bones news service reports. Rather, they tossed the Washington dispatches to staff writer Franklin. His job: localize the story and flesh it out.

Franklin's next graf quotes the head of a Chicago-based outplacement firm that tracks layoffs. The source says layoffs are way up. Now, the *Tribune* writer moves to the national scene—and, *for the first time,* to the Labor Department report that inspired the story:

> But the nation's jobless rate went down last month, falling from 4.6 to 4.4 percent in November, according to figures released Friday by the government. What's more, buoyed by seasonal retail hiring and the strong construction industry, the government reported a very positive gain of 267,000 jobs, a number that exceeded most economic forecasts.

Now, the *so what?* factor emerges—so what?, readers might ask. Is this good news or bad? How will business and finance interpret the figures? One measure is how Wall Street reacts, and writer Franklin turns immediately to that:

> Wall Street embraced the news, and the Dow Jones industrial average closed the day's trading at 9016.14, up 136.46 points.

—Stephen Franklin, *The Chicago Tribune*[6]

Note the *Tribune* writer's delay in mentioning the *news peg*—the Labor Department report. That's because the report was such hot news the day before, on Friday, that it was transmitted urgently as soon as it was announced. Bankers, brokers, business executives all got it immediately on private subscriber services, such as Dow Jones, Reuters and Bloomberg, via the Internet and cable TV. TV and radio stations got it immediately from AP and aired it Friday afternoon and evening for their general audiences.

How could the *Tribune* publish the next morning, on Saturday, the same version the world already had received? It couldn't. So, news service stories from Washington were given to staff writer Franklin to rewrite the story, localize it *and move it ahead,* with the result you saw above.

It will happen to you. Learn the publishing rhythm of your newspaper or magazine; study, *intently,* how quickly your competition can get to your audience. Then, write "around" your newspaper's time-delay limitation, as Franklin did so successfully.

A couple more factors to crank into your stories on the unemployment rate:

- Like other broad-based economic indicators we're studying, this one is controversial. Critics say the unemployment rate doesn't include the jobless who have given up searching for work.

- You should advise readers precisely who is counted and how. For one week, researchers check thousands of households and record the work status of anyone 16 or older. "Unemployed" are those who did not work during the survey week but tried in the prior four weeks to get a job, through employment agencies or direct application with employers. The unemployed do not include persons temporarily laid off; the employed are those who worked for pay for one or more hours during the survey week.
- State employment agencies keep unemployment statistics by county. They maintain offices in most county seats and major cities. They're good sources of comparative statistics you can use when localizing the national report.

Housing Starts

What happens when someone breaks ground for a new home on the outskirts of your town?

- A bank does new business in lending money to (perhaps) ***both*** the homebuyer and home builder.
- Carpenters go to work, alongside electricians, plumbers, roofers.
- New furniture, appliances, drapes are sold.
- A nursery sells lawn sod, trees and bushes.

On goes the economic ripple effect, as scores (hundreds!) of people find work and create wealth to build a single house.

Small wonder that economists, business executives, financiers—and business journalists—watch closely each month as the U.S. Commerce Department reports ***housing starts.***

Each month's figures include privately owned housing units and single-family housing and buildings with two or more units. Each is counted only when ground is broken.

You can localize this key economic indicator by reporting on construction activity in your town. Sources include construction companies, builders' associations, real estate firms, officers of banks and savings and loan associations that finance construction and city and county clerks who issue construction permits.

Index of Industrial Production

This indicator, issued monthly by the Federal Reserve Board, reflects nationwide production by factories, mines and electric and gas utilities.

It is localized easily because it measures production of autos, appliances, clothing, food, and you can contrast local production of any of those items against national ups or downs.

Retail Sales

This measures what you, I and all other Americans spend, and, for that reason, retail sales are closely watched as an indicator of the broader economy's health and consumer confidence.

Note below how AP related an August retail sales report (issued by the U.S. Commerce Department) to both a seasonal swing in spending and to the larger economy.

> Although American consumers continued to fill new homes with furniture and bought plenty of back-to-school clothes in August, analysts see signs of a slowdown in the shopping spree that has helped insulate U.S. companies from economic crises abroad.
>
> "There's no sign of a collapse here, but there is slowing, and factors abroad could brake spending even more," said Paul Kasriel, chief domestic economist for Northern Trust Co. in Chicago.

Once again you see, above, how writers tell you what the numbers mean **before** they give you the numbers. AP's characterization of meaning is followed by the specifics:

> Retail sales increased a mild 0.2 percent to a seasonally adjusted $224.8 billion in August, the Commerce Department said Tuesday.

Now, should the numbers be qualified or otherwise handled carefully? Yes, and AP explains:

> That looks at first glance like a big improvement from a 0.6 percent drop in July. . . . But a strike at General Motors knocked car sales way out of kilter, and sales of other retail goods have slowed. . . .

Are there wider implications in all that for the United States and, even, **global** economy? Yes, and AP finds them:

> Heavy spending by American consumers has been the most important factor keeping production by U.S. companies on the upswing in spite of big increases in the trade deficit. A spreading global financial crisis, which started in Asia, is drying up markets for American product overseas.
>
> The Associated Press[7]

Clearly, the interrelationship of global economic forces is tight and truly leads from distant capitals beyond the horizon right down to Main Street, **in your town.**

Drawing the Big Picture

How do you move from taking snapshots of the economy—writing localized sidebars—to drawing the big picture with analysis and interpretation?

How do you move up to the next level from straight hard-news reporting of the Five Ws and How?

Very carefully.

As you broaden the scope of your coverage of economics, it's essential to beware of this:

FIRST, we're into complicated stuff here, and building your personal expertise is a long-haul process. Start now with college courses in economics, business and finance—and reconcile yourself to a *career* of continuing self-education and inquiry.

SECOND, the "experts" to whom we normally turn for analysis and interpretation don't agree always on much of what we're covering. Economists are notorious for reading differently the same signals.

Nevertheless, even early in your career you can draw at least part of the big picture. Let's look at devices you can use.

Two-Plus-Two-Equals-Five Stories

Straight Five W and How treatment of a *single* economic indicator yields limited understanding of the big picture.

But, combine, in a single story, details of *two* or more indicators and the individual components of your story often will multiply into wider and, certainly, more meaningful interpretation for your readers.

For example, Reuters transmits this *single-element* report on an important indicator:

Washington—Consumer prices rose moderately in November as inflation remained subdued, the Government said today.

The Consumer Price Index, the Government's main inflation gauge, rose two-tenths of a percent last month after an identical increase in October, the Labor Department said. . . .

Reuters[8]

Note above the single stab at interpretation: "inflation remained subdued."

On the *same* day, Bloomberg News Service *combines* in a single dispatch the CPI report *and* a Commerce Department report on business inventories. Note that combination permits very substantial interpretation (emphasis added):

U.S. *inflation is on track for its smallest yearly increase* in 12 years and companies are keeping inventories lean, *suggesting manufacturing might pick up next year,* government reports said Tuesday.

The Consumer Price Index rose 0.2 percent in November, matching October's rise, as dropping fuel prices offset increases in the cost of housing, food and medical care, the Labor Department said. ***That put the CPI on course for a 1.6 percent increase*** for all of 1998—below last year's 1.7 percent increase and the lowest since a 1.1 percent increase in 1986.

The Commerce Department said businesses added inventories at a slower pace in October than a month earlier as robust retail sales caused retailers to pull merchandise out of warehouses to satisfy demand. . . .

Now—and it's a ***must*** in all business writing—Bloomberg turns to an expert for ***look-ahead analysis:***

"Low inflation is just part of this best-of-all-worlds scenario in the U.S.," said [John Jones], chief economist at John Hancock Mutual Life Insurance Co. in Boston. "We're probably going to have a Merry Christmas" and strong sales early next year.

Bloomberg News Service[9]

Yielding even more tentative analysis, AP covers ***three*** indicators in the same dispatch. Note how interpretation is woven into hard-news reporting (emphasis added):

New York—The manufacturing sector slowed for the sixth straight month in November as industrial companies felt the crunch of the global financial crisis, but a separate report Tuesday ***suggested that the economy will improve*** by mid-1999.

The National Association of Purchasing Management, which tracks the manufacturing sector through a survey of corporate purchasing executives, said new orders, exports and imports declined at many of the nation's factories . . .

The trade group's index of economic activity registered at 46.8 percent. . . . Any reading under 50 percent ***is a sign*** that the industrial sector is contracting.

The index also inched closer to the NAPM's benchmark of 43.6 percent, which it considers the point at which the broader economy is in recession. . . .

Now, AP moves to the second and third economic indicators:

In a separate report Tuesday, the Conference Board, a private research group, reported that its Index of Leading Economic Indicators rose 0.1 percent in October, to 105.6. The gain followed two months of flat results.

In a third report, the Commerce Department said U.S. construction spending rose a moderate 0.3 percent in October, the fifth consecutive increase.

The purchasing managers survey is closely watched because it is the freshest evidence of how the economy fared in the previous month. ***The leading indicators are widely viewed as a forecast of how the economy will fare six to nine months in the future.***

Deeper in the story, AP's writer quotes authoritative sources—among them an NAPM executive and an economist with Nikko Securities International Co. (on international implications for the U.S. economy). Then, as always with the pros, AP's writer moves to look-ahead analysis:

> [John Jones], director of business cycle research at the Conference Board, welcomed the advance after two months of flat numbers.
>
> "We are seeing some signs of economic growth being rekindled," he said, noting that consumer confidence is robust and employment is strong. "We can expect a very healthy economy in 1999."
>
> The Associated Press[10]

Sometimes, of course, you're forced to report **conflicting** indicators on the economy and your multiplication of two times two will yield only confusion if you're not careful.

Just remember in reporting the big picture that you're a journalist, not a soothsayer. You're not expected to know it all, particularly what's coming over the horizon. You **are** expected to offer strong, accurate reporting and, when it's available, an overlay of analysis from experts.

With that in mind, note how nicely a Dow Jones reporter handles conflicting indicators:

> Washington—The U.S. economy may be slowing somewhat, or perhaps it's chugging along nicely, based on new economic data released Thursday.
>
> "You can be pessimistic or optimistic," said Brown Brothers Harriman & Co. economist [John Smith].
>
> On the optimistic side: October housing starts surged 7.3 percent. . . .
>
> On the pessimistic side: Initial unemployment insurance claims rose by 9,000 to 332,000, for the week ended Nov. 14. . . .
>
> The housing starts data were the larger surprise to analysts. . . .
>
> Dow Jones News Service[11]

Put a Human Face on Economics

Washington policy-makers deliberate, bankers debate, global and national economic forces converge and diverge.

And hog prices fall in South Dakota.

Hog prices?

Yes, hog prices. And Ray Thomas, Springfield, S.D., hog farmer, is in trouble.

And for Randy Dockendorf, staff writer for *The Yankton (S.D.) Daily Press & Dakotan,* Ray Thomas is the human face on the story of economics. For Dockendorf and hundreds of small-town reporters across the nation, covering economics doesn't mean covering the Federal Reserve Board or the U.S. Labor Department or U.S. Department of Agriculture.

Rather, the story for them is in the farms and fields, the factories and mines, where ***real people*** are affected by the government policies and market forces we've been studying in this chapter.

Follow the chain of economic events to the logical end and put a human face on ***your*** coverage. Dockendorf does that:

> Springfield—Ray Thomas is reliving the "good old days" of farming, but he says he can't afford it any longer.
>
> He is selling hogs for 16 cents a pound—even less than the 18 cents a pound his family received in 1918. Hog prices are at their lowest level since 1972.
>
> Thomas says he always counted on his wife's income as a nurse to help pay their living expenses, but now her paycheck must pay the farm bills.
>
> "She has been working off the farm for 14 years to pay the taxes, the groceries, and the water and light bills—but never the farm expenses," Thomas said.
>
> "Even with my wife already working, I am looking to get a job for us to survive. This can't go on—I haven't made enough money to pay income taxes for five years."

Now, writer Dockendorf broadens his story to one very important dimension of the U.S. economy, federal subsidies:

> Thomas said he expects a number of hog producers will be driven off the farm unless prices turn around dramatically. "Something has to change, because people can't produce hogs for nothing."
>
> In response, Thomas and his neighbor, John Mesman, are proposing a one-time federal subsidy of $40 per head, up to 500 head, or $20,000 a farm. Congressmen from four states, along with the general public, will discuss the subsidy idea at a 10 a.m. forum today (Friday) at the Sioux Falls Stockyards.

Dockendorf now addresses the influence of banking policies laid down in distant cities and federal reluctance to intervene as "meatpackers and other large corporations nearly control an industry once the domain of the family farmers." . . .

It's the stuff of "big picture" economics, all right, but Dockendorf gives the last word to farmer Thomas:

> "We need to get the word out. Most city people talk about the good economy, but just lately they had layoffs in the steel industry and at Boeing," he said.
>
> "I think we are already in a recession as far as farmers go, but the city has not caught up with it. People don't realize it until it's in their backyard."
>
> —Randy Dockendorf, *The Daily Press & Dakotan*[12]

(*The Daily Press & Dakotan* was on the hog story early, but national press coverage quickly picked up momentum, and just weeks after Dockendorf's story on farmer Thomas, U.S. Agriculture Secretary Dan Glickman announced creation of a special task force to help hog farmers through their crisis.)

Summary

- You must learn to interpret distant signals for non-expert readers on the meaning of events in the production, distribution and consumption of wealth, which is what economics generally is about.
- Start by taking "snapshots"—writing localized stories—rather than trying to draw the "big picture" of global economics.
- Watch *current economic indicators,* such as gross domestic product, the total output of all goods and services within the United States, and gross national product, total output of all Americans, in or out of the country.
- *Lagging economic indicators* measure past economic performance, in such sectors as business inventories and long-term employment.
- *Leading economic indicators,* watched for signals on things to come, include new business enterprises, new orders for durable goods, construction contracts.
- Strive for the look-ahead angle, seeking authoritative sources on what, for example, a current measurement of the gross domestic product might mean for the national economy in months ahead.
- Three closely watched indicators are *gross domestic product, consumer price index* and *unemployment rate.*
- Other measurements—retail sales and housing starts, for example—lend themselves nicely to localized stories.
- Move very carefully from hard-news Five W and How reporting into writing "big picture" analysis and interpretation.
- Weaving two or more indicators into the same story—consumer price index and business inventories, for example—often creates an interpretative dimension for readers.
- As always, put a human face on economics—for example, the South Dakota hog farmer nearly driven out of business by national economic policies and global marketplace forces.

Recommended Reading

CNNfn and major newspapers make available, via the Internet, running coverage of the national and global economy that is fun—and educational—to watch.

Reading as AP, Dow Jones, Reuters and Bloomberg cover the daily breaking economic story can be of enormous value to beginners. Note particularly Washington coverage of the economic indicators discussed in this chapter.

For background: Jeremy Atack and Peter Passell, *A New Economic View of American History* (New York: W.W. Norton & Co., 1994), a look at the American economy from colonial days forward.

An excellent text: Gary M. Walton and Hugh Rockoff, *History of the American Economy,* 8th ed. (New York: The Dryden Press, 1998).

Also: Robert E. Hall and Marc Lieberman, *Microeconomic Principles and Applications* (Cincinnati: Southwestern College Publishing, 1998), and Robert J. Barro, *Macroeconomics,* 5th ed. (Cambridge: MIT Press, 1997).

Notes

1. "Early Warning," Nov. 20, 1998, p. A-1.
2. "Affluent Buyers Show Signs of Caution About Spending," Oct. 12, 1998, national edition, p. A-1.
3. "Housing Crunch Eases," Sept. 19, 1998, p. D-1.
4. "New Data Show That Economy Remains Strong," Nov. 25, 1998, national edition, p. A-1.
5. Dispatch for afternoon papers, Dec. 15, 1998.
6. "Signals Mixed in Job Sector," Dec. 5, 1998, Section 2, p. 1.
7. Dispatch for morning papers, Sept. 16, 1998.
8. Dispatch for morning papers, Dec. 16, 1998.
9. Dispatch for morning papers, Dec. 16, 1998.
10. Dispatch for morning papers, Dec. 2, 1998.
11. Dispatch for morning papers, Nov. 20, 1998.
12. "Area Farmers to Make Pitch for Hog Prices Subsidy," Dec. 4, 1998, p. A-1.

Exercises

1. By now, you should be reading business pages regularly, so over the next five days collect at least three examples of newspaper stories on the economic indicators or national economic developments discussed in this chapter. In 300 words, discuss the writing styles used. Are the stories straight hard-news Five Ws and How? Or, is there an element of interpretation and analysis? If there is analysis, is it by the writer or from authoritative sources who are quoted?

2. In 300 words, describe three localized story ideas for sidebars to news service accounts from Washington on the gross domestic product, unemployment rates or retail sales. What angles would your stories take? Which local experts would you interview?

3. Interview a local banker or business executive approved by your instructor. In 300-350 words, describe which economic indicators your source says are most important to the local economy. Which indicators does your source personally watch? Why?

4. The consumer price index represents, of course, a "market-basket" price survey by the U.S. Bureau of Labor Statistics of over 400 items nationwide. In 250 words, describe how you could establish a local "market-basket" index. Which 15 or 20 items could you price each month locally when the national CPI is received? Which items would you include to represent local buying habits (the price of heating oil in the North during winter, for example)?

5. Your instructor will designate a news development in the national economy, perhaps a new GDP or CPI report from Washington. ***Put a human face on that story.*** Interview local persons affected by the national news development. Illustrate how their lives felt impact. Weave in background information on the national news "peg" on which the story hangs. Write this in about 400 words.

7

Business: Walking the Main Street Beat

FINANCIAL COLLAPSE along the far-off Pacific Rim is big news. So are World Bank moves in Geneva and Federal Reserve pronouncements in Washington.

But have you ever been in small-town America on the day Wal-Mart or Kmart opens a new store?

Ever been at a city council meeting the night Eckerd Drugs asks permission to build a super store in a residential neighborhood?

After years in "big picture" journalism and as a foreign correspondent, I watched astounded in a small southern town as ***thousands*** of eager shoppers and the just plain curious turned out for a Kmart opening. I watched amazed as huge Eckerd Drugs retreated in disarray before angry residents screaming, "Not in our backyard!"[1]

All to say that here in Chapter 7, Walking the Main Street Beat, we are heading into—not away from—one of the hottest, most fun news beats in journalism. It is on Main Street—or just around the corner—where for many Americans *real* news lies.

Why? Because local businesses create local jobs and throw payrolls into local economies. Local businesses pay taxes that support local schools, roads, public services of all kinds. And, local businesses are "good citizens" or "bad citizens," helping or harming the local environment, the air we breathe, the water we drink—our daily way of life.

So, although "business" is defined broadly as the manufacturing, buying and selling of commodities and services, we'll discuss covering local business as it impacts your readers' lives—every day, in many ways. As always, you must learn to *translate* the esoterica of the business beat into terms meaningful to your readers.

We'll also discuss *company news,* reporting that's somewhat more complex in substance and more sophisticated in tone because it's designed to *inform business experts about business.* Here, obviously, you need a high degree of reporting and writing expertise to serve readers who themselves are business executives, investors and others who know a great deal—perhaps more than you—about your subject.

As always, remember that important decisions—whether to buy or sell, whether to invest or not—are made on what we write. Accuracy is paramount.

First, Cover the Big Picture

There's a lot of business action on Main Street, all right. But don't plod along simply looking for it in store windows. Watch also the wider story—your community's overall economic health—and write that, too.

And when you take that broader view, keep two things in mind:

FIRST, you need substantive *dollars-and-cents reporting.* Light features about curious people who grow unusually large pumpkins or who fashion unusually creative pottery aren't what your readers need in their *business* sections.

SECOND, you must seek interesting *news pegs* to catch reader interest, then write colorfully and vividly to get into your newspaper's crowded pages and into your readers' limited reading time.

Gail Kinsey Hill of the Portland *Sunday Oregonian* did that in a major takeout on the economy of the coastal town of Newport. Her news peg was, of all things, an *orca killer whale.*

Hill's whale wasn't just an ordinary whale, of course. It was a whale named Keiko, star of a popular movie titled *Free Willy,* who was moved to a Newport aquarium prior to being released in the North Atlantic.

Worldwide interest in this movie star is Hill's news peg as, in a story headlined "City's Economy Shipshape," she examines the impact on Newport's tourism, its fishing industry and general business economy. Her lead:

Newport—When Idea Print Works Inc. of Newport won a contract to silkscreen Keiko T-shirts, Vice President Victor Weitzel knew he had grabbed an economic behemoth by the tail.

He held on tight, and the ride was a wonder. Within months, business tripled.

"It was like going from 0 to 150 mph," he said.

He wasn't alone. As tourists rushed to Newport to gawk at the star of the movie "Free Willy," the business community flourished.

You'll recognize, from our Chapter 5 discussion, the writing structure—the "neck of the vase"—Hill selects for her profile of Newport's economy. With her first four grafs, Hill uses a single-anecdote intro to *characterize* the impact of Keiko's arrival. But, now Keiko is leaving. Hill's next three grafs:

> Now Keiko is leaving. He will head for Iceland and his new North Atlantic Ocean pen Sept. 9. After that Weitzel won't be printing any more Keiko shirts, and the rest of Newport, a town of 10,000 tucked into Oregon's central coastline, won't enjoy the killer cash the whale brought to town.
>
> Newport, heavily reliant on tourism, will feel Keiko's absence. The Oregon Coast Aquarium, Keiko's home, expects the visitor count to slow considerably, well into next year and perhaps longer. Many motel, restaurant and shop owners admit, sometimes reluctantly, that business growth may slacken.
>
> "We're not deluding ourselves," said Phyllis Bell, aquarium president. "Attendance will drop off; it will drop off quite a bit."

Note above how the writer quickly summarizes the views of motel, restaurant and shop owners. Note also that of this story's first seven grafs, two are devoted to full quotes. *People want to read what other people say.*

Now, writer Hill broadens her story, inserting *informed comment* from *authoritative sources* and gradually weaving in the hard facts—*the numbers*—so important in this type of reporting.

> Hans Radtke, a natural resource economist from Yachats and a member of the Governor's Council of Economic Advisors, estimated that tourism, which makes up about 15 percent of the area's economy, could slump by as much as 20 percent—should the extra visitors suddenly go elsewhere.
>
> "Keiko's a hard act to follow," Radtke said.
>
> Still, economists and business leaders agree, Newport will be better off economically than before Keiko arrived in January 1996.

But what does "better off" mean? In business writing you can't let such sweeping generalizations flap in the wind without tying them down to hard facts. And writer Hill does that:

> More than 200 motel rooms have been added to the town's lodging capacity in the past three years; restaurants, shops and small businesses have proliferated; and new attractions, such as the Yaquina Head interpretive center, have opened.
>
> Tourism along the central coast is much bigger than one orca. Tourism-related revenues have increased by 5 percent to 7 percent annually since the early 1990s. The new businesses and hotel rooms, and the publicity generated by Keiko's stay, increase the area's ability to attract and house tourists.

Writer Hill now quotes yet one more authoritative source, the executive director of Oregon's Tourism Commission. But, recall our need to focus not only on important people who make important decisions but also the "little people" affected by those decisions. Hill quotes one of the "little people" who live off summer tourism:

> "You see it build every year," said Carol Edwards, a waitress at Georgie's Beachside Grill, a new restaurant that overlooks the Pacific. "It's gotten so touristy, I don't think you're going to see it slow appreciably."

Now, understand that if you write for a highly technical business journal—a magazine read principally by bankers or brokers, for example—comments from a waitress who lives off tips would be regarded as entirely anecdotal, not solid, operative information for making important business decisions. But for readers of a general-circulation newspaper, the "human touch" is essential in business writing.

For that reason, writer Hill ends her story with a "kicker," returning to the T-shirt guy she opened with. Now he wonders about all the shirts, coffee mugs, amulets, refrigerator magnets and key chains he produced carrying the whale's image.

> "We have a ton of that stuff," he said. "I don't know what we're going to do with it."

> —Gail Kinsey Hill, *The Sunday Oregonian*[2]

Hill, incidentally, brings impressive credentials to business reporting, including a master's degree with emphasis in business journalism and experience on *The Portland Business Journal,* a weekly devoted exclusively to economic and financial news. She spent three days reporting the Newport story.[3]

LESSON: If you aspire to Big League business reporting, prepare professionally and invest the time necessary to do the job right.

Watch–Carefully–Real Estate

You can monitor your town's economy by watching *local business indicators,* just as you monitor the national economy by watching gross domestic product or retail sales.

One of your best local indicators is *real estate activity.*

In boom times, new homes, condos and business offices are thrown up. Property values and rents soar. Realtors, mortgage banks and construction firms flourish—and successive waves of prosperity sweep over much of your community.

In bad times, contraction in real estate is immediate. Construction firms lay off workers. Banks tighten lending. Realtors scratch for sales commissions. Home values plummet.

For every newspaper, the real estate story is big because it has compelling interest for both reader constituencies principally served by business pages—

general readers (the folks who own homes) and your business community (those folks who build and finance homes, offices and factory building).

Broadly, you must watch two types of real estate—***commercial*** (office space, factory buildings) and ***residential*** (homes, apartments, condos).

Commercial real estate activity is one of the most important ***and quickest*** indicators of general business trends in your town. Low vacancy of downtown office space means business is moving into your town; high rents mean businesses are prospering and able to pay more for space.

Below, a *Boston Globe* writer cites hard dollar-and-cents facts drawn from authoritative sources and sketches quickly a view of his city's commercial real estate market:

> Just how hot this city's commercial real estate market has become is summed up in a couple of superlatives found in a national survey released yesterday by Meredith & Grew Inc.
>
> As of mid-1998, Boston had the lowest downtown office vacancy rate in North America, along with the highest office rents, the survey said.
>
> The 2.5 percent vacancy rate compares with a nearly 20 percent rate in 1991, when the real estate market hit bottom in the midst of recession. The current average annual rent of $45 a square foot for first-class downtown office space is double what it was at that time.

Now, the writer cites an authoritative source on what all this says about Boston's overall economy:

> The information comes from real estate services firms such as Meredith & Grew that are affiliates of Oncor International, a network of 45 real estate companies.
>
> "These stats confirm that Boston has a very healthy economy in lots of ways, and additional supply [of office buildings] is warranted, particularly downtown," commented Thomas Hynes, Meredith & Grew's president.

Now, the *Globe* quotes a source as saying rents of $60 or more per square foot are "popping up" in downtown Boston and immediately compares that with rents elsewhere ($44 in San Francisco, $38 in Manhattan, and so forth). Remember: No stand-alone figure is meaningful. Compare!

So, the *Globe* writer nicely describes the ***what*** of Boston commercial real estate: office space is scarce. Is there a broader ***real what?*** Yes:

> The lack of new office space has become a concern for the city's planning agency, the Boston Redevelopment Authority, which is encouraging developers on their plans for several additional towers. The worry is that without space for growing Boston companies to move into, the companies will be tempted to move away or expand elsewhere. . . .
>
> —Richard Kindleberger, *The Boston Globe*[4]

The story above, incidentally, **led** the *Boston Globe*'s nationally prestigious business news section. Here's a small-town commercial real estate story that led the ***front page*** of *The Athens (Ga.) Daily News,* complete with banner headline ("Wal-mart Proposed for East Athens") and a color "locater" map showing the precise locations:

> Athens-Clarke County will boast two Wal-Mart stores—one of them a new "Supercenter"—if a shopping center project by the Bentonville, Ark.–based corporation and an Atlanta development company proceeds as planned.
>
> In a joint announcement Thursday, Wal-Mart Stores Inc. and JDN Realty Corp. revealed plans to build a 229,200 square-foot shopping center, anchored by a Wal-Mart Supercenter with a full grocery and garden center.
>
> The project is proposed for acreage in eastern Athens-Clarke County on U.S. Highway 78. . . .
>
> —Don Nelson, *The Athens Daily News* [5]

On the same day, *The Athens Daily News* granted No. 2 spot on its front page to another commercial real estate story (this one under a multi-column headline, "Downtown's Old Belk Building Soon to Be a Parking Lot"):

> The skyline and landscape in the eastern end of downtown Athens are about to change.
>
> Benson's Inc., the owner of the East Clayton Street building that once housed Belk department store, will demolish the 15,240 square-foot structure to make room for a parking lot, and eventually, an upscale hotel. . . .
>
> —Don Nelson, *The Athens Daily News* [6]

So, the **what** is that a small town's "skyline and landscape" are changing. And the **real what?** Jobs. Payroll. Prosperity.

The Anderson (S.C.) Independent-Mail sees that angle in reporting that a company will move into an empty building. This **tops** the front page:

> An Illinois company won't let the former Venture Packaging facility stay empty for long.
>
> Courtesy Corp., a plastics manufacturer that makes the tops of Gatorade sports drink bottles, plans to move into the empty building on Anderson's south side. . . .
>
> Courtesy plans to add 250 jobs over the next two years and contribute a $20 million investment. . . .
>
> —Naomi Snyder, *The Anderson (S.C.) Independent-Mail* [7]

Well, in newspapers large or small you don't sentence yourself to writing deadly dull briefs for deep inside pages when you cover commercial real estate. Indeed, you can get your copy—your byline—prominently displayed out front!

In covering **residential** real estate, remember this: For most Americans, buying a home is the largest single investment they ever make; for many renters, that check for the landlord is the month's largest single expenditure.

That is, you have **news** when anybody or anything affects the availability of housing, its value and cost, its financing, its care. Every significant socioeconomic development affects residential real estate.

- Industry moving in or out affects values throughout town.
- Street crime and quality of schools affect home values in individual neighborhoods.
- Highway construction, zoning changes, expanding business areas all affect home values.
- Mortgage loan availability can restrict or spur home construction and sales, drive values up or down.

When covering residential real estate, keep watch for such indicators of things to come.

Jobs, Unions, Workplace Issues

Local economic indicators important in one way or another to all your readers are found in this category.

Jobs—types available and their pay—are basic indicators of local business activity and, thus, crucial news on Main Street beats across America.

Unions are news because in many towns they represent huge numbers of local residents **and** they can assist or shut down some local businesses **and** help engender or endanger local economic prosperity.

Workplace issues such as equal opportunity and sexual harassment are of compelling interest because Americans are increasingly choosy about where and how they work and under what conditions.

Covering the Job Front

First look at the big picture—how many jobs there are (the what) and the overall impact on the local economy (the real what).

Don Nelson of *The Athens (Ga.) Daily News* leads with the **real what**— the impact—of job growth in his town:

> A university economic expert foresees Athens merchants faring much better than national retailers and even statewide businesses this holiday season.
>
> Jeff Humphreys, director of economic forecasting for the University of Georgia's Terry College of Business, said the fact that the metro Athens area enjoyed the nation's highest percentage of job growth should ensure busy cash registers for area merchants. . . .

Nelson now inserts crucial numbers: Athens-area employment increased 8.6 percent in the past year. Economist Humphreys predicts holiday spending will increase 4–6 percent over the previous year and disposable personal income (income minus taxes) will rise 4.5 percent.

Building on the specifics of those excellent indicators, Nelson turns to his authoritative source for a comprehensive overview:

> In terms of buying trends, Humphreys predicted that shoppers will be looking for better values and will gravitate toward practical items and inexpensive luxuries. He expects items related to home, health and travel to see above average sales growth. Favorable demographics will boost sales in toys and children's clothing. Likewise, sales of computers and books should see an increase. He said home improvement stores and discount retailers should fare very well.
>
> Areas that take a hit from lower sales are jewelry and automobiles, flowers and cards, he said.
>
> —Don Nelson, *The Athens Daily News*[8]

Excellent sources for job numbers and wage levels—and what they mean—include the state employment commission's office in your town, the local chamber of commerce and university economists. Contact also the personnel departments and economic forecasters of major local companies. And watch the "employment" category of your own newspaper's classified ad section. It's an excellent barometer of local economic health.

Covering the Union Beat

Just think of the enormous number of **stakeholders** vitally affected by trouble between, say, an airline and its unions:

- The traveling public.
- Businesses that sell fuel, food, maintenance and airplanes to the airline.
- The unions and their thousands of members plus businesses where those members spend their paychecks.
- The airlines, their customers **and investors.**
- Competing airlines, railroad companies, bus lines.

Clearly, organized labor and its impact on the local economy are important. Yet, many news organizations provide little ongoing coverage of organized labor as an important political and economic institution. Mostly, we jump in only when trouble erupts.

When you are assigned to this beat, keep a checklist for each story:

✔ **Explain precisely who is involved.** Your readers need the union's full title and national or international affiliations. How many members are involved? Which company operations are affected? All divisions or just local operations?

✔ *Define the issues.* And note the plural "issues." Even if the single shouted demand is "higher wages!" you'll find, beneath the surface, tension over company work rules, health and pension benefits and so forth.

✔ *State*—carefully—*both sides' positions, claims and countercharges.* Be fair and balanced. That's sometimes difficult when union-company skirmishing gets heated or even violent.

✔ *Describe how stakeholders are affected.* Will the wider public suffer? Local businesses? How about company shareholders? Is their stock value dropping? How about the company's marketplace image and position? Will the company's competitors benefit?

✔ *Report the status and techniques of the negotiating strategies employed by both sides.* Are outside mediators or the government involved? Report precise details of any settlement—wages, working conditions, benefits.

Note below how a *Chicago Tribune* pro weaves essential elements into his first two grafs:

> Increasing the pressure on Northwest Airlines Corp., which resumes negotiations Monday in hopes of heading off an imminent pilots' strike, the machinists union asked the Federal Mediation Board on Thursday to start the countdown on when it can strike the airline.
>
> A little more than a week after 27,000 mechanics, reservation and gate agents, and equipment service workers rejected a contract proposal, the International Association of Machinists and Aerospace Workers said negotiations with Eagan, Minn.–based Northwest are at an impasse because the airline has refused to resume bargaining on new contracts for the four groups it represents.

The *Tribune* writer adds vital details:

• A strike could strand as many as 144,000 passengers.
• Service would be particularly hard hit in Minneapolis, Detroit and Memphis and on flights to Japan.
• The pilots are "trying to win back some of the salary and benefits they gave up in 1993 when the airline was on the verge of bankruptcy."
• Northwest's competitors are "already banking on a strike" and have raised fares in cities where they compete with Northwest, "calculating that travelers will be willing to pay more to board their flights to avoid getting stranded if they book flights on Northwest."

Now, the *Tribune* writer moves to precise details on the meaning of all this for the largest group of stakeholders, the traveling public:

According to an airline newsletter that tracks air fares, United Airlines and Atlanta-based Delta Air Lines have boosted fares $20 to $60 on a round-trip ticket on routes where one or the other is the only Northwest competitor offering non-stop service.

—John Schmeltzer, *The Chicago Tribune*[9]

Below, a writer is precise in explaining to one group of stakeholders—investors—the meaning for them in the settlement of a strike against Bell Atlantic Corp.:

Bell Atlantic shares, traded on the New York Stock Exchange, fell to a nine-month low on Monday, the second day of the strike, then rebounded on news of the settlement. The shares closed yesterday at $41.75, up 56.3 cents on heavier-than-average volume of 2.53 million shares. . . .

—Henry J. Holcomb, *The Philadelphia Inquirer*[10]

LESSON: In reporting labor news, don't focus so intently on the quarreling parties that you overlook your responsibility to other stakeholders, particularly the wider public.

Covering Workplace Issues

This news sector has grown explosively and now is an important reporting beat. Broadly, two dimensions are hottest:

1. Who gets into the workplace and, once there, whether they are treated fairly—men and women, whites and minorities, the young and the old.
2. Workplace rules and conditions of employment and how they are evolving as Americans redefine what they will and won't do on the job.

Workplace opportunity draws major journalistic attention, particularly whether race, gender or age discrimination exists. Much of this reporting is straightforward:

Older women in the workforce can face the dual burden of age and sex discrimination, which presents daunting obstacles to getting ahead.

The issues facing older female workers are likely to get more attention as their numbers hit unprecedented levels.

"Age plays differently for women than it does for men," says Deborah Chalfie at the American Association of Retired Persons (AARP). "Baby boomers have a much stronger attachment to the workplace than . . . their grandmothers, so it's likely to become an increasing issue."

Some issues include . . .

—Stephanie Armour, *USA Today*[11]

A McClatchy Newspapers reporter does a straight reporting job on a dramatic increase in black-owned businesses and wins major display in newspapers nationwide:

> Washington—One of the strongest, most durable business expansions in American history is being led by a minority group that usually finds itself trailing the economic parade: the nation's 34 million African-Americans, whose incomes are suddenly rising at a remarkable pace.
>
> Over the last five years, as the vibrant economy pushed Americans back to the record-high living standards they reached a decade ago, African-Americans have not just kept pace. Their household incomes have skyrocketed, soaring three times faster than the nation as a whole.
>
> The 16.8 percent climb has added almost $3,600 a year in inflation-adjusted income to the average African-American household, which topped $25,000 for the first time last year. . . .
>
> —David Westphal, McClatchy Newspapers[12]

However, covering workplace issues doesn't stop with such straightforward and, frankly, ***predictable*** stories as discrimination, real or imagined. Note these workplace issues—and how nicely writers handle them:

New ways to dress . . .

> One of the last companies to insist on white shirts is waving the white flag.
> Electronic Data Systems Corp. is dumping its rules that required men to wear only white shirts and suits and ties, and limited women to dresses, suits and stockings.
>
> The change, announced Monday by the new executive vice president for human resources, Robert Mintz, should end the company's reputation as a fashion stick-in-the-mud in a high-tech industry. . . .
>
> —Aisha Sultan, *The Wall Street Journal*[13]

New ways to decide . . .

> Managers at Texas Instruments will soon begin taking a class on making decisions based not only on business needs—but on workers' needs.
>
> The effort is part of a growing realization by Corporate America that to be family-friendly, a company can't just set up programs on paper and wait for employees to sign up. . . .
>
> —The Associated Press[14]

New ways to inner peace . . .

> The phone is ringing, bosses are hovering, and the deadline is just about here.
> You can't prioritize, your muscles are tense, and all you can think about is how awful it all is. If only you could escape, maybe you could get it all together.

> Companies including Bethesda-based Acacia Life Insurance Co. and New York City's PT & Co. realized the need for mending the worker's soul, and both provide that escape in the form of a meditation room. . . .
>
> —Amy Joyce, *The Washington Post*[15]

New ways to fire . . .

> You walk into the office, and as the day goes on you realize that the guy who sat in the cubicle next to you for years isn't there. It's not just that he hasn't come in to work. There is no trace of him. The family pictures, the plants, the cartoons he liked to clip and post are simply gone. Office scuttlebutt has it that he has been dismissed. But there is no official word: no memo, no department e-mail.
>
> Welcome to the modern workplace, where companies are so concerned about wrongful-termination suits that silence often replaces honest communication. Most managers with power to dismiss have faced the problem: whether to let people know why a colleague has been let go or to lie low. . . .
>
> —Jeffrey L. Seglin, *The New York Times*[16]

LESSON: The workplace with its new ways is a happy hunting ground for an imaginative reporter with a gentle writing touch.

Adventures in Company News

News services report IBM's earnings (profits) are higher than Wall Street expects—but the company's stock immediately plunges $17.25 a share, and that drags down the Dow Jones Industrial Average by 143.41 points. Investors are stunned.[17]

A *Washington Post* reporter notes "dollar" stores are emerging as one of retailing's fastest-growing sectors. The stores sell stuff "that might be considered schlocky, such as Barbie knockoffs," but are very profitable and offer customers great bargains—including $19.99 leather work boots and out-of-season shirts and pants at $1 each.[18]

Forbes analyzes a drug gang and finds its profits plummet when gang war erupts and drug sellers knock off each other in the streets. Readers get "an inside peek into the numbers behind the crack business."[19]

Welcome to company news. And you thought it had to be dull!

Well, it isn't dull, for two reasons any journalist will recognize:

1. Covering company news involves delivering good news or bad news to readers, news of profit or loss, better or worse products and service. And what more could a reporter ask than to be covering news crucially important to readers?
2. As in covering war, politics or any other hot story, you'll find fascinating and, often, subtle or hidden interlockings of personalities, economic forces

and competitive factors running through company news. For truly inquis- itive reporters, company news is just plain fascinating stuff.

Take the IBM story, for example. Directly or through mutual funds and retirement plans, *millions* of Americans own IBM stock. An owner of 1,000 shares lost, of course, $17,250 in *moments* as that news story sped around the globe.

Even investors who owned *no* IBM shares suffered. Millions of dollars in market values disappeared when other computer-based companies were hit by the fallout of doubt surrounding IBM's performance.

No subtleties there? That's just obvious cause-and-effect journalism? Like covering a football game? Think again.

Why did IBM's share value *fall* when its profits *exceeded* expectations? Ah, therein are the fascinating subtleties.

It seems probing reporters sifted through IBM's profit report and dis- covered the company's sales of hardware (as contrasted with software and services) fell 1.5 percent, and *that* is what Wall Street analysts didn't like. Bang! Down went IBM stock.

The drop in stock value of other computer-based companies was heav- ily nuanced, too. Not only did the black cloud over IBM extend over them, but IBM was such an important component of the Dow Jones Industrial Average that IBM's price fall was responsible for about half of the average's 143.41-point drop.

Talk about facing challenges in journalism! Reporters covering Big League company news confront them daily.

And, want to get close to your readers? Want to talk to them about what *they* talk about with each other? Then, go where Stephanie Stoughton of *The Washington Post* goes on the company news beat. Here are the open- ing grafs for the story mentioned above:

> The variety store's obituary was written long ago, the cause of death listed as expansion of big-box discount chains such as Wal-Mart and Kmart. But from the ashes of the five-and-dime has emerged a breed of "dollar" stores that are, to the surprise of some analysts, becoming one of the fastest-growing sectors in retailing.
>
> They are the small Family Dollar and Dollar General stores tucked in small towns and downtowns across the nation. This generation of anything- you-need, quintessentially American store has filled a gap in the retail discount landscape in part by nestling in urban and rural areas that big discounters have overlooked as they've migrated to the more affluent suburbs. In the process, the dollar stores have proved it's possible not only to coexist with Wal-Mart but also sometimes to siphon off sales from the giant.

Those well-crafted grafs above nicely cast the writer's net wide enough to attract *three* reader constituencies—general-interest readers who are consumers, retailers (those in discount merchandising and those competing against it) **and,** third, investors wondering whether to plunk a few bucks into companies owning Wal-Mart, Kmart or the competing discount stores.

Now, the *Post* reporter turns to two requirements of **any** well-done company news story:

1. She must **localize** the story after her two-graf intro look at the national picture.
2. She must **serve all reader constituencies** that were promised, in the intro, details pertinent to them (general-interest consumers, retailers and investors).

In a decision sound for a reporter on a general-circulation paper, the *Post*'s Stoughton first turns, in her third graf, to localizing her story for Washington and her **consumer-readers:**

> The locations are often ostentatiously unostentatious, like the tiny, triangular-shaped shopping center on Michigan Avenue in Northeast Washington, unidentified by any sign, its name, if there is one, a mystery. On a recent Sunday, most of the center's stores were closed, protected by barriers resembling metal garage doors.
>
> This is exactly where Family Dollar Stores wants to be. In fact its Northeast store is one of the chain's best performers. Most days, it bustles with business as customers scour the packed shelves for deeply discounted items such as $19.99 leather work boots, rolls of paper towels for 50 cents each and the Bloopers brand of irregular underwear, a buck a pair.
>
> Up front, shoppers can sort through a selection of out-of-season shirts and pants—each going for $1. Bargains on everyday items are the store's bread and butter. . . .

Note above these factors:

- The writer creates a **word picture** of a store and locates it in Washington. Ah, readers say, **now** I know what we're talking about here!
- The time element is imprecise ("a recent Sunday"). No need to report a company profile such as this on one day, then rush to write it for publication the next.
- There is precise dollars-and-cents detail for consumer-readers. They may not understand discount merchandising but they **do** understand underwear at "a buck a pair."

After more consumer detail, the *Post* writer turns to a second reader constituency, her **business community readers.**

> The dollar stores are not new. They're experiencing a rebirth and an expansion, transforming themselves into more convenient, closer-to-home versions of Wal-Mart. They are much smaller than discount supercenters in floor space—generally about 10,000 square feet, vs. 200,000 square feet.

"Some people don't want to shop in a 150,000- or 200,000-square-foot store with groceries and everything else if all they're looking for is a tube of toothpaste or a T-shirt," said George Mahoney, senior vice president of Family Dollar Stores Inc. "We locate in the neighborhoods so they'll have to pass us on the way to these [discount] stores."

And, the third reader constituency, *the investors*? The *Post* writer notes Family Dollar's sales rose 9 percent in the year just ended and that economic indicators signal even better times ahead. She reports an executive of one dollar store company, Dollar Tree Stores Inc., is maneuvering to make the company even more attractive to investors. Then, this:

> Investors apparently like his company's formula. Dollar Tree's stock went public in 1995 at $6.67 and closed Friday at $39.87½. Like its competition, the chain is growing rapidly. It now operates about 1,000 stores, including 40 in the Baltimore-Washington region. Next year, it hopes to open 200 stores.
>
> —Stephanie Stoughton, *The Washington Post* [20]

And *Forbes'* analysis of the economics of drug pushing? It's an example of off-beat features that pop up on the company news beat. Some are deadly serious, some funny—but if you do them correctly, *all* must leave readers with a core understanding they didn't possess when they started reading.

That is, yes, profile the little old lady whose business has been selling newspapers and magazines in the lobby of the county building for 30 years and, yes, describe what a colorful, cheerful little person she is. But also report how much she makes for every *Wall Street Journal* she sells and how much of *Time* magazine's cover price she gets to keep.

Yes, profile the new arts and crafts shop on Main Street, but also give your readers details of how its owners organized their business, raised capital, bought inventory and, for certain, how their goods are priced.

Indeed, do an off-beat financial analysis of a drug gang, but quote authoritative sources and answer obvious questions:

> . . . Two economists discovered that the rule of economics applies to narcotics. So why do kids risk a bullet in the head for $3 an hour? Part of the lure is glamour: There's a certain prestige that goes with drug pushing. And there's the hope of promotion. The economists found that some neighborhood gang leaders can make $65 an hour, and the hope of reaching the top keeps the other pushers going.
>
> —Scott Woolley, *Forbes* [21]

In sum, a well-done company story generally has these characteristics:

- It is *localized,* written about a local company *or* a company which, even if distant, is of interest to our three principal reader constituencies: local consumers, business executives or investors.

- It is *timely,* with an interesting *news* peg—today's new store opening, perhaps, or tomorrow's new product launch—but need not be rushed hurriedly into print.
- It is *well written,* crafted to go far beyond the Five Ws and How by luring readers with color and detail not normally found in spot-news stories.
- It is *strongly reported* and contains dollars-and-cents facts, hard numbers that leave readers *informed* as well as amused or entertained.

Let's take a deeper look at the need for hard figures in reporting company news.

The Earnings Report

For many of your readers, particularly stock market investors, one of a business section's most valuable offerings is the *earnings report.*

This report can come in two parts—the *earnings digest* and an *explanatory story.*

The digest looks like this:

AMERITRADE HLDG (Nq)		AMTD
Quar Dec 31:	1998	1997
Revenues	$52,116,908	$25,675,693
Net income	3,741,507	(11,249,342)
Avg dil shs	29,133,444	a29,052,234
Shr earns:		
Net income	.13	a(.39)
a-Adjusted for a two-for-one stock split paid in August 1998.		

Here's how to read that earnings digest (which was published in *The Wall Street Journal*):

- Ameritrade Holding Corp. is traded on the Nasdaq (Nq) Stock Market. (Other exchanges are (N), New York Stock Exchange; (A), American Exchange; (Pa), Pacific; (C), Chicago; (P), Philadelphia; (B), Boston; (T), Toronto; (Mo), Montreal; (F), foreign.)
- Ameritrade's stock market symbol (which you can see scrolling across the bottom of financial news cable channels) is AMTD.
- This digest covers the quarter (three months) ended Dec. 31, 1998, compared to the *same* quarter in 1997.
- Revenues for the quarters were $52.1 million and $25.6 million, respectively.
- Net income (profit) was $3.7 million in 1998, compared to a *loss* (in brackets) of $11.2 million the year before.
- Average daily shares outstanding (shares held by banks, mutual funds, individual investors) were 29.1 million in 1998, compared to 29 million the year before.

- Net income was 13 cents per share in 1998, versus a loss of 39 cents in 1997.
- The footnote "a" (and **always** read the footnotes in reporting financial news) means the company's board of directors issued two shares of stock for every one share held by investors. Such "splits" are designed to keep the per-share market price low so investors will continue trading in the stock. Although investors get more shares, the dollar value of their holdings remains unchanged. That is, in a two-for-one split of a stock valued at $100, investors receive two shares worth $50 each.

Though packed with information, Ameritrade's earnings digest lacks the detail investors need. So, *The Wall Street Journal* presents, **on the same day,** a lengthy story by staff writer Rebecca Buckman. Her intro:

> Despite technology problems stemming from the fast growth of online stock trading, online broker Ameritrade Holding Corp. said revenue more than doubled for the fiscal first quarter, helping it handily beat analysts' profit expectations.

Note, above, how Buckman **opens** with, "Despite technology problems . . ." **That** analytical dimension simply cannot be drawn from the bare-bones earnings digest.

Now, the *Journal* writer expands on information in the earnings digest:

> Ameritrade, of Omaha, Neb., rode investors' continuing fascination with online stock trading—and Internet stocks themselves—to net income of $3.7 million, or 13 cents a diluted share, for the period ended Dec. 31. Wall Street had been expecting earnings of nine cents a share, according to First Call Corp.
>
> Last year, the company had a loss of $11.2 million, or 39 cents a share, as it spent much more heavily on advertising to attract customers.

The writer now switches to deeper analysis:

> But Ameritrade's rapid growth has a big downside, this quarter's earnings show: lost profits from overloaded and poorly performing computer systems.
>
> The company took charges of $5.1 million, or 11 cents a share after taxes, to upgrade its technology and reimburse customers who received bad trade executions when Ameritrade's systems were slow or not working at all. Although all on-line-brokerage firms have been struggling with bogged-down systems during the wild market volatility of the past several weeks, analysts say Ameritrade's problems have been especially acute.

Now come quotes from an outside authoritative source **and** the company chairman:

> "Even though they've had a great quarter, it's painfully obvious that the technology problems are starting to hurt the bottom line," said Stephen

C. Franco, an electronic-commerce analyst who covers Ameritrade for Piper Jaffray Inc.

Ameritrade Chairman and Chief Executive J. Joe Ricketts acknowledged that his firm, which snared hordes of new customers last year through an expensive ad campaign, is "struggling to get the infrastructure for the technology in place."

—Rebecca Buckman, *The Wall Street Journal*[22]

Buckman provides even more on information in the earnings digest plus further analysis. Result: readers know the ***what***—the numbers—and the ***real what*** of the numbers' meaning!

Learning to sort through company financial reports for the crucial numbers and their meaning is so important that I asked Steven M. Sears, senior writer with Dow Jones News Service, to walk you through the process. See his hints in Box 7-1.

Box 7-1

How to Handle the Numbers
By Steven M. Sears

The first rule in dealing with numbers is not to be afraid of numbers. Many people are intimidated by financial reports, but they are easy to analyze no matter how complicated they appear.

The second rule is to be completely accurate. Double-check all numbers. Your articles have immediate impact on financial markets. Investors buy or sell stock based on what they read—so get it right.

Corporate earnings reports are one of the most common financial statements handled by business reporters. Every three months—a financial quarter—publicly traded corporations release earnings reports that tell investors if the company made or lost money. Investors use this information to decide if a business is growing or shrinking.

Wall Street is obsessed with corporate earnings. A good quarter can set off frenzied bidding that increases a stock's price. A bad earnings report can prompt investors to quickly sell stock, causing the price to fall.

Once you become familiar with basic terms like ***revenue*** (amounts received for sale of products and services), ***net income*** (revenue less expenses), ***earnings per share*** (profit accruing to shareholders), a 10-page report filled with numbers and graphs is simple to write about.

All financial statements, from corporate earnings to economic forecasts, have one purpose: they measure something—and that can cause millions, and even ***billions,*** of dollars to move in the financial markets.

This is what you need to know when writing about corporate earnings:

First, check if earnings meet or beat the consensus estimate, a widely available number published by First Call Inc. This is the number that Wall Street expected the company to report. If Wall Street expected $1 a share and the company earned 80 cents, expect the stock to sell off. But if the same company reported $1.25 a share, the stock could race higher.

The current quarter's earnings must be compared to the same year-ago quarter's results. ***All financial reports are useless unless compared with the year-ago quarter.*** Investors look for trends and patterns to track the growth, or decline, of a corporation.

You also must write about how much money flowed into the company during the quarter—revenue. You want to see if revenue rose or fell in the quarter compared to the previous quarter and why.

Wall Street is filled with people who do nothing but follow companies and measure every dime and dollar made or spent. These analysts work at securities firms that buy and sell stocks and bonds.

Analysts are good sources for earnings stories. After you learn from the company how much it earned during the quarter, call analysts to add perspective to the numbers. After much study of earnings reports, analysts assign investment ratings such as buy, sell or hold, that are used by investors to decide what to do about the stock.

To pull everything together, let's look at an imaginary company—Widget Inc.'s fourth quarter earnings report. A few weeks after the quarter ended Dec. 31, the company released a report to tell investors about its financial condition in the previous three months.

The report is filled with pages of numbers, but you're going straight to the heart of the matter by looking for revenue and net income.

The following is how you might write a story on Widget after finding out the company's net income, revenue, analysts' consensus estimate, sales and expenses. (Remember, things are not always what they appear to be.)

Widget Inc. surprised Wall Street today by reporting that net income increased 25% in the fourth quarter because the holiday season created strong demand.

The company reported net income of $1.25 a share on revenue of $750 million, compared with $1 a share on revenue of $700 million in the year-ago period. The analysts' consensus estimate was $1.05 a share.

"This is the best quarter we've had since 1952 and it's only going to get better from here," Chairman I.M. Rich said. "People understand how important widgets are."

But Tom Bear, an analyst at Greed Inc., said investors may not want to buy Widget stock. He said fourth-quarter results benefitted from aggressive price cuts that reduced the company's gross profit margin to 10% from 60%.

"This will catch up with the company. They can't grow their business if they don't make more of a profit on their products because the cost of making widgets has increased," said Bear, who lowered his investment rating to sell from strong buy.

Widget's expenses increased 700% in the fourth-quarter, compared to the year-ago period. Chairman Rich said the increase was caused by the cost of new machines that ultimately will let the company make widgets for almost nothing.

"Everyone needs widgets," he said. "Our sales figures have grown every quarter since 1952 and we set a record in the fourth quarter. Profits will only increase from here."

Widget's future earnings probably will decrease in the future because the company will take a charge, or deduct money from earnings, to pay for the new machines, said Joe Bull, an analyst at Make Money & Co. The machinery costs $12 billion.

But Bull said the machines will revolutionize the Widget business even though it may depress earnings for the coming year.

"This is a great opportunity. Short-sighted investors are fleeing, but the stock is a bargain at its current price," said Bull, who raised his investment rating to strong buy from hold.

Widget's stock fell 2 to 32⅜, off its low of 28, on volume of 1.2 million shares, compared with average daily volume of 435,000 shares.

"Widget is a solid company, but the new machines are extremely expensive and it's not even clear they will actually work," Bear said. "Money talks and everything else is just commentary."

As this sample article shows, numbers tell a story, but the story may not always be what it seems. Widget appeared to have a good quarter. It beat analysts' estimates, earnings per share and revenue were higher quarter over quarter. But expenses increased and that changed everything.

The analysts disagreed on the effects of the new machines and so did investors. Widget's stock price fell sharply on the news, but the price rebounded, showing that people initially sold Widget stock because they thought the earnings report was bad. But some investors bought the stock, lifting the share price, because they thought the new machines would ultimately increase the price of the stock.

The impact of a corporate earnings story is felt far beyond Wall Street. Many reporters work in cities where companies maintain headquarters or major factories.

Local, state and regional reporters should be aware of the financial condition of major employers. If a company has a couple of good quarters, it might hire more employees because business improved. Several bad quarters could lead to layoffs or even factory closings.

Reporters often joke that they get into journalism to avoid math. Many reporters will do anything to avoid dealing with numbers in earnings reports or even government and school board budgets.

But reporters who take time to learn about finance and accounting have a great advantage over their colleagues that will add perspective and depth to any newspaper beat.

Follow the numbers and you'll be surprised where that takes you.

Interpreting Financial Highlights

To perform well in business reporting you'll need to master basic financial documents that report on the condition of companies.

My advice: Study accounting in college, or in a nearby community college if you're already working in a newsroom. *Or* launch serious self-directed study—*NOW.*

(How to read balance sheets and income statements is explained superbly for beginners in "How to Read a Financial Report," a comprehensive booklet published by Merrill Lynch, Pierce, Fenner & Smith Inc., Response Center, P.O. Box 20200, New Brunswick, NJ 08968-0200. Ask for "Document Code 10006-0197." Telephone: 1-800-637-7455, ext. 1745.)

A *balance sheet* is a statement—a "snapshot"—of a company's assets and liabilities on a given date.   To be reliable, a balance sheet must conform to specifications laid down by the American Institute of Accountants.

An *income statement,* known often as a "profit and loss statement" or a "P&L," is a summary of a company's income and expenses over a specified period and, of course, shows the resulting profit or loss. This, obviously, is of keen interest to investors, and you *must* learn to read and interpret a P&L.

Let's start by looking at a few numbers in a company annual report.

Annual reports are issued by publicly owned companies—those, of course, whose shares are traded by the public. To protect shareholder rights, a federal agency, the Securities and Exchange Commission (SEC), requires periodic disclosure of pertinent financial and operational details by all publicly owned companies. The underlying mission is to protect investors against malpractice and ensure they have equal access to verified data about company operations.

Highly detailed financial data are available in the so-called 10-K Report, also required by the SEC. It's to the annual report, however, that most reporters turn first.

Box 7-2   ## SEC: A Source for Crucial Numbers

Federal law requires publicly owned companies to reveal detailed information on their operations and financial strength.

Corporate compliance is monitored by the Securities and Exchange Commission, 450 Fifth St., NW, Washington, DC, 20549. The SEC's mission is to ensure all investors have equal access to information about publicly owned companies.

A company's *annual report* and *quarterly reports* normally are mailed to all shareholders and made available to reporters by each company's corporate secretary or, often, a corporate relations executive. The SEC also will provide the documents.

Annual reports contain detailed financial information, reports on operations and, importantly, management's discussion of the company's performance. Knight Ridder Newspapers, for example, issues a slick and colorful report of nearly 100 pages covering all aspects of operations.

Company stockholders also receive a separate *proxy statement* or *letter to shareholders,* which reports on salaries and benefits paid executives. Biographical sketches of directors, their compensation and their other corporate ties normally are included in the letter, along with where and when the annual meeting will be held.

Form 10-K, available from the SEC or each publicly owned company, provides additional financial data. *Form 10-Q* is a quarterly report, filed with the

SEC and mailed to shareholders. ***Form 8-K*** is filed with the SEC on interim changes in the company's ownership, resignations of directors, or financial developments that might have material effect on company operations.

Many privately held companies issue annual reports but strip them of financial data that publicly owned companies are required to publish.

Something else to watch: ***Tender offers*** are offers from one company to acquire the shares of another. Shareholders of the target company are asked to ***tender*** their shares, either for cash or for stock in the acquiring company. Federal law requires full disclosure by the acquiring company to the target company, its shareholders and the SEC.

Below are numbers I plucked from the annual report of Knight Ridder, a leading newspaper publisher. The numbers are modified for our discussion of a company's ***income statement*** (Table7.1).

Table 7.1.   Knight Ridder financial highlights (in thousands, except per share data and ratios)

	Dec. 28, 1997	Dec. 29, 1996
Summary of Operations		
Operation Revenue		
Advertising	$2,202,251	$1,793,424
Circulation	567,757	501,826
Other	106,777	78,974
Total Operating Revenue	2,876,785	2,374,224
Operating Costs		
Labor, newsprint and other operating costs	2,214,026	1,920,444
Depreciation and amortization	156,731	120,647
Total Operating Costs	2,370,757	2,041,091
Operating Income	506,028	333,133
Interest expense	(102,662)	(73,137)
Other, net	290,486	50,213
Income taxes, net	(297,348)	(124,829)
Income from continuing operations	396,504	185,380
Discontinued BIS operations	16,511	82,493
Net Income	$ 413,015	$ 267,873
Operating income percentage (profit margin)	17.6%	14.0%
Share Data		
Basic weighted-average number of shares	88,475	96,021
Diluted weighted-average number of shares	101,314	97,420
Earnings per share		
Basic: Continuing operations	$4.48	$1.93
Discounted BIS operations	0.19	0.86
Net income	4.67	2.79

Table 7.1. Knight Ridder financial highlights cont'd

Earnings per share *(cont'd)*			
Diluted:	Continuing operations	$3.91	$1.90
	Discounted BIS operations	0.17	0.85
	Net income	4.08	2.75
Dividends declared per common share		0.80	0.58½
Common stock price			
High		57⅛	42
Low		35¾	29⅞
Close		50 3/16	39¼
Shareholders' equity per common share		$15.65	$12.12
Price/earnings ratio		21.8:1	21.6:1

Note first, above, that most data are in thousands. *Always* read bracketed material (and footnotes) in financial documents.

Total operating revenue includes subscription fees and single-copy sales for Knight Ridder papers, but, as you can see, most revenue comes from advertisers. (Advertisers provide about 80 percent of revenue at most newspapers.) Note the $2.8 *billion* in 1997 is up substantially from 1996. *That*'s the kind of trend information to look for in annual reports: How is the company performing against last year?

Total operating costs also are up, to $2.2 billion—but not so much that the company doesn't show handsome improvement in operating income, to $506 *million* from $333 million.

Note the distinction between *operating income* and *income from continuing operations.* During the year, Knight Ridder sold Business Information Services (BIS), so that is broken out as a "discontinued" operation.

Note *operating income percentage (profit margin).* Most investors (and business reporters) would look first—and hardest—at this line, which represents *pre-tax profit.* Operating income is regarded by many analysts as *the* most important indicator of how a company is being managed.

In this case, Knight Ridder's 17.6 percent profit margin shows substantial increase from 14 percent the year before. *However,* to properly report on Knight Ridder you must know how it performs relative to other companies, *particularly peer publishing companies.*

That is, to protect your readers' interests, you must build general expertise in business but, particularly in the industry of the company on which you're reporting. Reporters covering the newspaper industry know—at a glance—that even though Knight Ridder has improved operating income, it still is underperforming its peer group (which, at the time, averaged more than 19 percent, with some newspapers delivering 20–25 percent margins or even more).

In *share data,* Knight Ridder's financial highlights single out, among other things, these facts:

- *Basic weighted-average number of shares* represents the number of "primary" shares—88.4 million in 1997—owned by individual and corporate investors. The "diluted" share figure is the number that would result if convertible securities, bonds, debentures and other instruments were converted into shares.

- *Earnings per share* figures are extremely important. They illustrate for shareholders how the company performs. Note 1997's *net income per share* was $4.67, a whopping improvement over the year before.

- *Dividends declared per common share* shows what investors received— 80 cents per share in 1997, up from 58½ cents the previous year. Why didn't investors get *all* the net income per share—$4.67? Because Knight Ridder's board of directors used some of the funds to buy new plants and equipment or to expand the company by acquiring other newspapers. Your readers obviously will want full and fast word on dividends declared. It's the dividend check in the mail they wait for.

- Knight Ridder's common stock is traded on the New York Stock Exchange. In *common stock price,* Knight Ridder notes its stock traded during 1997 at a high of 57⅛ (or, roughly, $57.12), a low of 35¾ ($35.75), then closed for the year at 50³/₁₆ ($50.18).

    (Above, incidentally, is the key to your personal fortune: buy a stock at the low point and sell at the high. And precisely *where* are the highs and lows? Ah, as the Bard said, there's the rub!)

- *Shareholders' equity per common share.* A company's *net worth* is its assets minus liabilities. Shareholders' equity is the interest of all shareholders in the company's net worth. Knight Ridder expresses that in a per-share figure—$15.65, up from $12.12 the year before.

- *Price/earnings ratio* is the market price of the stock, divided by total earnings per share reported over the past four quarters. Many investors view it as an important indicator of how a stock is priced relative to its earnings and, thus, whether the market price is attractive.

De-Mystifying the Balance Sheet

The *balance sheet* is a snapshot of what a company owns and owes on a specific date. It has two parts: *assets* and *liabilities and shareholders' equity.*

Table 7.2 is a Knight Ridder balance sheet for Dec. 28, 1997, drawn from the same annual report we studied earlier in this chapter. The numbers below are modified for our discussion.

Table 7.2. Knight Ridder consolidated balance sheet

(in thousands of dollars, except share data)	Dec. 28, 1997
ASSETS	
Current Assets	
Cash	$ 160,291
Accounts receivable	374,746
Inventories	50,332
Prepaid expense	15,844
Other current assets	39,902
Total Current Assets	641,115
Investments and Other Assets	
Equity in joint ventures	197,585
Net assets of discontinued BIS operations	24,673
Other	172,859
Total Investments and Other Assets	395,117
Property, Plant and Equipment	
Land and improvements	89,375
Buildings and improvements	444,952
Equipment	1,127,875
Construction and equipment installations in progress	111,883
	1,774,085
Less accumulated depreciation	(727,571)
Net Property, Plant and Equipment	1,046,514
Excess of Cost Over Net Assets Acquired and Other Intangibles	2,272,396
Total	$4,355,142

LIABILITIES AND SHAREHOLDERS' EQUITY

Current Liabilities	
Accounts payable	$ 172,021
Accrued expenses and other liabilities	131,491
Accrued compensation for employees	119,036
Federal, state income taxes	33,920
Deferred revenue	72,491
Short-term borrowings and current portion of long-term debt	69,697
Total Current Liabilities	598,656
Noncurrent Liabilities	
Long-term debt	1,599,133
Deferred federal, state income taxes	282,695
Postretirement benefits other than pensions	150,485
Employment benefits, other noncurrent liabilities	171,225
Total Noncurrent Liabilities	2,203,538

Table 7.2. Knight Ridder consolidated balance sheet (cont'd)

Minority Interests in Consolidated Subsidiaries	1,275
Shareholder's Equity	
Preferred stock, $1 par value; shares authorized—	
2,000,000; shares issued—1,754,930 in 1997	1,755
Common stock, $.02 ¹/₁₂ par value; shares authorized	
250,000,000 shares issued—81,597,631 in 1997	1,700
Additional capital	911,572
Retained earnings	636,646
Total Shareholder's Equity	1,551,673
Total	$4,355,142

Here's how to read that Knight Ridder balance sheet:

Current assets are cash and other assets such as marketable securities that normally are turned into cash within a year.

Accounts receivable are amounts owed by customers but not yet collected; *inventories* are items on hand for later sale (such as newsprint in storage at *The Miami Herald,* a Knight Ridder newspaper); *prepaid expenses* include such things as insurance premiums paid a year ahead.

Equity in joint ventures includes Knight Ridder's minority ownership of the company that publishes *The Seattle Times* and various newsprint-producing firms. In Investments and Other Assets, "discontinued BIS operations" refers to assets Knight Ridder retained after selling its Business Information Services division.

Note the huge investment in *property, plant and equipment.* These *fixed assets* demonstrate that newspaper publishing is a *capital-intensive* industry.

Depreciation is the bookkeeping practice of charging against income the cost of a fixed asset over its useful life. For example, if a $20,000 company car has an estimated useful life of five years due to wear and tear, the company will charge $4,000 annually against income over those five years. Come income tax time each year, the company will be able to shelter $4,000 in income against taxes, so depreciation is a major asset. And, the 1997 portion of that car's depreciation—$4,000—would be among assets listed in this balance sheet.

Note *excess of cost of net assets acquired and other intangibles.* Knight Ridder's acquisitions include *tangible assets,* such as buildings, and *intangible assets,* which are nonphysical valuables, such as patents, copyrights or licenses to do business.

The cost of acquisitions is established through negotiations as ***fair market value***—what a willing buyer will pay a willing seller. That fair market value often exceeds the value of the assets acquired because the buyer pays for the company name, its management's skills and workers' expertise, and so forth. The difference between fair market value— what was paid—and the value of assets is ***goodwill,*** which on Knight Ridder's balance sheet is included as an asset in *Excess of Cost Over Net Assets Acquired and Other Intangibles.*

So, Knight Ridder states its ***total assets*** at $4.3 billion. On the other side of the balance sheet—"balancing" the assets—are ***liabilities.***

Current liabilities are obligations that must be paid within 12 months.

Accounts payable are amounts owed to creditors for goods and services purchased. ***Accrued expenses*** are those owed for past purchases and which also must be paid within 12 months. ***Accrued compensation*** includes salaries owed employees on the day the balance sheet is "struck," or calculated.

Note ***taxes*** owed—$33.9 million. To ***really*** understand business, understand tax law.

Deferred revenue includes newspaper subscriptions collected in advance. The revenue is recognized in the period in which it is earned.

Short-term borrowings covers repayment required on 12-month notes. In the same period, Knight Ridder must repay 12-month portions of notes covering loans of, say, 5 or 10 years. In many balance sheets, this category is titled ***notes payable.***

Noncurrent liabilities, such as ***long-term debt*** and ***deferred taxes,*** are amounts payable beyond the 12-month period of current liabilities.

Minority interests in consolidated subsidiaries reports Knight Ridder's liability to minority shareholders in the company's newspapers in Miami and Fort Wayne, Ind.

Retained earnings (sometimes called, "earnings surplus") is retention of profits. Knight Ridder accumulated this amount out of after-tax profits and has not distributed it to shareholders through dividends. It is a sum held for later use.

Shareholders' equity is Knight Ridder's ***net worth***—its assets minus liabilities. The shareholders' equity—the interest of all shareholders in the company—is $1,551,673,000.

Note total assets ***balance*** total liabilities.

Now, what can a reporter deduce from all this? Well, with additional in-depth study of balance sheet analysis, you'll be able to report on a company's basic financial strength.

- You can calculate, for example, *working capital,* which is used in conducting business—in purchasing, say, materials (as distinguished from *fixed capital,* which is invested in buildings or equipment). Subtract total current liabilities from total current assets to arrive at working capital. That subtraction yields the *current ratio,* the relationship of current assets to current liabilities. Many experts say a company should have a 2:1 ratio, or, that is, $2 in current assets for every $1 in current liabilities, if it is to meet its debt and expand.
- You can calculate the *debt-to-equity ratio.* Divide total shareholders' equity into total liabilities. Experts say the ratio should be under 1:1 or, that is, debt level should be less than the owners' investment in the business.
- You can calculate *net book* (or *net asset*) *value,* which is all assets minus all liabilities. This measures the assets backing company shares and bonds. *Book value per share of common stock* is what each share would receive if the company were liquidated.

CAUTION: Always check whether financial statements are endorsed by independent certified public accountants. A leading firm, Ernst & Young, signs off on the Knight Ridder annual report in a section titled "Report of Independent Public Accountants." This language, in the Ernst & Young statement, must be present (emphasis added): "We conducted our audits *in accordance with general accepted auditing standards*" . . . and, "in our opinion, the financial statements . . . *present fairly, in all material respects, the consolidated financial position* of Knight Ridder and its subsidiaries at Dec. 28, 1997." . . .

Beware of passing to your readers company information—on which they might trade—unless you have such assurances.

| Box 7-3 | Reading Stock Tables |

Here's how to interpret stock tables, those storehouses of crucial information published in the business sections of all major newspapers:

Table 7.3.   Example of a stock table

52 Week High/Low	Stock	Div	Yld %	P/E	Sales 100s	High	Low	Last	Chg
59⅝/40½	KnightR	.80	1.7	13	2622	47⅜	46⅝	47	-³/₁₆

Reading from the left:

- During the past 52 weeks, the stock traded at a high price of 59⅝ (or $59.62) and a low of 40½ ($40.50). Note this is a *trailing* 52-week period that changes daily; it is *not* the past calendar year.
- The *stock,* of course, is Knight Ridder, a leading U.S. publisher of newspapers. (Its stock ticker symbol is "KRI".)
- *Div* is the current *annual* rate of dividend payment, in this case 80 cents *per share.*
- *Yld* or *yield,* is the ratio of the annual dividend to the closing price—1.7 percent. You can get 5 percent or so guaranteed on a savings account at your local bank, so why buy a stock that yields 1.7 percent? Because you hope the value of your stock will rise. Investors calculate whether yield *and* value appreciation combined will return appropriate reward for their investment.
- *P/E* is the price/earnings ratio, or the price of the stock divided by earnings per share reported over the past four quarters. This relationship of price to earnings is an important indicator to many investors of whether the market value of the stock is high or low.
- *Sales* is the number of shares traded in the previous trading day—in Knight Ridder's case, on the New York Stock Exchange. Note the "100s." Add two zeros: 262,200 shares of KnightRidder were traded.

The last four columns detail trading action on the *previous day:*

During the day, KnightRidder traded at a high of 47⅜, a low of 46⅝ and the final or last price *at closing* was 47. That last price means the stock price dropped (-³⁄₁₆) from the day before. It wasn't a good day for KnightRidder shareholders, but not a disastrous one, either.

Now you can follow daily the marketplace fortunes of media companies that interest you—or, perhaps, that might offer you a job in the future.

More importantly, though, if you learn to read these tables you add to your professionalism and your ability to report knowledgeably for your readers.

Summary

- Financial collapse along the Pacific Rim and World Bank moves in Geneva are big news, but for small-town America, the opening of a new Wal-Mart or Kmart store is big news, too.
- Covering Main Street business can take you into, not away from, one of the hottest, most fun reporting beats in journalism.
- *"Business,"* broadly defined, is the manufacturing, buying and selling of commodities and services, but beginners should concentrate on covering local businesses and their impact on readers' lives.
- In reporting company news, you often are writing for readers who know more about the subject than you do, so you'll need a high degree of reporting and writing expertise.
- First cover the local big picture—your community's overall economic health—with substantive dollars-and-cents reporting.

- *Real estate*—residential and commercial—is an important local business indicator because in boom times, construction soars; in bad times, construction halts, unemployment increases, property values plummet.
- *Jobs*—types available and their pay—are basic indicators of local business activity, and covering the employment picture is a major responsibility of business reporters.
- *Unions* are news because in many towns they represent many local residents *and* they can assist or shut down local businesses and thus affect local economic conditions.
- *Workplace issues,* such as equal opportunity and sexual harassment, have compelling news value because Americans are increasingly choosy about where and how they work.
- In covering jobs, unions and workplace issues be certain you report the effects on stakeholders—often the wider public that feels the impact of unemployment or strikes.
- Covering *company news* includes reporting profit performance by companies and writing about local retail establishments; a *Forbes* reporter even did a fascinating financial analysis of a drug gang's business!
- *Earnings reports* are crucial news because they detail, in digests, the revenue and profit figures investors need and, in explanatory stories, the analytical details that explain the dollars-and-cents facts.
- *Quarterly* or *annual reports* show the fabled bottom line—profit or loss—and thus are awaited eagerly by reader-investors.
- A *balance sheet* is a statement—a "snapshot"—of a company's assets and liabilities on a given date, and can be analyzed to show the company's basic financial strength.
- Always check whether financial statements are endorsed by independent certified public accountants before you pass to your readers information found in them.

Recommended Reading

Strong reporting of local business news is featured in many major metropolitan papers, among them *The Boston Globe, New York Times, Newsday, Philadelphia Inquirer, Washington Post, Atlanta Journal and Constitution, Dallas Morning News, Los Angeles Times, Seattle Times, Portland Oregonian, Chicago Tribune.* Beginners in business news can spend hours profitably in their pages.

Forbes publishes the best quick-hit profiles of businesses and business leaders I've ever seen. They are models of excellence. For a beginner, an hour in front of a supermarket's magazine rack—reading *Business Week, Money* and others—is an investment in professionalism.

The Wall Street Journal is must reading, of course, for students of any subject raised in this book. Its front-page profiles of companies and their leaders are excellent. Watch, too, the paper's shorter company stories and earnings reports.

Study the annual report of a leading company (why not a media company?) for a "feel" of the financial and operational information it contains. Annual reports are available at most libraries or from the secretary of the corporation.

Notes

1. Both incidents occurred in Athens, Ga.
2. "City's Economy Shipshape," Aug. 16, 1998, p. B-1.
3. Gail Kinsey Hill, telephone interview, Jan. 20, 1999.
4. "Business Real Estate Hot in Hub," Sept. 10, 1998, p. D-1.
5. "Wal-Mart Proposed for East Athens," Oct. 23, 1998, p. A-1.
6. "Downtown's Old Belk Building Soon to Be a Parking Lot," Oct. 23, 1998, p. A-1.
7. "250 Jobs Coming as Company Moves Into Now-Empty Plant," Aug. 19, 1998, p. A-1.
8. "Significant Job Growth in Past Year Means Athens Retail Market Will Be Even Stronger," Nov. 8, 1998, p. F-4.
9. "Northwest Machinists Ask to Start Strike Countdown," Aug. 14, 1998, Section 3, p. 1.
10. "Bell, Union Agree on Contract," Aug. 12, 1998, p. A-1.
11. "Women in Workplace Encounter Obstacles," Sept. 16, 1998, p. B-5.
12. Dispatch for Oct. 11, 1998.
13. "What Next? A Ponytail Perot? EDS Ditches Stuffy White Shirts," Sept. 16, 1998, p. B-1.
14. Dispatch for Sept. 8, 1998.
15. "A Spot to Work Out the Stress," Sept. 27, 1998, p. H-4.
16. "In Dismissals, Silence Has Its Perils," Oct. 18, 1998, p. B-4.
17. AP dispatch for Jan. 23, 1999.
18. Stephanie Stoughton, "After the Dime Store, 'Dollar' Explosion," *The Washington Post,* Nov. 15, 1998, p. H-1.
19. "Greedy Bosses," Aug. 24, 1998, p. 53.
20. "After the Dime Store, a 'Dollar' Explosion," op cit.
21. Scott Woolley, "Greedy Bosses," op cit.
22. "Ameritrade Has $3.7 Million Net on Sales Surge," Jan. 21, 1999, p. C-22.

Exercises

1. Examine for five consecutive days the business section of a local paper designated by your instructor. In about 400 words analyze (1) coverage of your community's overall economic health and (2) reports of businesses and business personalities in the community. Is the newspaper presenting solid information on the state of local business? Can a reader grasp the strength or weakness of the local economy? Is business news personalized and localized?

2. Interview at least two local realtors, a banker and a construction company executive, then write an overview of the local real estate market. Are sales and construction expanding or contracting? Are home values and rents rising or falling?

What do your authoritative sources predict for the next 12 months? Write this in 500–600 words.

3. Interview the manager of the state unemployment office responsible for your city. Also interview personnel managers for at least two local firms. Talk to any university economist who tracks local job figures. In 350–400 words, report on the present employment picture **and** what your experts predict for the next six months.

4. Interview the director of personnel (or human relations) at your college. Obtain the college's guidelines on workplace rules and regulations. Ascertain whether there have been complaints or official grievances about workplace unfairness or discrimination. Write a "state of our workplace" article in about 350 words.

5. Obtain from your college library or business school the annual report of a major firm, preferably a media company. Study the company's income statement, balance sheet and the opinions of the company's top executives (usually expressed in "Letter to Shareholders"). In about 500 words, analyze the company's position. Is it strong? Weak? Expanding? Poised to expand?

8

Finance: It's Their Pocketbooks That Count

Entire books (indeed, *libraries*) are written about finance—the supply, regulation and management of money, credit and capital.

And, everywhere in journalism you see the "big picture":

The Economist comments solemnly about "enforced flotation of Brazil's currency." . . .

Investor's Business Daily jumps to report that "The benchmark 30-year Treasury bond suffered its fifth straight loss." . . .

The Boston Globe notes "Russian Ruble in Free Fall."

In even small-town journalism, the big picture of finance is covered: *The Harrisonburg (Va.) Daily News-Record,* circulation about 33,000, is, thanks to its AP service, right on top of Russia's debt default. *The Anderson (S.C.) Independent-Mail* (42,000) keeps readers abreast of Japan's financial woes.

Heavy stuff! So, where can you, the beginner, begin?

Begin by recognizing that panoramic study of finance is far too ambitious for this chapter (or, even, book) and that, anyway, the complexities of Russia's ruble problems are for senior, strongly experienced financial writers, as are the esoterica of 30-year Treasury bonds and the interaction of Europe's new currency, the euro, with the U.S. dollar.

That is, you can—you *should*—begin by edging carefully into writing about finance and by concentrating first on subjects you understand intimately. Look first at the dollars and cents of your own pocketbook, your own financial challenges, your own efforts to earn more, save more, spend more wisely.

These same challenges confront your readers. Write about them and you'll get close to your readers—as close as their pocketbooks.

Let's look in Chapter 8 at how the pros do that with three types of stories:

- The "quick alert" on spot-news developments in finance that readers need to know about *right now.*
- The "on-guard" warning that scam artists and other assorted bad guys are doing awful things to nice people out there.
- The "how-to-do-it" story that walks readers through ways to earn more, save more, spend more wisely.

What's News in Personal Finance?

Newspaper editors long ago redefined "business news" to require major focus on personal finance. A study way back in 1982 for The Associated Press Managing Editors put it this way:

> Changes in society have meant that everybody has to be interested in money and the economy. Education is part of the reason. But rising expectations for what we get in life are mainly the cause.
>
> Materialism is respectable. The result: Kids want to know what jobs and careers pay best, how to prepare for them and how to land them. Job satisfaction is still based on intangibles, but the roar of the consumer credit economy makes every jobholder conscious of his salary, his benefits package and the best tax strategy for his situation.[1] . . .

Magazines also plunge into personal finance. Some specialize in the subject, such as *Money, Forbes, Fortune.* Even magazines with broader news horizons emphasize it. By 1998, for example, *U.S. News & World Report* was devoting about 6.4 percent of its total newshole to personal finance.[2]

Television and cable channels on finance are proliferating. CNNfn, CNBC and others attract millions of viewers with news about personal finance and investing.[3]

The Internet combines strengths of the new and old media, offering vast information resources once the sole province of print plus the speed of electronic delivery. The Internet is a big player in personal finance, with biz.yahoo.com/news, www.fool.com and others now being regular stopping points for hints on how to make, save and spend money.[4]

And for all these media players, reporting breaking news—"spot news," in media parlance—clearly is the first responsibility.

Give Readers the Quick Alert

More than anything, readers need from you fast word on developments that will affect their personal finances.

Here is how a *Boston Globe* reporter meets that obligation in a story (on p. A-1, incidentally) about a news break affecting hundreds of thousands of Bostonians:

> Many Massachusetts consumers will begin feeling the pinch today of automated teller machine surcharges, as Fleet Financial Group starts charging non-customers 75 cents each time they use one of the bank's 475 machines.
>
> Surcharging is expected to spread rapidly across the state over the next several weeks. BankBoston, with 1,295 ATMs in Massachusetts, launches a $1 fee on Sept. 24. Citizens Bank, the Springfield Institution for Savings, and Salem Five Cents Savings Bank all plan to follow suit at most of their ATMs.
>
> According to filings with the state Division of Banks, 63 percent of the state's 3,708 ATMs will be surcharging by the end of October.

Well, fine so far. That's a good wrap-up of the big picture. But what about the question each reader asks in personal finance: "How about *my* pocketbook?" The *Globe* writer turns to that quickly:

> Most of the surcharges are $1, although some banks are varying the charge depending on the ATM location. Salem Five, for example, is imposing a 50-cent surcharge at ATMs it co-owns at 13 BJ's Wholesale stores and 80 7-Eleven stores. It plans to charge $1 at ATMs it owns . . .
>
> —Bruce Mohl, *The Boston Globe*[5]

Incidentally, as a "sidebar" to his story above, writer Mohl produced a chart showing the competitive surcharges on ATM usage at 20 Boston-area banks. That's **news readers can use!**

Giving your readers the quick alert in personal finance doesn't always require the hard-hitting, Five W and How approach—the **today** angle—of *The Boston Globe* story above. Here's how a *Dallas Morning News* writer uses a feature-like **but still timely** approach:

> These days, grocery store checkout clerks don't just ask customers whether they prefer paper or plastic. Often they add: "Credit or debit?"
>
> For [John Jones] of Dallas, using his debit card is the most convenient—and cost-effective—way to go. Standing in the checkout line at Minyard's in Lakewood last week, he used the card to pay for his groceries and get $50 cash back from the cashier—skipping a trip to the bank and cutting out the time it takes to pay with a check.
>
> "I don't have to take money out of the ATM machine," he said, "and I avoid service charges."

Yes, the *Morning News* writer uses a modified "neck-of-vase" structure, such as we discussed in Chapter 5—a focus on a real human being that personalizes and warms up the story.

Now, the writer broadens the story structure to illustrate how many debit card users are following the "John Jones" model:

> Like [Mr. Jones], an increasing number of consumers are choosing to pay with debit cards at grocery stores, gas stations and a wide variety of other retail outlets. But as the number of debit card users rises, so do concerns about the ability of consumers to handle what is essentially a whole new way to spend money.

Now, a fast quote from an authoritative source:

> "They're just now beginning to take off, . . . but there's been a lot of confusion about them," said Gail Liberman, co-author of *Improving Your Credit, Decreasing Your Debt.*

At this point, the *Morning News* story reaches what might be called a "writer's fork in the road": take the story in one direction, and write in industryspeak for bankers and finance experts; or go in another direction, and write as a translator for non-expert readers who need help in sorting out the complexities of debit card use.

As is essential in reporting personal finance, the writer wisely writes for non-experts and inserts a "housekeeping" or "nut" graf of explanation:

> Debit cards look much like automated teller machine cards—embossed plastic cards issued by banks with the cardholders' names on the front and magnetic stripes on the back. The cards enable customers to pay for purchases with money from their checking accounts without using checks. Cards branded with MasterCard or Visa logos can be used wherever merchants accept major credit cards. Others require personal identification numbers and can only be used at specified debit terminals, such as those found on gas pumps and in grocery checkout lanes. . . .
>
> —Anne Marie Borrego, *The Dallas Morning News* [6]

But there's more: Anne Marie Borrego poses a question her readers might ask: Is there a danger in using debit cards? Yes, and she answers the question with a sidebar:

> It looks like a credit card. It is accepted like a credit card. But when somebody steals it, it doesn't always protect like a credit card.
>
> Just ask Mike Kidwell, vice president of the Debt Counselors of America. He paints a frightening picture of what could happen to a consumer whose debit card is stolen.
>
> "I encountered somebody who had . . . [a debit card] that was stolen out of the mailbox," Mr. Kidwell said. "Next thing they knew, somebody had

used all the money in their checking account." And then it started rolling into the victim's other bank accounts.

As the use of debit cards becomes more common, Americans are finding out—often the hard way—that their potential liability from lost or stolen cards can be greater than with credit cards. . . .

—Anne Marie Borrego, *The Dallas Morning News*[7]

Now, *The Dallas Morning News* story and sidebar have sprawled across two pages of the paper. They total thousands of words. Is there any way to digest all that in a handy list of tips for readers? Read on:

Tips for Debit Card Users

As debit cards' use skyrockets, consumer credit specialists are urging cardholders to follow some simple precautions:

—Talk to your bank officer about the right checking account for your transaction habits.

—Record all transactions in the same place.

—If you lose your card, call your bank immediately to cancel the card. Write the bank within two business days, using certified mail as well.

—Don't share your pin number with anyone.

—Monitor your statement for hidden fees.

Boxed sidebar, *The Dallas Morning News*[8]

That is, in reporting personal finance you should ***package*** information in easily accessible ways. Use main leads, sidebars, boxes, graphs, charts—whatever it takes to ***translate*** a complex story for non-expert readers.

The "quick alert" is a favorite of columnists who specialize in dispensing financial advice. Below, one of the best, Jane Bryant Quinn, a *Newsweek* columnist also syndicated in newspapers nationwide, alerts readers to a forthcoming deadline:

Are you currently paying off an education loan—either a student loan or a PLUS loan taken out by parents? Time is running out for refinancing at a lower rate. You have until Jan. 31 to apply.

Immediately, in her second graf, Quinn starts ***outlining the solution:***

At least two major lenders are competing for your business—the federal government, through its loan-consolidation plan, and the private lender, Sallie Mae.

Note, the warmth in Quinn's writing as she ***talks,*** as if across the kitchen table, with "you," her reader:

Normally you consolidate to get a single monthly payment for your various loans. Also, you can lower your payments by stretching out the due date of the loan.

Now there's a bonus. By consolidating your loans, you can also cop a lower rate of interest.

Which lender you choose depends on what you want. The government starts you out with a lower monthly payment—ideal for borrowers who feel squeezed. But Sallie May might cost you less in the long run. Here's how the programs work:

Now, Quinn begins a highly detailed examination of the various programs:

1. The feds. The government will consolidate one or more student loans. . . .
2. Sallie Mae. This private lender consolidates two or more loans worth at least $7,500. . . .

An essential of this type of reporting is detailed dollars-and-cents information. For example, in explaining the federal government's program, Quinn points out:

Under previous consolidation plans, the interest rate formula generally left you with a loan at 8.25 percent. Until Jan. 31, however, you can consolidate at just 7.46 percent—a bargain for almost everyone carrying student loans today. Repayment terms range from 10 to 30 years.

The new, low rate is variable. Every July 1, your interest rate—hence your monthly payment—will rise or fall, depending on the level of Treasury bill rates. (You're charged 2.3 percentage points over the rate on three-month Treasuries.)

A second essential of the quick-alert story is explaining how readers can act—find solutions—on information you've provided. Quinn does this:

For information and an application call 1-800-557-7392 or apply by Web at http://www.ed.gov/directloan. Your application must be in by Jan. 31, says Deputy Secretary Marshall Smith of the U.S. Department of Education. The government is currently getting 10,000 calls a week. Processing the loans takes 30 to 60 days. . . .

—Jane Bryant Quinn, syndicated columnist[9]

Now, anything strike you about the Quinn story? It essentially provides only **Quinn's** thinking. The passing reference to Deputy Secretary Marshall Smith is the only quotation of an authoritative source.

Few beginners in personal finance journalism are ready to start dispensing their own advice on how readers can make, save or spend money. Your challenge is to report, in lively, warm and personalized writing, **_the views of experts._**

Below, Rob Kitchel, a first-year reporter just out of journalism school, moves cautiously—quoting authoritative sources along the way—in alerting *The Macon (Ga.) Telegraph* readers they can save money by using the Internet to plan travel. Note Kitchel's feature-like, neck-of-vase intro:

[Joan Jones] is planning her honeymoon, but instead of calling a travel agent, she's doing it on the World Wide Web.

[Jones], a sales representative in Macon, has been checking prices on the web for months now, but she hasn't made a purchase.

"It's interesting to price on the Internet," [Jones] said. "I don't know if we'll book our plans on the Internet, but it gives us some good ideas. It's hard to tell how legit some of these companies are. I don't want to spend my honeymoon in a shack."

In his fourth graf, Kitchel inserts the views of authoritative sources. Note particularly how Kitchel warns readers his sources have their own axes to grind (emphasis added):

It's no surprise that local travel agents agree with [Jones]. ***Not wanting to erode their customer base, they say it's wise to do research on the web but still recommend going through an agent to actually book vacations.***

"It hasn't been there that long, and I don't think there are a lot of people who feel really comfortable doing it themselves," said [Mary Doe], co-owner of [Acme Travel]. "I don't think anyone really knows where it's going because it's so new, but it's certainly interesting."

Now, with good old-fashioned reporting, Kitchel quotes an array of authoritative sources: a Delta Airlines spokesman, more travel agency executives, a computer expert who outlines how to search the Internet for the best travel deals. (In a sidebar, Kitchel lists Internet addresses of nine web sites offering information.)

To exit his story, Kitchel returns to [Joan Jones], whose honeymoon planning provided his neck-of-vase intro. The writer's "kicker":

[Jones] definitely sees the advantages of high-tech travel planning, just not for the special trip she's about to go on.

"I'm just not sure I want it to be my honeymoon," she said. "But it seems like a good way to find a cheap flight."

—Rob Kitchel, *The Macon (Ga.) Telegraph*[10]

Whereas the *Telegraph*'s Kitchel wrote his quick alert for a wider audience of general-interest readers, effective reporting can be done also for narrow niche audiences of experts. Below, a writer alerts ***business executives*** to a spot-news development affecting business travel:

Now that fall is approaching, many corporate travel managers (and even a few travelers) are preparing budgets for 1999.

According to Runzheimer International, the news isn't so bad. The firm is expecting a modest 4.8 percent increase in business travel costs for the upcoming year.

The Rochester, Wis., consulting firm says there will be some market resistance to price increases in all categories of travel expenses because travel price inflation has consistently outpaced general inflation for the past three years. . . .

Note above how tightly the writer ties those three grafs to an authoritative source—a consulting firm. Now, he provides the dollars-and-cents specifics so necessary to effective "quick-alert" stories:

Here's a breakdown of the firm's forecast:
—Air travel: Up 5.1 percent . . .
—Lodging: Up 4.9 percent . . .
—Meals: Up 3.5 percent . . .
—Car rental: Up 4.8 percent . . .

—Christopher McGinnis, *Atlanta Journal-Constitution*[11]

Want to give *your* readers meaningful quick alerts? Follow the Kitchel and McGinnis models. They have these characteristics:

- "Quick-alert" stories are *timely,* rushing to readers with news of developments that will affect their financial affairs immediately or in the near future.
- They contain hard dollars-and-cents specifics—precise dates of deadlines, percentages up or down, dollars to be saved or spent.
- Authoritative sources are quoted to lend credibility—*believability*—to the story, and only with years of experience do writers such as Jane Bryant Quinn begin dispensing advice on their own.
- A well-done quick alert gives readers specific sources for follow-up—telephone numbers, addresses, Internet web sites.

Your Crucial Responsibility: "On-guard" Stories

Sometimes it seems a financial reporter's world is divided roughly into two groups of people: Those with money and those trying to get it.

There's nothing wrong, of course, with people trying to make money *legitimately* by offering valid service or products for reasonable prices. That's business, and we fill our news pages with it each day.

More infrequently—but not rarely—business reporters turn to *illegitimate* and unscrupulous scam artists who cheat, steal and rip off the unsuspecting. And when we do this, when we find and tell and put our readers "on guard," we may reach the ultimate goal of principled, effective journalism.

Below is an "on-guard" story by AP that *The Dallas Morning News* ran in 17 column-inches, under the headline "Scam Artists Try Currency Schemes."

Washington—Move over, pennystock scams.
The hottest new telemarketing fraud plays on people's vague awareness of Asian economic turmoil and hunger for hefty returns to get them to invest in super-risky foreign currency schemes, state securities regulators say.

Note, above, two factors:

1. The AP writer uses a swinging, easily understood style that eases readers into what is going to be a complex, highly technical story. To reach readers you must be open, engaging, **smooth** in your writing.
2. The scam is outlined quickly in language attributed to "state securities regulators," the authoritative sources always needed in financial reporting, and the scam is **characterized** as "super-risky."

Now, AP's writer elaborates on the scam and how it revolves around "futures contracts"—which are explained immediately (emphasis added). Remember your role as a **translator.**

> With the long-running bull market on Wall Street seeming to peak and law enforcers cracking down on small-stock fraud, the investment rip-off wave appears to have rolled into foreign currency scams. The Asian crisis, marked by sudden devaluations of regional currencies, has made foreign exchange markets more volatile.
>
> Instead of the latest hot stock, fast-talking telemarketers are touting get-rich-quick investments in futures contracts on Japanese yen, German marks and many other currencies in overseas markets. **A futures contract obligates a trader to buy or sell a currency at a fixed price at a specific time in the future.**
>
> In most cases, the investment schemes—modeled after legitimate currency-market trading done by financial institutions—are just a come-on and none of the money handed over is actually invested, according to the regulators.

Deeper in the story, AP's writer notes the targets chosen by scam artists:

> Modest investors around the country are losing thousands of dollars, lured by a type of investment that when it is legitimate is among the riskiest and not suitable for the average person. In some cases, notably in California and the New York City area, the telemarketers are exploiting Asian-Americans' penchant for tangible assets such as currencies and their close family ties.
>
> In other areas, the targets of the unsolicited phone calls are the same as those in other investment swindles: unsophisticated consumers, especially the elderly. The bull market in stocks has made many small investors accustomed to high returns and hungry for even bigger ones. . . .
>
> The Associated Press[12]

Let me suggest something: If **you** look back, at the end of a day as a financial journalist, and see that you might have saved some elderly, perhaps unsophisticated person from a scam artist, you will have had a very good day, indeed!

A very good day was had by Susan Harrigan, a *Newsday* writer, when she took on a scam artist in a story headlined "Many Unhappy Returns." Her story, which led *Newsday*'s "Money & Careers" section, was written to be irresistible:

There are times when the stress of trying to get his money back wakes [John Jones] up at night, unable to breathe.

[Jones], 58, said he lost his life savings of $62,000, along with $60,000 of his parents' money, in late 1996 when a salesman from [Acme Co.], a brokerage based in Lake Success, disobeyed [Jones'] orders to sell his stocks before they plunged in value.

The broker, [Jones] said, sold him the risky, volatile stocks—an [Acme] speciality—by making constant, aggressive sales calls when [Jones] was distracted by his wife's death from lung cancer. Once, the broker woke [Jones] up with a call at 5:30 a.m.

But when [Jones] decided to sell the stocks, the broker was "at lunch, at the chiropractor or at a staff meeting," and never returned his calls, [Jones] said.

After regulators closed [Acme] for fraud on Dec. 5, 1996 . . .

—Susan Harrigan, *Newsday*[13]

Harrigan, of course, writes the sad story of vulnerable people cheated of their life savings—including a Florida man, 86, and his wife, 85, who lost $252,000. The story runs for pages, with Harrigan smoothly laying out sordid details of a nationwide scam.

The *Newsday* story is such good reading that Harrigan's audience undoubtedly numbered tens of thousands—that's tens of thousands who, at the end of Harrigan's work day, were better equipped to protect themselves from scam artists.

A warning: scam-busting in stories that hit hard and name names can lead you into dangerous territory. More on this later in the book, but inaccurate reporting can damage reputations—of individuals *and* corporations—and that, of course, can open you to libel action. So, proceed carefully, involving senior editors in your work and, if necessary, your newspaper's libel attorney. In fact, if you're a beginner you probably should eliminate the word "expose" from your reporter's vocabulary and forget trying, at least right away, to rampage across town as journalism's white knight out to skewer bad guys. Better to take a careful *reporter's* approach to a less complicated story you can master, then pin the whole thing on authoritative sources. Jennifer Files does that for *The Dallas Morning News:*

Unless you run a company in a big office building and spend megabucks on business calls and Internet service, there's only one sure way to become a target for local-telephone competition in Texas.

Stop paying your phone bills.

Get disconnected, and the phone companies will fight for your business. "Phoneless? Don't fret—call us!" says one ad.

No credit check! No deposit! No questions asked, promise others.

Needless to say, no bargains either.

Like other businesses that cater to people with below-average incomes, these alternative local-phone companies, sometimes called "phone sharks," charge above-average rates.

Monthly bills for local-phone service run about $50—three times what Southwestern Bell or GTE charges.

Subscribers must pay in advance, and no long-distance service is included.

"To a certain extent, they are meeting customer needs. The other side of it is, yes, they are taking advantage of people," said [Joan Jones], spokeswoman for the Public Utility Commission of Texas.

—Jennifer Files, *The Dallas Morning News* [14]

You noted above, of course, that the writer appealed to virtually all *Morning News* readers with telephones plus those who don't have one but who wish they did. Her audience was wider than the stock market investors who were subjects of our other examples of "on-guard" stories.

That is, your biggest audience can be attracted to those "little" personal finance stories that surface every day—stories about telephone costs, electric and gas charges, real estate taxes, auto license fees.

Incidentally, the *Morning News* writer went to elaborate lengths in her telephone story to quote all sides in the controversy over so-called "phone sharks." One executive was given the opportunity to state his case: His company serves low-income people without the credit ratings or bank accounts required to get regular telephone service.

Fairness, objectivity, balance—all are characteristics of a well-done "on-guard" story.

Serve Readers With "How-To" Stories

A good reporter goes places readers can't go, to see and do things readers can't see or do—all to help them understand a little bit better, live a little bit better.

No story form is better for that mission than the "how-to" story.

Particularly in personal finance, the "how-to" structure is a splendid vehicle for showing readers how to do something important—buy a car, read a lease, get a credit card, select a bank or an attorney. On and on go the possibilities.

The "how-to" structure is wonderful for another reason: It lets you bust out of writing inhibitions and free yourself for creative wordsmithing. And, it's perfect for using the perpendicular pronoun—"I"—which is the best device for personalizing your writing and "talking" to readers.

Here is how a *Philadelphia Inquirer* specialist in personal finance starts that type of "how-to" story:

When I set out last fall to replace my decrepit, 13-year-old pickup, I had every intention of following my long-standing practice: to buy a stripped-down, used, modestly sized vehicle, and pay cash.

At the end of the search. I had bought a brand-new, loaded, full-size truck, and had a three-year loan.

Now, I don't know about you, but I couldn't resist that story after reading those first two grafs. Neither could *Inquirer* editors; they gave it important front-page play in a Sunday business section.

Why are those two grafs so alluring?

FIRST, they instantly portray for the reader a dilemma we all face, one time or another: Setting forth determined to spend less, then straggling home having spent more. I chuckled when first reading that intro, thinking, "So, I'm not the only guy who overspent. . . ."

SECOND, the language is informal, chatty—the style you'd use in ***telling*** a friend about buying a new truck. The intro is open, warm, inviting and ***not*** jammed with forbidding facts and figures.

THIRD, and most importantly, the intro promises help, deeper in the story, on ***how*** to buy a vehicle. And, that ultimately is the mission of the "how-to" story—telling readers how to handle life's complexities.

The *Inquirer* writer, Jeff Brown, a specialist in personal finance, now tugs readers ahead by expanding on the basic dilemma of whether to buy downscale for cash or let 'er rip and buy upscale, even if you have to borrow money (and that, again, is a dilemma many readers have faced).

At the time, I rationalized that smaller, used trucks were so expensive they offered little savings. A few options such as an extended cab don't sting so much if you figure you'll own the truck for 10 years. And when a dealer offers 1.9 percent financing, why spend cash that could be earning more in an investment?

Now, four-and-a-half months later, I have to confess it's awfully nice to have a new vehicle. Everything works, and there's the warranty to fall back on. And my baby looks so great I even keep it clean.

The *Inquirer*'s Brown now injects an endearing note, the tone of a little boy in a candy store: Are there more goodies to be had?

So what's next as I skid down this slippery slope? A lease?

With a lease, you can have a new vehicle every two or three years, and you're always on warranty. The monthly payments can be much lower than those of a loan, since you're not paying off the full value of the car, just the depreciation—the decline in the value—over the term of the lease. With a lease, I could have paid about $200 a month for my new truck, half the cost of the three-year loan.

How do you figure whether buying or leasing is best?

Now, of course, after his little romp through used versus old, cash versus loan, writer Brown takes his readers, step by step, through how to figure whether buying or leasing is best. The writing takes on a serious tone as Brown describes the relative merits of both purchasing plans, including translation of lawyer jargon in leases.

For example, that across-the-kitchen-table writing tone in Brown's intro gives way to this type of hard-fact writing:

> Your monthly payment is interest on the capitalized cost plus a monthly portion of the depreciation calculated over the term of the loan. If the vehicle will lose $10,000 in value over three years, the monthly depreciation cost will be $10,000 divided by 36 months, or $278. (Money factors can be converted to annual interest rates by multiplying by 24. A money factor of .00333 equals 8 percent.)
>
> —Jeff Brown, *The Philadelphia Inquirer*[15]

Yes, you must write "how-to" stories engagingly. You won't be read otherwise. But *always* include the hard facts and figures readers need for their own decision-making.

Although the "how-to" structure is widely used for general audiences— on subjects such as car buying or reading leases— it also is used in specialized publications for narrow niche audiences.

For example, a writer for *Forbes,* a magazine for executives, does a piece on security training for international business executives in an age of terrorism. The story describes the training, under this intro:

> New York Consultant [John Doe] knew he'd made a wrong turn into a bad neighborhood in Dilley, Tex. when he passed his fifth rusting car hulk. Before he could turn around, a man with a rifle popped up from behind a junked Cadillac and fired directly at his windshield.
>
> The bullets exploded into pink globs of paint when they hit the glass. [John Doe] was on a training course on how to deal with thugs and terrorists. His assailants were instructors from International Training Inc., and [Doe] was their student. Not your standard training for international consultants, but it's becoming that at a time when corporate executives' work take them to dangerous places.
>
> —Jay Akasie, *Forbes*[16]

Now, the reporter turns to a sidebar, using a story structure that might be termed *"the walk-through."* The reporter *walks* readers through an antiterrorist training experience:

> This Forbes reporter got a taste of the stuff. I was finishing my second day of classes at ITI, and there was one final test: driving a course on which my teachers would be the attackers.
>
> [John Doe] left me on the track with a walkie-talkie and a 1978 Chevy Malibu. When they gave the signal, I pulled onto the track. Suddenly I saw a car behind me. Another puffed out from the brush and passed me. When it was in front of me, the first car pulled alongside.

Sweat beaded on my forehead as the car in front stopped. As I tried to figure out what to do, an instructor in the car to my left fired three paint pellets into my window. Goodbye, world . . .

—Jay Akasie, *Forbes*[17]

As must all writers in personal finance, the *Forbes* reporter turns to dollars-and-cents details: how much it costs to take the antiterrorist training, where to go and how to do it.

Writing for *The Orange County (Calif.) Register,* Jan Norman does a "how-to" for entrepreneurs trying to start a small business. Note the anecdotal intro:

[Jane Doe] started [Acme Business Services and Resume Service] in Irvine, Calif., with $1,000 in vacation pay from her previous employer.

[Doe] had to make her own fliers and pound the pavement to deliver them to potential clients.

It wasn't easy, but it also wasn't a disaster. [Doe] celebrates her 20th business anniversary in January.

Now, writer Norman broadens her story:

I've interviewed thousands of small-business owners, and just about every one tells a tale of misconceptions and miscues about starting and running their companies. I've compiled 101 of them—including [Doe's]. . . .

—Jan Norman, *The Orange County Register*[18]

But, ***precisely how*** do you start a business? A list of 10 hints follows: "Hobbies aren't businesses," "failure IS an option," "persistence is essential," and so forth.

Below, a writer uses the familiar ***question lead*** to pull readers into a "how-to" on retirement:

Can you ever afford to retire?

More and more people are worrying about just that question. One out of three working people think the answer is no. Their edginess came to mind last week as . . . top-drawer politicians and money managers came together in Washington to encourage Americans to save more for their retirements.

Note how quickly the writer above elaborates on the question posed in the lead. Make it a rule in using question leads: ***answer*** the question quickly.

Now the writer "sets up" his "how-to" story:

. . . It is important to remember a couple of things:

—Most people can work out an estimate of how much they'll need to save toward retirement.

—Most people can, without overwhelming strain, build a nest egg for themselves. It helps if you start young, and it helps to keep saving something from every paycheck.

Finally, the story moves into dollar details on how to lay down a financial plan for retirement:

> If you start young, invest $20 weekly for 30 years and earn an 8 percent return, you would have more than $127,000. If you got a bit more ambitious—assuming you get regular pay raises and increase your savings by $5 a week each year—your 30-year savings plan would grow to more than $419,000. . . .
>
> —Hank Ezell, syndicated columnist[19]

Included in the story above, incidentally, were Internet addresses and telephone numbers readers can use to seek more information.

Visualize the "how-to" story structure as looking like this:

Figure 8.1.   Example of how-to story structure.

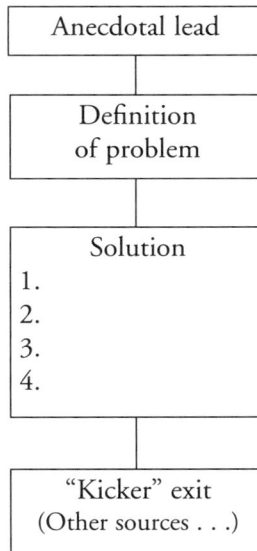

But, What Else Is Out There?

Writing "how-to" or "on-guard" stories is a fine way to edge into financial reporting. But after years of experience where can a reporter turn?

Steve Sears, senior writer for Dow Jones News Service, leaves no doubt where he thinks the action will be:

> Wall Street will be to the 21st century what Washington was to the 20th century. Billions of dollars flow each day through a world without financial borders.

The global trading cycle moves money from New York to Europe and Asia, leaving in its wake buildings, factories and capital that are needed to sustain nations and industries. The demand for money is great, and the demand for reporters who can see stories beneath numbers is perhaps even greater.

As Baby Boomers near retirement age, they are increasingly concerned with providing for themselves in their old age. The stock market has become a national obsession because no one is depending on Social Security checks for a comfortable retirement.

Sears also says the financial news beat carries adventure—and enormous responsibility:

The financial markets provide a fascinating window to view America, the world and human nature. The markets have their own values and rituals and an intricate society, ruled by chieftains and high priests.

Some of these people are as influential as prime ministers and presidents. Business reporters play a crucial role. Reliable information is the most valuable commodity on Wall Street—after money.

A headline published by a financial news service, such as Dow Jones Newswires, can unleash millions of dollars into the stock market, instantly sending a stock's price up or down. An article about an industry or company can influence the outlook and stock prices of an entire industrial sector. . . .

Financial journalism is demanding. Reporters converse with sources in a specialized language describing complex transactions. Beneath the numbers are issues that truly affect people, that influence how people live, in ways far beyond the palavering of feuding politicians. These issues are not subsiding, which insures that Wall Street will remain the best story—in the same way Washington was for previous generations of reporters.[20]

Those issues Sears mentions surface far beyond Wall Street, of course. Here are just a few of the areas fertile for journalists who eventually move beyond personal finance and into broader issues:

- *Monetary policy,* a news beat that revolves around the central bank of the United States, the Federal Reserve, in Washington. Decisions made there drive trading in Wall Street—and around the world (*see* Box 8-1).

| Box 8-1 | He Speaks, Markets Move |

Greenspan: the Sequel should keep investors on the edge of their seats Wednesday after the Fed chairman gave a mixed review to stock prices after Monday's big rally.

Such is the power of Federal Reserve Chairman Alan Greenspan that his brief mention to Congress Tuesday that stocks might be overvalued sent the Dow down 79 points, though it later recovered to end off 8 at 9,544.

Wall Street will also be watching . . .

CNNfn dispatch, Feb. 24, 1999

- *Supply of money and credit,* which the Fed influences by setting interest rates, buying and selling U.S. securities and, even, "jawboning"—as when the Fed chairman comments negatively or positively on the economic outlook or stock market values.
- *Banking,* or "depository institutions," as the experts say. Much of the nation's money is held by them, of course, and they link monetary policy to the financial markets and borrowers to lenders.
- *Financial markets,* where reporters cover the huge number of instruments and techniques through which we buy, sell, invest, spend. *The Philadelphia Inquirer,* like many newspapers, devotes pages to those instruments—certificates of deposit, money market accounts, bonds and so forth. (The *Inquirer*'s coverage is titled "Places to Stash Your Cash.")
- *International monetary policy and markets,* which takes reporters into the fascinating interlocking of financial and economic developments abroad with those that drive the U.S. economy.

Well, those are just a few of the areas open to skilled financial journalists. "Dullsville," you say? Not so. Just skip through any issue of *The Wall Street Journal* or any other leading newspaper and you'll see evidence of meaningful information relayed to readers by skilled, imaginative writers. Take, for example, this *Wall Street Journal* front-page headline:

> How Some Bum Bonds,
> Buried for a Century,
> Bankrolled a '90s Scam[21]

Doesn't writing that type of stuff sound like a fascinating—and meaningful—way to make a living?

Summary

- All major media define *"business news"* to include a strong focus on personal finance and helping readers understand how to earn more and save and spend better.
- More than anything, readers need fast word on developments that immediately affect their personal finances.
- The *"quick-alert" story* gives readers fast word on spot-news developments, and you can write either a hard-news approach with a today angle or a feature-like but still timely intro.
- On most finance stories you must take one of two directions—writing in industryspeak for experts, such as bankers, or writing as a translator for non-expert readers, the people who need your help.
- Sidebars, graphs, charts and boxes can be used in a package to add effectively to the totality of information you present readers.
- Each story must be written carefully to engage readers, present dollars-

and-cents information **and** advise readers on how to solve their problems or, at least, where to pursue authoritative sources who can provide solutions.

- The *"on-guard" story* serves to warn readers of unscrupulous scam artists trying to cheat, steal from and rip off unsuspecting and perhaps unsophisticated readers.
- Stories alleging wrongdoing can defame individuals or corporations, so be sure to involve senior editors or your newspaper's libel attorney if your reporting and writing does so.
- Beginners in financial reporting probably should eliminate "expose" from their writer's vocabulary and, instead, concentrate on careful, old-fashioned reporting that quotes authoritative sources.
- *"How-to" stories* are wonderful writing structures for showing readers how to do something important—buy a car, read a lease, get a credit card, select a bank or attorney.
- "How-to" stories enable you to break out of your writer's inhibitions and, particularly, use the perpendicular pronoun—"I"—to personalize your writing.
- After edging into financial reporting by writing personal finance stories you can aspire to one day cover **monetary policy,** the **supply of money and credit** or **banking** and the **financial markets,** which are among news beats enjoyed by skilled experienced journalists.

Recommended Reading

See excellent personal finance writing in *The New York Times, Wall Street Journal, Philadelphia Inquirer, Boston Globe, Chicago Tribune, Los Angeles Times* and *Dallas Morning News,* among other major newspapers.

The Wall Street Journal is one of the most effective learning tools for a beginning reporter/writer. For how to use the *Journal* effectively, see Michael B. Lehmann, *The Dow Jones–Irwin Guide to Using the Wall Street Journal* (Homewood, Ill.: Dow Jones-Irwin, Inc., 1984). This "how-to" book takes you step by step through understanding and using the *Journal's* daily coverage.

For writers ready to move into covering monetary policy, the financial markets and banking, see Ann-Marie Meulendyke, *U.S. Monetary Policy and Financial Markets,* published by the Federal Reserve Bank of New York. This bank, at 33 Liberty Street, New York, NY 10045, has published a series of excellent guides to understanding monetary policy. Also, many helpful books and newsletters are available through the Board of Governors of the Federal Reserve System, Washington, DC 20051.

Notes

1. Chris Waddle of *The Kansas City Times,* "The New Business Sections," 1982 Associated Press Managing Editors report by Business and Economics Committee, p. 2.

2. "Less Entertainment, More Advice," *The New York Times,* Aug. 3, 1998, p. D-5.

3. For details on burgeoning channels and viewership, *see* "Guns, Butter and TV," *The New York Times,* national edition, Oct. 21, 1998, p. B-7.

4. An excellent summary of such activity is in Steve Kichen, "Time to Get Hooked," *Forbes,* Sept. 26, 1994, p. 158, and Steven Kichen, "Site for Investors' Eyes," *Forbes,* June 15, 1998, p. 264.

5. "Many Banks Soon to Begin ATM Fees for Non-clients," Sept. 14, 1994, p. A-1.

6. "Checking on Debit," Aug. 17, 1998, p. D-1.

7. "'Check Cards' Couple Convenience with Potential Problems," Aug. 17, 1998, p. D-2.

8. Ibid.

9. Syndicated column for Jan. 3, 1999.

10. "Cruising Through Cyberspace," Nov. 8, 1998, C-1.

11. "Increase in 1999 Costs Projected as Moderate," Sept. 7, 1998, p. E-4.

12. Dispatch for morning papers, July 23, 1998.

13. "Many Unhappy Returns," Dec. 20, 1998, p. F-6.

14. "Pay Now, Call Later," Aug. 9, 1998, p. H-1.

15. "To Buy a Car or to Lease: Is the Decision Strictly Financial?" Feb. 14, 1999, p. D-1.

16. "Thwarting Terrorists," Sept. 21, 1998, p. 184.

17. Ibid.

18. Dispatch for Sunday papers, Nov. 29, 1998.

19. Dispatch for Sunday papers, June 7, 1998.

20. Steve Sears, letter to author, Dec. 7, 1998.

21. Headline on story by Richard B. Schmitt, Feb. 25, 1999, p. A-1.

Exercises

1. Study your local daily newspaper (or another newspaper your instructor designates) for three consecutive days, including a Sunday issue. List each example of personal finance reporting you encounter. In about 50 words each, evaluate the examples for (1) writing form/structure, (2) content, and (3) whether the story generally meets **your** standards for effective personal finance reporting. Outline your personal standards.

2. Study front-page stories in *The Wall Street Journal* (or another paper designated by your instructor) for three consecutive days. Note **spot-news** developments that you believe warrant "quick-alert" stories on personal finance, as we studied in Chapter 8. Select one news development, and outline, in about 200 words, how you would write a "quick-alert" story about it. What would be the thrust of your story? Which **local** authoritative sources would you contact? What helpful hints would you provide readers.

3. Review the Chapter 8 segment about "on-guard" stories. Which local events or developments warrant "on-guard" stories for **students on your campus?** Are there advertisements in your campus newspaper, for example, that promise fantastic spring break vacations at costs that may be too good to be true (and may **not** be true)? Are there other products or services offered students that may be questionable and thus may warrant "on-guard" analysis? Do this in about 300 words.

4. With your instructor's approval, do a "how-to" story on either (1) obtaining a credit card under the best possible terms, or (2) reading an apartment lease for traps and pitfalls. Remember the basic mission of a "how-to" story and write in a manner designed to help your readers live their lives just a little bit better! Do this story in 350-400 words.

5. With your instructor's approval, do a "how-to" story on the cost of eating off campus, in your own apartment, compared with the cost of your college's dining hall meal plan. Make certain your story contains hard dollars-and-cents information and quotes authoritative sources. Write this story in about 400 words and use a personalized neck-of-vase intro.

PART FIVE

You, the Law and Ethics

GET USED TO it: A lot of folks out there don't like what we journalists do for a living.

We've never been the most-liked people in the public eye, of course. But, reporters today are at or near a low in public esteem, depending on whose poll you read.

Taking criticism always has come with the territory in journalism, but our critics now seem more numerous than ever and, importantly, they are willing to do more than complain. In increasing numbers, they are suing for libel.

Libel law is used frequently as a club by persons with real or imagined complaints about the media, and that willingness to sue reflects widespread public unhappiness over media performance. One poll even shows 50 percent of respondents support rewriting libel law to make it easier to sue the media, and 70 percent support fines for inaccurate or biased reporting.[1]

In courts, juries—reflecting attitudes of the public from which they are drawn—find often against the media in libel cases and levy judgments sometimes in the millions of dollars against them (in 1997, the *average* jury award for damages was $588,700).[2] And, I should emphasize, *reporters* often are sued, along with their newspapers or magazines.

And that's the central point of Part Five: It's *legally dangerous* out there for reporters, and you shouldn't touch a keyboard without understanding libel law.

In Chapter 9, the single chapter of Part Five, we'll look particularly at how you can report and write **defensively** without detracting from your basic mission of finding and telling what your readers have a right and a need to know.

Then, we'll look at ethics and social responsibility—particularly how you can fine-tune a personal code of ethics on what, law aside, is the *right* thing to do.

Ethics is discussed nationwide by editors and reporters wrestling with our obvious need to do better journalistically and somehow reverse the decline in public esteem. That decline inevitably creates more problems on the legal front.

Two warnings:

- As important as it is that you understand libel law, nothing in this chapter should weaken your resolve to practice aggressive, hard-hitting journalism. Rather, my intent is to **embolden** you by building a basic understanding of the law that can strengthen your self-confidence and free you from the doubt and worry that cause some reporters to pull their punches.

- I am not a lawyer, and this chapter should be just a beginning point for your study of libel law. Start with a fine textbook: Kent R. Middleton, Bill F. Chamberlin and Matthew D. Bunker, *The Law of Public Communication*, 4th ed. (New York: Longman 1997), and the 1999 update of that book, by Middleton and Robert Trager.[3]

Now, libel law from the reporter's perspective.

| Box 9-1 | Good Reporter, Bad Person? |

The good news is that the public regards journalists as motivated and intelligent. The bad news, according to some in . . . focus groups: journalists "like to see adverse things happen to people." They enjoy their "power." Saddest of all, perhaps, is the belief of one focus group participant: "You wouldn't be a good reporter if you were a nice person."

—Alex Kuczynski, "Media Talk," *The New York Times*, national edition, Dec. 28, 1998, p. C-6

9

Be Fair,
Be Accurate

Instinct born of 45 years in journalism tells me this about avoiding libel suits:

- Your first (perhaps, **best**) defense against libel trouble is to report fairly, accurately and with balance. Simply put, doing the job **journalistically** as it should be done is the best way to keep the lawyers away.

   It's my experience that libel suits rise mostly from sloppy journalism—inaccuracies large and small, stories that treat people unfairly, stories that accuse but don't give the accused right of response.

   It's poor journalism more often than malice in writers' hearts that offends and harms those we write about.

- Reporters tend to relax—get sloppy—on "little" stories, those of a couple hundred words that not even editors spend much time reading. And those "little" stories, for that reason, are dangerous. Your huge investigative takeout—the three-part series on how Acme Smokestacks illegally pollutes the environment—will be read by every editor in the newsroom, perhaps twice, and maybe even by the newspaper's libel attorney **because the series looks dangerous.**

   For you, however, that "little" story you're writing is just as important because at that moment it is the one story for which you are professionally, ethically and legally responsible. Handle it carefully.

- The manner in which you respond to hurt feelings or yelps of outrage over what you've written can help determine whether you get sued.

   You dramatically **increase** your chances of getting sued if, when a complainer calls, you snarl, "Ever hear of the First Amendment, buddy?" and slam down the telephone.

   Many people sue **because that's the only way to get our at-**

tention. Listen when that telephone call comes; ***let 'em vent.*** (We'll discuss later the need to be very careful not to say anything that can dig you into a deeper legal hole.)

But, of course, good journalism and compassionate listening to complaints don't always prevent legal problems, so ***make sure you understand the law.***

Defamation: The Basics

Media law has grown hugely complex since the First Amendment to the U.S. Constitution, with its foundation directive that "Congress shall make no law . . . abridging the freedom of speech, or the press. . . ."

Of the complexities, one is of utmost importance to reporters: the law of defamation.

*   *Defamation* is *injury to reputation,* a false communication that tends to harm people's reputation and thus lower them in the estimation of their community or deter others from associating with them. Defamation exposes a ***person*** or ***business*** or ***business product*** to dislike, hatred, ridicule, disgrace.
*   *Slander* rises from injury to reputation through the *spoken word.*
*   *Libel* concerns us here—*writing, pictures, cartoons* or a *message* via other tangible media that injures reputation.

Be alert if anything in your story—including facts or quotes from outside sources—alleges criminal behavior or incompetency, inefficiency, immoral, fraudulent or other dishonorable conduct. Particularly dangerous are stories that harm ***professional reputations*** and cause financial loss to individuals or businesses.

The Burden of Proof

To succeed against you, the person who brings a suit—the ***plaintiff***—must prove these factors:

*   *That libel was published, that someone other than the writer and the target saw the libel.* But that doesn't mean proving a story was seen by thousands in a newspaper or magazine. Libel can be disseminated to one person in a memo, a note, a letter, an internal advisory to your editor. And those "private" e-mails on the Internet? That's like publishing a libel on a billboard in blinking lights. GOOD RULE: If you're in doubt, don't put it on paper or screen—in any form, for anyone.
*   *That the published language indeed was defamatory.* A judge will decide if language—even a single word—is capable of defaming; a jury will decide

whether the language defamed the plaintiff. It's not only *literal* language that can defame. If your story leaves an overall impression that defames, you could be in trouble. Watch also the context of a statement that might lead a reasonable person to reach an unfair, defamatory conclusion about your subject. That is, don't write about a business executive in generalities but leave the impression—which a jury could draw—that the executive is a person of bad moral character who makes shady business deals.

- *That the plaintiff was identified.* Don't think you're safe if you omit the name of your subject. If identity can be inferred from your story, identification is complete. Don't write untruthfully about a "certain Local Biggie" who made his money in shady real estate deals and now is ripping off widows if only one "certain Local Biggie" fits that description.
- *That the statement was false.* You have one unconditional defense in a libel suit: That your facts are *provably true.* If the plaintiff proves your statement is false, you're in trouble. Note *your* burden of proof is proving, to a jury's satisfaction, that your facts are true. *This includes facts or quotes given you by sources.*
- *That you were at fault.* Plaintiff must prove you published defamation through negligence or recklessness or, of course, that you *intended* to defame.
- *That the plaintiff suffered personal harm.* This can include emotional distress, loss of reputation or loss of business revenues.

Aside from provable truth, you have other lines of defense:

Qualified privilege gives you some protection in reporting fairly, accurately and without malice official proceedings. This can cover even false or damaging information *if* you indeed are reporting official proceedings, which can include court hearings or legislative sessions or most official public records. But you must be certain your reporting is from privileged proceedings or sources. State laws vary somewhat on what is official.

Fair comment and criticism is strong protection if you're commenting on people or issues of public interest and importance. But note: Facts in your opinion writing must be provably true. Ensure your opinion is based on provable facts.

Words to Watch

The list is long—*bankrupt, blackmailer, crook, double-crosser, grafter, incompetent, liar, profiteer, shyster.*

Each of those words is on the long list of words reporters wish they never had used in a story. Each was central to a libel action. That's the power of a word, a single word.

Rather than memorizing a long list of potentially actionable words, remember this: Words (and phrases) are most dangerous if they suggest ***criminal activity, incompetence*** in business or professional life or ***serious moral failing.***

A Stanford University law professor, Marc A. Franklin, studied 400 libel cases and found that 320 involved statements or implications of criminality, immorality or incompetence.

Of particular concern to business news reporters is Franklin's finding that nearly 40 percent of plaintiffs worked in manufacturing or general business. More than three-quarters of the libel cases involved allegations of criminal activity, unethical practices and ***incompetence related to work.***[4]

You can draw two reasonable conclusions:

1. People might be strongly inclined to seek redress in libel law if you falsely charge or imply that they lack the intelligence, ability or credentials to do their jobs. If you can't prove it, don't allege that a chief executive officer is incompetent in running a company or that a banker is unethical in dealing with widows.
2. In business news reporting you're often dealing with people—entrepreneurs, executives, professionals—who have the force of personality and financial backing to launch a libel action. We're not talking here about impoverished, uneducated people who don't know libel law and, anyway, can't afford a lawyer.

Another conclusion from my years of watching people in the news: An executive needs great self-confidence to run a multibillion dollar company. That builds strong, often egotistical belief in self ***and*** conviction that good name and a recognized record of accomplishment are crucial to continued business success.

If your reporting impairs a business executive's reputation, you are attacking the very basis of that continued success. And, you can expect reaction much more vigorous than you would get from similarly offended public officials or public figures.

Public officials are more familiar with being covered by the press and, anyway, have a much heavier burden of proof if they wish to succeed in a libel action. So do public figures who thrust themselves into the public limelight.

Many business executives, despite their prominence in business circles, are not used to seeing their name in print. They have no traditional or legal responsibility, as some public officials do, to answer to the people and, thus, open themselves to the press. Private or public, people you write about will scrutinize—carefully and critically—your every word.

But it's not only chief executive officers who are sensitive about reputation. Increasingly, ***companies*** are, too.

Businesses Sue for Libel, Too

The equation is simple:

A company's success depends on its reputation for providing good products and service.

If you write a story accusing that company of providing *poor* service or products, business suffers and company officers are likely to be very upset.

If your story is journalistically sloppy, unfair, unbalanced, you may draw a lawsuit.

If your story is *untruthful*, you stand a good chance of losing.

So, don't commit the error of some reporters: Don't think that because you are writing about a *company*, rather than a *person*, defamation can't occur.

You *can* libel a company, and there is an increasing tendency in corporate America to use the law to protect the reputations of businesses. For many companies, the strategy seems aimed at creating a "chilling effect"—sue or threaten to sue in hopes reporters and editors will pull their journalistic punches.

This strategy sometimes is effective because the cost of defending against libel suits can be prohibitively high—even when you're on solid legal ground. Legal costs alone can run into hundreds of thousands of dollars—millions, even—when news organizations are forced into court.

Box 9-2   ### Business on the Attack

Aggressive, well-funded business interests, public figures and celebrities of every stripe are using a new array of [laws] to attack enterprise reporting. The assaults on newsgathering are finding receptive audiences in court. Judges, it should come as no surprise, harbor the same deepening contempt for the news media that is abroad in the land.

—Bruce Sanford, libel expert, Baker & Hostetler, in "Mortification,"
The American Editor, September 1998, p. 17

Corporate America and its lawyers understand that adding the threat of such huge legal costs to the possibility of judgments in the millions of dollars can cause some editors to wonder whether aggressive, hard-hitting journalism is "cost effective."

So, even a tobacco company sues (and wins) over a news report that it tried to sell cigarettes to young people through a special ad campaign.[5]

So, a construction company sues (and wins) over a report that it filed for bankruptcy, which the company said could damage its bank credit.[6]

That is, look back over your story and ask:

- Have I alleged poor service or faulty products or that the company is deceptive in what it sells?
- Have I alleged commission of a crime by the company, or that it intentionally sells harmful or ineffective products?
- Have I reported the company is financially insolvent?

If so, consult a senior editor and discuss *your* burden of proof—***provable accuracy.***

There's More: Trade Libel

Trade libel (or "product disparagement") arises from defaming not an individual, not a company but, rather, a ***product.***

In *The Law of Communication,* Middleton, Chamberlin and Bunker point out:

> Stories suggesting that a brand of scissors cannot cut, a manufacturer's basketball does not bounce, or a prescription drug causes cancer are examples of product disparagement.[7]

To be dangerous under the laws of trade libel, your story need not allege illegal or immoral conduct by a company or individual; it's enough to defame the usefulness or quality of the product. However, the same story can draw fire as ***both*** business defamation and product disparagement if, for example, disparaging the product implies the company is incompetent, dishonest or fraudulent.

In trade libel, the plaintiff carries an extra burden of proof—***proving financial loss and malice.*** That is, the plaintiff must prove your story financially damaged the business and that you wrote it with malice—with intent to harm or with reckless disregard of the truth or with knowledge that it contained false information.

A Defensive Checklist

When you complete a story, lean back and run through a defensive checklist:

Are Your Facts Provably Correct?

Is everything in that story, including information from outside sources, provably correct? Is the story ***journalistically sound?*** Your reporting and writing are balanced, fair?

Is there ***any error,*** even if seemingly insignificant, that might give an opposing lawyer opportunity to convince a jury your entire story is inaccurate? There are no "little" errors in our business.

Does the Story Contain Accusations?

Do you charge illegal or immoral conduct? *Or could your story lead a jury to perceive it as accusing such conduct?* Double-check any language that might allege criminal activity, misconduct or dereliction of duty.

Beware, particularly, of language, structure or context that might cause financial loss.

Review "Privilege"

Yes, quoting privileged information is a defense. *But* under your state's laws is the information in your story from truly privileged sources?

Also note: Even if you quote from official and public records, you have the defense of privilege only if your reporting is fair, accurate, balanced.

Is "Neutral Reportage" Operative?

Some courts permit the argument that a story has privilege in reporting, say, accusations, charges or damaging statements by responsible sources *if* the circumstances are newsworthy and *if* you impartially and with balance report opposing views. For example, if a chief executive officer comes under fire at a company annual meeting, you might claim the defense of "neutral reportage" in reporting charge and countercharge by shareholders critical of how the company is being run.

However, some courts reject "neutral reportage" on grounds reporters can hide behind it while reporting damaging charges they know to be false. Check legal precedent in your state.

Discard the "Fair Game" Tradition

Some journalists regard public officials and figures—and business executives—as "fair game" because they are prominent, influential, wealthy.

That's unfortunate because (1) it implies we reporters are big game hunters who unfairly shoot first and ask questions later, and because (2) it's untrue anyone is "fair game" under the law and, thus, the hunter-killer mentality is legally dangerous.

The law is clear: Everyone has a right to defend reputation. Our polls show the public agrees. And so do juries drawn from that public.

The "fair game" mentality implies vigilante journalism—good guys mercilessly tracking down bad guys. Life and journalism are more complicated than that.

Beware of "Humorous" Writing

A little "cute" writing can liven up a story, all right. It also can get you in big trouble if your idea of funny isn't funny to the target of your story (ever tell a joke that fell flat?). And, juries tend to be rather solemn in libel cases!

So, look again at language you think is humorous. Would your target and a jury agree?

What to Do When Trouble Erupts

Picture it: That executive you interviewed explodes in anger when your story is printed. Your facts are wrong! Your quotes are wrong! And, dammit, you've committed libel!

At this point, it's not clear you did commit libel, of course. But the executive snatches up the telephone and calls you.

How should you react? *Very carefully.*

How you act now can influence whether a lawsuit is filed and, if one is, whether you add to the problems you'll face in court.

Understand, first, that many libel suits are filed by people who think they have no other way to vent their anger. The public has no legal right of access to the media to complain about our rights and wrongs, real or imagined, and many newspapers don't voluntarily create an openness that exactly welcomes complainers.

Ever try to telephone a newspaper editor? Many stay hidden behind impenetrable automatic switchboards ("Press one if . . ."), secretaries ("Sorry . . .") and voice mail ("I'm away from my desk . . ."). And, if the complainer persists and actually gets through, too often the response is unsympathetic ("Write a letter . . .") or, even (and in my actual experience), a nasty reference to the caller's apparent canine ancestry.

When *you* get such a call—and in a newspaper career you will—display polite professionalism. A few hints:

1. If your caller is a lawyer, *get off the telephone.* Only lawyers talk to lawyers. There is danger that you might be enticed into saying something damaging. ("Gee, now that you mention it, I guess that paragraph *is* libelous. It sure didn't look that way last night when I wrote it. . . .")

   Libel law is complex, and regardless of how defamatory your writing might look the morning after, it may *not* be libelous. *Never* acknowledge you committed libel.

2. When your angry executive is on the telephone, *limit yourself to a gentle throwaway line* ("I am sorry you are upset. . . . Give me full details of your thinking."). Let the caller rage. **But make no comment on who is right, who is wrong.** Simply getting you—anybody—to listen can give a complainer satisfaction ("Well, I sure told off that reporter!").

3. *Immediately go to a senior editor:* "**We** have a problem." Editors are paid to keep you—and, thus, the newspaper and themselves—out of trouble. Make the problem a corporate, not your personal, problem. Do not—ever—try to sort out your problem without advising your supervisor.

The temptation (I know from experience) will be to try to handle things quietly by, for example, promising the complainer, "I'll do another story tomorrow and straighten all this out." It's only human to consider hiding the complaint from supervisors who, after all, judge your career potential on, among other things, your ability to write libel-free copy. But such self-help remedies create a likelihood that you'll thus acknowledge libel was committed or, even, repeat one in a corrective story.

4. *Be fully forthcoming with your editor* and, if it gets to that, your newspaper's libel attorney. Only with full details on what was wrong in your story as well as right can they mount a proper defense. And you'll note they take their time in doing so. Nothing is gained in the law—and much can be lost—by rushing haphazardly into print with a revision, correction or apology.

Incidentally, many newspapers have libel insurance, and it's accepted practice for newspapers to cover and defend reporters. After all, if you're allowed to swing by yourself, and are found to have committed libel, the newspaper, as the transmitter of the libel, is in trouble, too.

Of course, the best way to handle a libel suit is to prevent it from happening. Make it your writer's mantra: "Fairness, balance, provable accuracy, provable accuracy, provable . . ."

Beware of Insider Trading

Has it occurred to you that if your reporting can move millions of dollars in world markets, it could move a couple bucks into your pocket, too?

Well, you're not alone in recognizing the linkage between news and profit or loss, and that people who possess "inside" information can profit before the general public is even aware of it.

So, there are laws against misuse of inside information.

Mostly, such laws cover ***corporate insiders***—a firm's executives, for example, who learn through their work of developments that will affect the company's stock price, then trade for their own benefit before the public is informed. That's the key: Securities law is designed to ensure ***all*** investors have equal access to material information about a stock.

Reporters in some instances also are obliged to disclose still-unpublished information they intend to profit from. Financial journalists, along with newsletter publishers, public relations practitioners and others, are considered ***market insiders*** because they handle sensitive market-moving information.

Market insiders have been found guilty of fraud for misappropriating information owned by their employers and using it for personal gain. A *Wall Street Journal* reporter was convicted of securities fraud for using *Journal* information for personal profit and passing it to friends. The reporter also was convicted of wire fraud in using the *Journal*'s confidential information in violation of the paper's conflict-of-interest policy. Like the *Journal,* most newspapers claim ownership of all news and information collected by their staffs.

Passing nonpublic information to others so they can trade is called "tipping." Both giver and taker of information are open to fraud charges. "Scalping" is manipulating a market by, for example, buying a stock, then reporting favorably on it—and selling at a profit when the price rises.

Note another dimension of that *Wall Street Journal* incident: The reporter was convicted of fraud on grounds his misuse of information sullied the newspaper's reputation for ethical journalism.

It's to ethics—what, law aside, is ***right and wrong***—that we now turn.

Ethics: Serving a Higher Principle

Journalists argue a lot about the ethics of our craft because, despite what moral absolutists might say, what's right or wrong in journalism isn't always clear.

However, journalists agree on one point of concern in business news: Reporters must serve a higher principle—the people's right and need to know—and must not use their power as reporters for personal gain and must not profit from information they collect before readers can.

You saw earlier that society considers insider trading illegal and can punish journalists for such conflict of interest. Professional journalism societies and news organizations also are united in their condemnation of it.

Under codes of ethics developed by journalists' groups, you betray a higher principle if you unfairly or, certainly, illegally profit from misusing your power as a reporter. Newspapers will fire you for it.

Box 9-3	Code of Ethics for the Society of American Business Editors and Writers, Inc.

Statement of Purpose—It is not enough that we be incorruptible and act with honest motives. We must conduct all aspects of our lives in a manner that averts even the appearance of conflict of interest or misuse of the power of the press.

A business, financial and economics writer should:

1. Recognize the trust, confidence and responsibility placed in him or her by the publication's readers and do nothing to abuse this obligation. To this end, a clear-cut delineation between advertising and editorial matters should be maintained at all times.
2. Avoid any practice which might compromise or appear to compromise his or her objectivity or fairness. He or she should not let any personal investments influence what he or she writes. On some occasions, it may be desirable for him or her to disclose his or her investment positions to a superior.

3. Avoid active trading and other short-term profit-seeking opportunities. Active participation in the markets which such activities require is not compatible with the role of the business and financial journalists as disinterested trustees of the public interest.

4. Not take advantage in his or her personal investing of any inside information and be sure any relevant information he or she may have is widely disseminated before he or she buys or sells.

5. Make every effort to insure the confidentiality of information held for publication to keep such information from finding its way to those who might use it for gain before it becomes available to the public.

6. Accept no gift, special treatment or any other thing of more than token value given in the course of his professional activities. In addition, he or she will accept no out-of-town travel paid for by anyone other than his or her employer for the ostensible purpose of covering or backgrounding news. Free-lance writing opportunities and honoraria for speeches should be examined carefully to assure that they are not in fact disguised gratuities. Food and refreshments of ordinary value may be accepted where necessary during the normal course of business.

7. Encourage the observance of these minimum standards by all business writers.

Addendum to Code of Ethics

Guidelines to Ensure Integrity of Business News Coverage

1. A clear-cut delineation between advertising and editorial matters should be maintained at all times.

2. Material produced by an editorial staff or news service should be used only in sections controlled by editorial departments.

3. Sections controlled by advertising departments should be distinctly different from news sections in typeface, layout and design.

4. Promising a story in exchange for advertising is unethical.

5. Publishers, broadcasters and top newsroom editors should establish policies and guidelines to protect the integrity of business news coverage.

Cautions on Use of Non-Journalists with Conflicts of Interest in the Subject Matter

Using articles or columns written by non-journalists is potentially deceptive and poses inherent conflicts of interest that editors should guard against. This does not apply to clearly labeled op-ed or viewpoint sections or "Letters to the Editor."

In its ethics code, the Society of American Business Editors and Writers warns that writers abuse "the power of the press" if they misuse, for personal profit, information collected on the news beat.

A leading professional group, the American Society of Newspaper Editors, puts it this way in its "Statement of Principles":

> The primary purpose of gathering and distributing news and opinion is to serve the general welfare by informing the people and enabling them to make judgments on the issues of the time. Newspaper men and women who abuse the power of their professional role for selfish motives or unworthy purposes are faithless to that public trust. . . .
>
> Journalists must avoid impropriety and the appearance of impropriety as well as any conflict of interest or the appearance of conflict. They should neither accept anything nor pursue any activity that might compromise or seem to compromise their integrity.[8]

The Society of Professional Journalists says in its "Code of Ethics" that "the duty of journalists is to serve the truth." The Code hits hard on where our principal duties lie:

> The public's right to know of events of public importance and interest is the overriding mission of the mass media. The purpose of distributing news and enlightened opinion is to serve the general welfare. Journalists who use their professional status as representatives of the public for selfish or other unworthy motives violate a high trust.

The code adds that accepting gifts, special treatment or privileges "can compromise the integrity of journalists and their employers" and "nothing of value should be accepted." And that, says the Society of Professional Journalists, covers your life off the job, too:

> Journalists and their employers should conduct their personal lives in a manner which protects them from conflict of interest, real or apparent.

Newspaper codes of ethics similarly express concern over any conduct, personal or professional, that constitutes conflict of interest or might give even the appearance of conflict. One difference: Unlike professional codes, newspaper codes make it clear that violating this principle can warrant dismissal.

The Wall Street Journal, whose entire success is built on journalistic integrity, is particularly strong on the point in its code:

> It is important for all employees to keep in mind the tremendous embarrassment and damage to the Company's reputation and that of fellow employees that could come about through a lapse in judgment by one person, or someone closely associated with that person, no matter how well-intended that person may be. Because we think it is so essential that every employee be above suspicion, we consider any slip in judgment in the areas covered in this policy statement to be serious enough to warrant dismissal.

The *Journal*'s code warns:

• Don't use for personal profit any information gained on the job about the *Journal* or its parent company, Dow Jones. (News in ***tomorrow***'s

Journal will move markets; just think how the unscrupulous could gain by trading on that news ***today***!)

- Each employee "must bend over backward" to avoid even suspicion of engaging unethically in stock trading to personal advantage on information gained in working for the *Journal.*
- *Journal* employees may trade in stocks but not in a manner that gives them advantages because of what they learn as journalists. All stocks must be held for six months, for example, to eliminate possibility of short-term trading based on news gathering daily by reporters.
- Reporters are forbidden from investing in specific industries they cover.
- All news and information collected by reporters "is deemed to be strictly the Company's property."

| Box 9-4 | Conflicts of Interest Policy |

As a condition of employment, each employee of Dow Jones & Co., publisher of *The Wall Street Journal,* must agree to adhere to a detailed conflicts of interest policy. Excerpts:

> This policy statement is designed to provide all employees with guidelines which will enable them to avoid conflicts of interest that might be construed to be detrimental to the best interests of Dow Jones. It is important for all employees to keep in mind the tremendous embarrassment and damage to the Company's reputation and that of fellow employees that could come about through a lapse in judgment by one person, or someone closely associated with that person, no matter how well-intended that person may be. Because we think it is so essential that every employee be above suspicion, we consider any slip in judgment in the areas covered in this policy statement to be serious enough to warrant dismissal.

Confidential Information

1. Employees should not use, directly or indirectly, for their own or any other person's financial gain, any information about Dow Jones which the employee obtained in connection with Dow Jones employment. Further, employees should not disclose to anyone confidential information obtained in connection with Dow Jones employment until such information has been made available to the public. . . .

Security Transactions

6. Dow Jones has always had a strict policy on security transactions by employees who have access to inside information regarding unpublished stories or advertising schedules. It also has had a strict related policy on the conduct of news and advertising staff members dealing with corporations we cover or

whose advertising we carry. Each employee is expected to bend over backwards to avoid any action, no matter how well-intentioned, that could provide grounds for suspicion:

    a. that an employee, his family or others close to the employee made financial gains by acting on the basis of inside information gained through a position on our staff, before it was available to the general public. Such information includes hold-for-release material, our plans for running stories, items that may affect price movements, or projected advertising campaigns;

    b. that the writing of a news story or item or scheduling of advertising was influenced by a desire to affect the stock's prices;

    c. that an employee is financially committed in the market so deeply or in other ways to create a temptation to biased writing or scheduling of advertising;

    d. that an employee is beholden to brokers or any other group we cover or advertisers. Such indebtedness could arise through acceptance of favors, gifts or payments for performing writing assignments or other services for them;

    e. that an employee is beholden for any tips, allocations or underwritten new issues or in any other way to anyone in the financial community.

We do not want to penalize our staff members by suggesting that they not buy stocks or make other investments. We do, however, want employees to avoid speculation or the appearance of speculation. Members of the Management Committee, national department heads, and members of the news and advertising departments must not engage in short-term trading; they must hold securities a minimum of six (6) months, unless they get approval from the Vice President/Legal or his designee to meet some special need. They must not buy or sell basically speculative instruments such as futures or options. No employee of the Company should engage in short selling of securities.

We reiterate that it is not enough to be incorruptible and act with honest motives. It is equally important to use good judgment and conduct one's outside activities so that no one—management, our editors, an SEC investigator, or a political critic of the Company—has any ground for even raising the suspicion that an employee misused a position with the Company.

With these general propositions in mind, here are some further specific guidelines:

    i. First and foremost, all material gleaned by you in the course of your work for Dow Jones is deemed to be strictly the Company's property. This includes not only the fruits of your own and your colleagues's work, but also information on plans for running items and articles on particular companies and industries and advertising schedules in future issues. Such material must never be disclosed to anyone outside the Company, including friends and relatives. Viewing information as the Company's property should avoid a great many of the obvious pitfalls.

    ii. No employee regularly assigned to a specific industry should invest, nor should his family, in any company engaged in whole or significant part in that industry.

iii. No employee with knowledge of a forthcoming article, item or advertisement concerning a company or industry should, prior to the publication of such article, item or advertisement, invest or in any way encourage or assist any other person in selling a security in that company prior to publication without the approval of the appropriate Management Committee member.

iv. Further, any employee having prior knowledge of a forthcoming article, item or advertisement, should delay buying or selling the securities of the company involved, as should his family, until the general public has an opportunity to read and digest the information contained in any Dow Jones publication or news service. Employees should wait two full trading days after an article or advertisement first appears in a Dow Jones publication or news service.

v. If an employee thinks there is a possibility he or a family member may have inadvertently violated any of the above guidelines, or if an employee should buy a security prior to publication, and then acquire knowledge of a proposed article, item or advertisement, the employee should notify his or her department head as soon as practical. In the case of a purchase, the employee or family member should hold the security for six months.

Serving on the Board of Directors of Other Companies

7. Dow Jones' employees are prohibited except with written approval of the chief executive officer from serving as directors or officers of any other company
devoted to profit-making. . . . If an employee is involved in a family-owned profit-making business, clearance should be obtained from the appropriate member of the Management Committee. . . .

Should any question ever arise in your mind as to propriety of your activity, you are urged to consult in confidence with your national department head or any Dow Jones officer.

We would like to emphasize that we have complete confidence in all our employees. It is essential, however, that all of us maintain the highest standards of ethics in the conduct of Dow Jones' business in actuality and also in appearances by acting within the framework of these guidelines. Please retain this policy statement in your files.

The Washington Post's statement of "Standards and Ethics" goes even further in monitoring employee activity:

To avoid real or apparent conflicts of interest in the coverage of business and financial markets, all members of the Business and Financial staff are required to disclose their financial holdings and investments to the assistant managing editor in charge of the section. . . .

All reporters and editors, wherever they may work, are required to disclose to their department head any financial interests that may be in conflict or give the appearance of conflict in their reporting and editing duties. Department heads will make their own financial disclosures to the managing editor.

Like *The Wall Street Journal,* the *Post* prohibits gifts, outside employment and other activities, ***on the job or off,*** that might create conflict of interest or the appearance of it. The *Post,* like the *Journal,* extends its concern beyond its employees. The *Post's* code states:

> Relatives cannot fairly be made subject to *Post* rules, but it should be recognized that their employment or their involvement in cases can at least appear to compromise our integrity. The business and professional ties of traditional family members or other members of your household must be disclosed to department heads.

Like other newspapers with codes, the *Post* and the *Journal* create in their statements of principle an ethical context wider than only issues specific to reporting business news.

The Wider Ethical Context

You have a responsibility to investigate the wider ethical context of journalism today and develop your ***personal*** approach to the rights and wrongs of business news reporting.

Note the emphasis on *personal.* Newspaper codes often are designed primarily to protect ***institutional*** integrity and marketplace image. Many corporate codes give little guidance to an individual reporter trying to sort out his or her own code of ethical conduct.

It's not the stuff of daily conversation in newsrooms, but serious study of ethics will take you back to the ancient Greeks, Socrates (who died in 399 B.C.), who discussed "justice," and his student, Plato (who died in 347 B.C.), who discussed "good", and ***his*** student, Aristotle, who spoke of the individual's responsibility for acting with virtue.

From that came the idea that the individual (read that, ***reporter***) sometimes must act with virtue ***even*** if personal sacrifice and unhappiness are the price.

Development of Judeo-Christian ethics sharpened the concept of the individual's responsibility for doing the right thing, and you can relate current thinking on media ethics to that and to subsequent philosophers.

Thomas Hobbes (1588–1679) was an early advocate of the idea that the people, not their sovereigns, possess true power. It follows that the people must be informed, and thus is born our sense that journalism's fundamental responsibility is to serve the people's right and need to know.

John Milton (1608–1674) suggested truth would emerge and false ideas would be vanquished if everyone were permitted to express ideas freely in an "open marketplace of ideas." We know, in this age of propaganda and "spin artists," that the ideas marketplace is a bit more complex than that suggests. But Milton's basic idea underscores journalism's tradition of placing ideas and facts before the people, who ascertain truth.

David Hume (1711–1776) identified usefulness—"utility"—as the measure of value for ethical principle. Justice is utilitarian because it serves the good of humanity. John Stuart Mill (1806–1873) identified *utilitarianism* as ethical conduct aimed at serving the well-being of the greatest number of people. And that ties, of course, directly to what many journalists would say, for example, about examining the personal life of a political leader: Revealing even intimate and embarrassing details is necessary if that serves the greater public's need and right to know.

So, then, does the historic evolution of philosophical and religious thinking tie directly to our discussion today of individual responsibility in media ethics.

Basic Ethical Concepts

Ethics codes written by and for journalists (as contrasted with those written by newspapers for employees) include those of the American Society of Newspaper Editors and the Society of Professional Journalists. Among their commonalities are basic ethical concepts:

- Journalists have special responsibilities because the First Amendment's guarantee of free expression is a people's constitutional right expressed through the press.
- Service to the people is the journalist's basic responsibility, and our overriding mission is to meet the public's right to know about events of public importance and interest.
- Any journalist who abuses the power of our professional role for selfish motives or unworthy purposes is faithless to that public trust.
- Truth is the ultimate goal, and accurate, fair and objective reporting, the mark of a professional journalist, is how we strive toward it.
- Independence of thought and action and freedom from conflict of interest or the perception of it are essential to fair, impartial journalism.

Well, you might think, those are wonderful generalities, but how do I sort out a personal approach to all that? Carefully. And, as you proceed, keep two things in mind:

- Unlike corporate codes, the codes of professional journalism societies don't carry punitive power. You can't be drummed out of journalism for being an unfair reporter. It's to your very personal sense of right and wrong that you must be true.
- Doing what *you* consider the right thing might take you into conflict with,

say, an editor who orders a story done a certain way—and you, after all, *are* paid to do as bidden and help get the paper on the street. That is, there can be pain associated with insisting on doing what you think is ethically right. You can get fired.

So, how *do* you decide what's right?

A Decision-Making Process

A five-step process might help you sort through ethical dilemmas:

1. *Assemble all facts.* This requires deep-dig reporting to peel back layers of facts until you reach the ***real what*** of an ethical problem.
2. *Identify the ethical issue(s).* A business executive is involved in a shady deal? What's the ethical issue? His privacy versus the public's right to know? Is there ***need*** to know? Will covering the story inflict pain on innocents—his wife and family? Most of the time, what you think is a single ethical issue will balloon to several at least.
3. *Consider alternative solutions.* Is there a way to meet the public's right and need to know about that executive ***and*** protect his innocent family?
4. *Decide which course you will follow.* Don't waffle, don't evade. Decide.
5. *Act.* Don't walk away from your responsibility, from your public's right to know—or, indeed, from the rights of the executive. Act.

Consider Societal Values

Basic societal values generally are accepted by all of us as important characteristics of civilized society. Consider them as you sort through ethical problems.

Truth-telling is fundamental to an orderly, just society, of course, and to lie or blur the truth is a cardinal sin in journalism.

Civilized society must guarantee ***justice,*** the impartial and fair treatment of all. Journalists must be just ***and*** must monitor whether society accords justice to all.

Humaneness is basic to civilized society, and journalists, who are very powerful people, must strive to help, not harm people.

Call it independence, autonomy, liberty—***freedom*** is basic to the American way. Journalists must protect it for others (called ***stewardship***) and ensure they stay independent themselves from any association that might restrict their ability to cover the news fairly and impartially.

Serve Basic Journalistic Principles

Adapting societal values to our craft, journalists long ago identified principles as essential to our mission:

- Serve the public.
- Monitor the powerful.
- Be balanced and fair.
- Be compassionate.
- Guard the First Amendment.
- Be courageous and independent.

As you move through the decision-making process you'll often encounter conflicting *loyalties.*

In any personal code of ethics you'll owe first loyalty to yourself and your conscience. It's that conscience, not memory of some editor barking at you, that will awaken you in the middle of the night years later if you've made a bad call in handling an issue of ethics.

Your conscience can be an early warning system. If something you're writing *seems* wrong, stop and consider—carefully—whether it *is* wrong.

Conflict can arise as you consider your loyalty to society and your loyalty to the hand that feeds you—your employer. What, for example, do you decide when orders from your editor conflict with your concept of loyalty to readers—to society?

Ah, that's where courage enters the equation!

Summary

- Journalists work in a legally dangerous environment, so understanding libel law is necessary in practicing aggressive, hard-hitting journalism.
- Your first *(best)* defense against libel trouble is to report fairly, accurately, with balance.
- *Defamation* is injury to reputation—false communication that harms reputation; *libel* is written defamation.
- Businesses and products can be defamed just like individuals; particularly dangerous are stories that harm professional reputations.
- To succeed, those filing libel suits—plaintiffs—must *prove* libel was published, language was defamatory, it was disseminated, the plaintiff was identified, the statement was false, you published through negligence or recklessness and the plaintiff suffered personal harm.
- Your single unqualified defense is that your facts—including those from sources—are *provably true.*
- Libel suits have been filed (and won) over language suggesting criminal activity, incompetence in business or professional life, or serious moral failing.
- Business news reporters cover executives and others who have the force of personality and financial backing to launch libel actions.
- Enormous defense costs plus threat of huge judgments in libel cases create a "chilling effect" that leads some editors to pull their journalistic punches.

- *Trade libel* ("product disparagement") rises from defaming usefulness or quality of a product or service.
- When you receive a complaint about a story, take facts and listen; don't comment on whether libel was committed; then consult a senior editor.
- Under securities law, business news reporters can be considered "market insiders" because they handle sensitive market-moving information and, thus, you can be subject to strict laws on how you use information for your own gain.
- Ethical questions often are unclear in journalism but the media and journalists' societies agree on this: Your duty is to serve the public, not your personal profit.
- Leading newspapers require adherence to ethics codes as a condition of employment and will fire you for misusing information for personal gain.
- In resolving ethical dilemmas, follow a five-step process: assemble all facts, identify the issue(s), consider alternative solutions, decide and act.
- Societal values to consider: truth-telling, humaneness, justice, freedom.
- Journalistic principles: serve the public, monitor the powerful, be balanced and fair, compassionate, independent and a defender of the First Amendment.
- In all questions of ethics, be *__courageous.__*

Recommended Reading

For a quick study of libel law, see *The Associated Press Stylebook and Libel Manual.* Its section on defamation—and how to protect against it—is basic and easily understood.

More in-depth understanding is in Kent R. Middleton, Bill F. Chamberlin and Matthew D. Bunker, *The Law of Public Communication,* 4th ed. (New York: Longman 1997) and subsequent updates, particularly the 1999 version by Middleton and Robert Trager.

I discuss media law in a variety of newsroom and management scenarios: *Introduction to Professional Newswriting* 2nd ed. (New York: Longman, 1998); *Writing Opinion for Impact* (Ames: Iowa State University Press, 1999); *Introduction to Magazine Writing* (New York: Macmillan, 1994); and *Strategic Newspaper Management* (Boston: Allyn and Bacon, 1996).

Current journalistic dialogue on ethics is in the American Society of Newspaper Editors' *Bulletin, Content, American Journalism Review* and other periodicals covering the media. I discuss personal and corporate ethics in *Media Ethics* (Boston: Allyn and Bacon, 1995).

Notes

1. *See* particularly Ken Liebeskind, "Credibility Problems Plague All Media," *Editor & Publisher,* Dec. 13, 1997, p. 23.

2. David B. Martens, "Libel Protection," *presstime,* December 1998, p. 27.

3. In the spirit of full disclosure, I should note that Prof. Middleton is my colleague at the University of Georgia. I like his book very much, nevertheless.

4. Kent R. Middleton, Bill F. Chamberlin and Matthew D. Bunker, *The Law of Public Communication,* 4th ed. (New York: Longman, 1997), p. 81.

5. Ibid, p. 84.

6. Ibid, p. 83.

7. Ibid, p. 84.

8. Full texts of this and other codes are reprinted in Conrad Fink, *Media Ethics* (Boston: Allyn and Bacon, 1995).

Exercises

1. Your instructor will invite the editor (or a leading reporter) of a local newspaper to appear before your class. Interview this person about (a) the defensive measures taken in the newsroom to prevent defamatory copy from being published and (b) whether the "chilling effect" is felt in that newsroom. Write your observations in 350-400 words.

2. Read the front page of *The Wall Street Journal* (or the business section of another paper designated by your instructor) for three consecutive days and, in about 300 words, comment on this: Is the reporting aggressive and hard-hitting or has the "chilling effect" settled in? Do any stories appear legally dangerous? Can you see defensive journalism in how stories are written and in language selected?

3. Apply this chapter's "defensive checklist" to the lead story in today's *The Wall Street Journal* (or another story designated by your instructor). In about 350 words comment on whether facts seem provably correct. Are accusations made? Is privileged information used? Does neutral reportage seem operative?

4. Read again this chapter's excerpts of *The Wall Street Journal* and *The Washington Post* codes of ethics. In about 350 words, comment on whether it is right for an employer to (a) so tightly monitor the personal investments of an employee and (b) whether a newspaper should extend its concern to an employee's relatives.

5. Of all the ethical issues facing journalists today, which concerns you the most? Is it invasion of privacy, lack of humaneness, people's right to know versus individual rights? In about 350 words, and using the five-step, decision-making process, describe how you personally resolve that troublesome issue.

PART SIX

Your Future on Campus and Beyond

YOU'VE STUDIED BUSINESS news reporting and read how the pros cover economics and personal finance.

What's next? ***Doing it yourself!***

Getting started—now—in writing about these news specialities should be your next step. Take it, and you'll get valuable experience and build that essential clip file all job interviewers want to see.

Campus journalism is your perfect starting place. Many university newspapers and magazines are thinly staffed and desperate for reporters. In return, campus publications offer you ink and newsprint—newshole for display of your reporting and writing skills (and, ***your byline***).

Of all sectors of journalism, none is as underdeveloped in campus publications as business news. Few, indeed, are the collegiate newspapers that regularly provide readers with dollars-and-cents reporting.

Yet, on every campus are many student readers badly in need of dollars-and-cents guidance.

Are ***your*** classmates counting their pennies as costs escalate for tuition, books, computers, rent, food?

Of course they are—and that's why you have great journalistic opportunity to help them with how-to-do-it stories on personal finance.

Another important reason for plunging in: Trying your hand now in this news speciality can help you sort out potential career paths, help you assess your personal reporting and writing strengths and your weaknesses.

Intrigued at perhaps covering "big picture" economics for, say, *The New York Times, Washington Post* or *Forbes* or *Fortune?* Start on the campus big picture—your university's budget or its five-year construction plan. Look at athletic department spending. Trace the big picture's impact to where it counts—student pocketbooks.

How about writing company news one day? Start now reporting on those intriguing entrepreneurs who set up shop around every campus—the graduate who stays in town to open a used book store; the business school student who is a part-time computer programming consultant. Tell other students how they can do it.

Writing personal finance is a possible career? Start now on pocketbook issues of deep concern to those readers you know best—your fellow students.

10

Starting Today Toward Tomorrow

You NOTED throughout this book efforts by professional business writers to engage readers by selecting topics crucial to them, reporting facts they need, writing at their level to lure them into reading.

You can do that in campus journalism only if you stay focused on basic guidelines.

Basic Guidelines for Campus Journalism

Stay Local

You're not yet at *The New York Times* or *Forbes*. And your readers aren't yet on Wall Street or managing international conglomerates.

So, focus your reporting on local campus news that's crucial right now to student readers *and* that you, a beginner, reasonably can handle.

That is, the Fed chairman's testimony before Congress on interest rates isn't your story. Your story is what the president of your university says is capital spending planned for next year—new dorms, new classrooms, new athletic buildings.

Your story isn't the latest Paris fashion show. Your story is the latest campus clothing fad—and where off campus that special clothing can be bought and, especially, at what prices.

Your story isn't Washington's latest figures on the Consumer Price Index; rather, it's comparison shopping at five local supermarkets for a story informing students where to find the lowest prices on food.

Listen to Your Audience

When you *do* reach *The New York Times* or *Forbes,* you'll have available massive amounts of reader research. All major newspapers and magazines use scientific focus groups and surveys to determine what news readers need and want.

In campus journalism, do-it-yourself research is required—but that's not as difficult as you might think.

First, your editors should seek help from research faculty in business, marketing, advertising, journalism. Many willingly supervise low-cost but highly effective research, and grad students ***need*** thesis or dissertation projects!

Second, you can conduct your own research—though unscientific and superficial it may be—***by listening.*** Take off the headset, turn off the boom box and ***listen*** to your roommate; listen on the bus, in the cafeteria, in the hallways before and after class. What money issues are students talking about? What they're talking about is what you need to write about.

Focus on Core Issues

Much of journalism is aimed at reaching the largest possible number of targeted readers.

Thus do newspapers and magazines reach for the reader support required to get, in turn, the advertiser support that's needed to stay in business.

For a reporter, aiming at the largest possible readership focuses your resources—your personal time and energy and your publication's newshole—on doing the best you can for more rather than fewer.

That doesn't mean, of course, we never write intentionally for small audiences. Economics reporters for *The Wall Street Journal, Washington Post, Forbes* know they're appealing to limited numbers of readers with stories on highly esoteric developments in global finance. However, those reporters also know they are reaching highly influential decision-makers.

In campus journalism, your reader target mostly has to be the largest number of students you can reach. And you reach them by covering ***core issues.***

Yes, your informal hallway research will pick up grumbling about, say, the cost of a hamburger. But that is only anecdotal evidence of the larger core issue—the cost of eating in campus dining halls versus off-campus apartments.

You'll hear a single student complain about having to work two off-campus jobs to pay bills. The core issue here is not that one student's travails. Rather, it is steadily rising costs of tuition, books, rent, food that are forcing many students to work part-time, even if grades suffer. (But do consider that single complainer as the human element for a neck-of-vase intro on your story!)

Stay Timely

Well, here it is September. Classes are starting, and graduation is 10 months ahead.

Is it time for a story on job availability for June graduates? No.

Is it time for a story on where to buy textbooks at the lowest price? Yes.

Is it time for a story on where students can get the best terms for personal loans to get them through the next 10 months? Yes. Time to explain how to understand an apartment lease? How to rent or buy a computer? Yes, again and again.

Save the job story for a couple months before graduation, when updated employment figures out of Washington will give you national context for your local view—and when campus economists and placement officials have more timely information.

Sharpen your sense of timeliness. Do as the pros do: offer a story when editors likely will be receptive, when readers have a ***need to know.***

Report Strongly and Authoritatively

Ever read a "news" story with no news? A story filled with gaseous writing but no facts?

Sure you have, and you felt cheated, didn't you? You likely threw down the newspaper or magazine in disgust.

Don't cheat your readers. Give them hard facts, dollars-and-cents figures—news they can use, information that leaves them better prepared to face the world than they were before reading your piece.

Watch the great reporters for clues. They may wax poetic about a football game, but the statistics—yardage won, yardage lost—are in the story. Their writing may soar as they take you on a trip fantastic to far-off places—but precisely how to get there and how much it costs will be in the story.

In no form of journalism are facts and figures more needed than in business news writing. We're talking here about ***service journalism***—helping readers lead better, more fulfilling lives.

Seek authoritative sources:

- Placement officials, academic counselors and employment executives to back up the anecdotal musings of that student whose grades suffer from working two off-campus jobs.
- Loan officers of local banks and financial advisors on campus for the ***facts and figures*** on where best terms are available for student loans.
- Law school faculty, local lawyers and realtors for your story on understanding apartment leases.

Learning to seek out authoritative sources and extract crucial information is a skill you should start developing now. And a bit of advice: In a job interview, don't put before the hiring editor a story on personal finance with just one or two figures in it and no authoritative sourcing. That signals amateurism.

Write Alluringly

It's old (but sound) guidance: There are no dull stories, only dull writers.

There is *magic* in journalism, excitement and adventure, the thrill of finding and telling—for the betterment of your readers.

If you don't feel that and can't reflect it in your writing, maybe you should consider another line of work. If you report grudgingly and write dully, you'll not appeal to readers and your career will be a nonstarter.

Not to say, of course, that you should "pump" your story beyond its intrinsic value with exaggerated reporting and high-flying writing. Your basic mission in business news reporting is to transmit operative, reliable information in clear, understandable language.

But *do* use everything you learned about strong writing in this book—and tricks of the writing trade you'll learn in the future. Enliven your writing. Only if you attract readers can you communicate essential information.

And now, in campus journalism, is the time to spread your writer's wings and fly a little. Use this time in the minor leagues to sharpen writing skills that one day will carry you into the majors.

Remember: People, Not Issues

It's people we write about and for, not issues or concepts.

All those "important" pronouncements by "important" officials in Washington? Those "global developments?" They're news only if they affect people—our readers—and we prioritize their news value strictly based on how important the effect will be.

So, your news story isn't the high unemployment rate; it's Dick and Jane, rising June graduates who may have difficulty finding jobs. The news isn't a soaring Consumer Price Index; it's Bill and Bertha, among the students on your campus who will face a cost squeeze in months ahead.

News is reflected in people; mirror the impact in your writing.

Campus Journalism's Fertile Fields

At *any* college newspaper or magazine, on *any* campus, you are blessed with fertile fields for learning the business of business writing. You are surrounded by fascinating stories—and students who need to know about them.

Big Picture Reporting

As excellent training for eventual wide-view reporting as a professional, seek the *student angle* in these broader stories:

Tuition trends. Interview the university's vice president for finance and admission officials on next year's expected levels. Establish a three-year track record for past increases. Report in both dollars and percentages. Is the gap between in-state and out-of-state tuition changing? Why?

Student fees. Exactly how does your university use all those dollars you and your fellow students pay each time you register? Interview the vice president for finance for a breakdown of dollar allocations between, for example, student activities, bus passes, computer labs and so forth. Are students paying for things or services not widely used?

University budget. Go to the top: Interview the university president and, again, vice president for finance. Compare next year's budget against this year's. Where will spending increase/decrease? Focus on items of particular interest to students—spending on new classrooms, for example, or computer labs. Handle this big picture story well and you're very likely to catch the eye of a hiring editor. Incidentally, any educational institution that receives state or federal funding is required to make these figures available. Most have line budgets on permanent display in their library's public records room.

Faculty salaries. Want to catch ***everybody***'s attention? Compare salaries for faculty, ***by name and department.*** They're in the line budget and by law open to your inspection. Interview the director of personnel of vice president for finance for an overview of salaries and explanation of any apparent disparities. Are women paid more or less than men? Note some salaries are for nine-month teaching contracts, some for 12 months. Always interesting: a comparison of the football coach's salary with the president's.

Parking services. Aside from a losing season on the gridiron, does anything cause more campus unrest than parking? Are too few spaces available and fees too high? And, why are those parking fines so high, and what is done with all the money collected, anyway? Report in depth on the finances of parking services. Be sure to ascertain how many spaces are rented and how many are actually available.

Intramural sports spending. Compare how much is spent on athletic facilities and events for the general student body with spending by the athletic department on the big ticket sports—football and basketball. Do those sports fund intramural sports?

University fund raising. Students generally aren't aware that a huge share of university spending is funded by nontaxpayer sources. Outside money generally is raised by the "development office." Interview its director on which portion of your university's budget is funded from outside sources, and how this year's fund raising compares with that of the past three years (***always*** look for trends in such reporting).

How-To-Do-It Reporting

As you noted throughout this book, outlining a problem isn't enough in Big League business writing. You've got to provide solutions, too.

You can prepare for a career in that kind of journalism by writing how-to stories of compelling interest to your student readers. Suggestions:

Buying textbooks. Students spend thousands of dollars on books en route to a degree. Think of the service you provide if you show them how to reduce that cost by even a few percentage points! Interview book store managers on and off campus. Do any offer special deals or volume discounts? How do prices compare for new and used books? Compare shelf prices for selected texts in a number of stores. Does Amazon.com offer better prices?

Buying computers. How can your readers find bargains? Are the best prices on campus or off? Are used (but reliable) computers available? Where? At what price? Can computers be leased? Are university labs available 24 hours for students who cannot afford their own computer? How much computer power is enough for most students? Do some students spend more than necessary? Consult computer science faculty.

Selecting credit cards. Every credit card company in America writes me three times annually and telephones twice, or so it seems. You, too? Why not sort through the competitive (and often conflicting) claims of credit card companies and report for your fellow students on how to get the best terms? Business school faculty, local bank officials and your university's student financial advisors are authoritative sources.

Student loans. You'll be well read if you report how to get the best terms. Your university has loan advisors on its administrative staff. Local banks are sources, too. Be certain to report specifics—where the loan office is, when it's open, its telephone number. Explain the process of loan applications.

Establishing credit. Bouncing checks at a local pub is part of a jolly Saturday night for some students. And even years later, "bad credit risk" pops out of some computer as those students try to get a loan, buy a car on credit or apply for a home mortgage. Interview officials of the local credit bureau (most towns have them) and local bankers on the importance of establishing good credit ratings, even as an undergraduate.

Choosing telephone service. Students are heavy spenders for telephone services, and communications companies compete vigorously for their business. Consult competing telephone companies on the many special services. You can help readers save real dollars.

Stretch for the Unusual

Campus journalism is perfect for trying your skills as a creative, imaginative writer. Take a stab at these ideas:

The profile. Many students work late night jobs or do the strangest tasks to help pay their college expenses. Profile a student who, for example, has the midnight-to-8 A.M. shift at a convenience store, or a student who babysits sick animals at the veterinary hospital. Include the availability of such jobs, wages, hours, how to get one.

The financial planner. Try a series of stories on how to do what all students do—only cheaper and better. For example, plan an alternative spring break that doesn't cost hundreds (thousands?) of dollars. Check local restaurants, bars and clubs, then report on, say, how to have a perfect date for $50 or less.

How to start investing. Most students agonize over simply paying current bills, let alone starting a lifetime investment program. But, financial planners say, *now* indeed is the time to start investing, even if only for small sums each month. Check local brokerage firms for their plans. Look also at bank plans and U.S. Savings Bonds.

On Campus Today

Economic, business and financial reporting is an underdeveloped artform in campus journalism. But some college papers offer it with considerable success.

For example, *The Iowa State Daily* in Ames runs the full range, from big picture coverage of economics to personalized how-to finance stories.

The *Daily,* which covers—and sells to—an off-campus "civilian" audience in Ames, as well as students, offers this type of broad-view coverage:

Although 1998 was a tough year for farmers across Iowa, the downward trend in commodity prices may be changing.

This is the consensus of two members of Iowa State's faculty in the economics department: Jim Kliebenstein, professor of agricultural economics, and John Lawrence, Extension livestock economist.

According to the Iowa Agricultural Statistics Service's (IASS) Web site, the prices Iowa farmers have received for corn, soybeans and hogs are among the lowest in a decade.

Lawrence said . . .

—Olivia Ogren, *The Iowa State Daily*[1]

Note above how tightly the writer ties the story—including lead—to *campus experts.* A typical faculty includes many experts in many subjects. Find them, use them.

The Iowa State Daily is excellent in finding *local pegs* for distant stories—for bringing home to the Ames campus the meaning of distant events. Note:

> The Asian economic crisis continues to pose financial problems for international students, causing decreased enrollment and threatening Iowa State's international diversity.
>
> For the past 14 months, the values of currency in Indonesia, Malaysia, Korea and Thailand have dropped.
>
> Deborah Vance, program coordinator for the Office of International Students and Scholars, said Indonesian currency, which was hit the worst, has lost 70 percent of its value.
>
> "I'd liken it to if someone went into your bank account and grabs 70 percent and told you to live on the remainder; that's what's happened to these students," she said.
>
> Vance said paying tuition poses the largest problem for students whose home countries are in economic crisis.
>
> According to the fall 1997 and 1998 ISU Fact Books, Indonesian student enrollment is down 24 from 252 in 1997; Malaysian student enrollment is down 70 . . .
>
> —Arlene Birt, *The Iowa State Daily*[2]

At *The Red & Black,* an independent student-run newspaper that targets University of Georgia-Athens students, Jeff Montemayor leads readers through the mysteries of how to select a bank. Note his swingin' intro:

> Students are as notorious for being broke as they are for spending money. So banks in Athens offer checking that won't bust a student's wallet.
>
> At SunTrust, students mostly choose the free checking account called "SmartChoice," said Heidi Spratlin, the marketing manager of SunTrust.
>
> The "SmartChoice" checking account provides students with free checking, so students don't have to pay additional check fees, Spratlin said.
>
> "If you're a student who doesn't like to use debit or charge cards, and you write a lot of checks, then you'll want the SmartChoice account," Spratlin said.
>
> The account includes a $10 monthly maintenance fee that covers ATM use, unlimited checking and filing used checks. . . .

Now, writer Montemayor reports dollars-and-cents terms offered by three other banks courting student business. And, he then breaks out those details in a stand-alone box:

STUDENT CHECKING IN ATHENS

SunTrust:
—Free checking with the "SmartChoice" account; $50 to open
—$10 monthly maintenance fee to file used checks

Main Street Bank:
—Unlimited checking and no service charges; $50 to open

NationsBank:
—$50 to open an account; first 50 checks are free
—$5 monthly maintenance fee if balance falls below $500

Wachovia:
—Free checking and no minimum balance; $50 to open
—$5 monthly maintenance fee, starting April, for more than two teller-assisted transactions

—Jeff Montemayor, *The Red & Black* [3]

At the University of Southern Mississippi, Christina Gates, executive editor of *The Student Printz,* personalizes her writing with the perpendicular pronoun:

Yesterday, I looked in my campus mail box and found yet another credit card application.

I wouldn't mind junk mail so much except that I get applications weekly. And I know I am not alone—creditors target students with deals that seem too good to be true.

College is a time that students need to start working toward a good credit record; however, this is not as easy as it sounds.

[Alisha Jones], a senior public relations major, had a first-hand experience with credit hassles.

She received a letter from a bank saying she was denied a credit card she hadn't even requested. When she called the issuing bank, she was told she owed over $20,000. . . .

—Christina Gates, *The Student Printz* [4]

Writer Gates now walks readers through the credit card travails of [Alisha Jones], then quickly goes to an authoritative source—the manager of a consumer credit counseling service—for advice on how student readers can solve their own credit problems. The story includes the service's address and other how-to information student readers need.

Now, ***that***'s outstanding personal finance reporting!

Tomorrow, Beyond Spot News

One day, but *only* when you've earned solid credentials in spot-news reporting, an editor somewhere might be persuaded to let you write what *you* think, not only what your sources say.

And that will be your ticket into truly Big League business journalism.

It also will move you into an entirely new realm of journalistic responsibility, for then you will be placing *your* opinions and *your* guidance in the marketplace of ideas where readers seek help on dollars-and-cents decisions that will decide their financial futures.

Begin thinking now about how to gain the experience necessary for a future move out of *objective* reporting and into three dimensions of *subjective* writing:

> *Analytical reporting,* a careful, limited departure from straightforward reporting of the Five Ws and How into reporting not only what happened, but what it likely means; not only that it occurred, but why—reporting, that is, not only what was said or done last night but what the possible outcome will be tomorrow.

> *Column writing,* a highly subjective and personalized form of journalism in which experienced reporters 1) establish reputations of being careful, reliable, accurate *experts* in their subject, then 2) overlay their expert reporting with their personal opinions.

> *Editorial writing,* which involves representing the *institutional attitudes* of your newspaper or magazine. That can require you to expound a viewpoint dictated by your publication's owner or an editorial board of your peers —and sometimes their position is contrary to yours!

Let's look more closely at these three forms:

Analytical Reporting

Print journalism has moved strongly into analytical reporting for two principal reasons:

- Competitors, including radio, television and electronic news services, are faster in delivering the who, what, when and where—the spot news. For competitive purposes, newspapers and magazines long ago revised their mission to include not only reporting the what, but the *real what*—the deeper meaning, the why and how of news developments.
- Simply put, events we cover today can be so terribly complicated that our readers, busy with their own lives and preoccupied with jobs and crabgrass in their lawns, need interpretation and analysis to comprehend what the news means to them.

That, of course, places enormous responsibility on reporters to be correct in understanding the deeper meanings of the news and to be precise in how they write it.

Most newspapers and magazines, therefore, let reporters edge only gradually into analytical writing. Permission sometimes is not even voiced; senior reporters who become more confident in their expertise begin to insert carefully sourced interpretation into their writing—and their editors accept it.

Sometimes the interpretation so helpful to readers takes just a few words (emphasis added):

> Washington—U.S. consumer prices rose at a subdued pace in July, ***suggesting inflation is under wraps.***
>
> The consumer price index, the nation's main inflation gauge, rose 0.2 percent last month after rising 0.1 percent in June, the Labor Department reported Tuesday. The CPI's core rate, which strips out volatile food and energy costs, rose 0.2 percent after rising 0.1 percent in June.
>
> "Inflation has bottomed, and if it's going to go back up, it's going to be a gradual climb," said Cary Leahey, chief U.S. economist at High Frequency Economics in Valhalla, N.Y. "The Fed is on hold until at least the end of the year." The Federal Reserve policy makers meeting Tuesday left the overnight bank lending rate unchanged, suggesting they're confident inflation will stay low in coming months. . . .
>
> —Laura Cohn, Bloomberg News[5]

Note these factors about the story above:

- The way this story is written, folks, that's ***Laura Cohn of Bloomberg News*** stating in the first graf that events suggest inflation "is under wraps."
- ***However,*** her analytical language is solidly based on authoritative sources— the third-graf reference to an expert economist.
- And, without writer Cohn's interpretive lead, the second graf—the CPI statistical report—is unintelligible to many readers.

Do ***you*** understand what's happening in the nation's health-insurance system? I don't, and Anita Sharpe (and her editors) of *The Wall Street Journal* assume many of their readers don't either. So, she ***opens*** a news story with a characterization (emphasis added) that's designed to help readers interpret what follows:

> ***In a sign of how unwieldy the nation's health-insurance system has become*** some doctors are actually agreeing to cut their fees for patients who pay upfront.
>
> Many of these doctors say dealing with insurers' red tape is so time-consuming and cumbersome they would rather work at a discount than battle the bureaucracy.
>
> "It's like Wal-Mart. You get your service, you pay your money." says [John Jones], a family physician in Athens, Tex. . . .

[Jane Doe], a Fresno, Calif., internist who specializes in preventive medicine, began offering discounts on services such as smoking cessation for upfront payments several years ago. . . .

Note, above, the first graf's interpretative language quickly gives way to sound, authoritative reporting—references in the third and fourth grafs to expert sources.

Now, the *Journal* writer inserts a full graf explaining the story's "what" and "why":

Most such cut-rate programs are aimed at patients who don't have health insurance or have a high deductible and would otherwise have to pay a doctor's full fee on their own. Insurance companies and HMOs generally negotiate their own discounts with health-care providers, sometimes at reimbursement rates that barely cover the physician's costs. ***It is no wonder then, that some doctors like the cash up-front idea.*** They not only get paid faster—they often get paid more than under managed-care plans, without the administrative headaches.

—Anita Sharpe, *The Wall Street Journal*[6]

The Associated Press, whose byword is objective reporting, permits—indeed, demands—analytical writing on the hugely complicated economic issues of our days. AP's Jeffrey Ulbrich landed on the front page of *The Richmond (Va.) Times-Dispatch* (and many other papers) with this characterization of a complicated European story:

Brussels, Belgium—The European Union launched more than a single currency yesterday—it launched hope. Hope for a more prosperous Europe. A stronger, united Europe. And, ultimately, a more peaceful Europe.

Currency, as European Central Bank President Wim Duisenberg put it, goes beyond money. The franc is France. The mark is Germany. The lira is Italy. Now, he hopes, the euro will become Europe.

"A currency is part of the identity of a people," said Duisenberg, a Dutchman.

"It reflects what they have in common, now and in the future. May the euro become a unifying symbol for the people of Europe."

—Jeffrey Ulbrich, The Associated Press[7]

Note how cautiously even experienced reporters insert interpretation. In a story dominating the front page of *The New York Times* business section, a veteran reporter stacks up impressive evidence that Bell Atlantic Corporation faces a bad year ahead. However, the reporter carefully qualifies the evidence (emphasis added):

This year is only a month old, ***but by some measures it already seems*** that 1999 will not be kind to the Bell Atlantic corporation, the nation's biggest local phone company.

Last month, Bell Atlantic—which serves 21.5 million households and more than 2 million businesses from Maine to Virginia—lost out in the bidding to acquire Airtouch Communications Inc., one of the world's top wireless phone companies. Then the AT&T corporation unveiled a uniform 10-cents-a-minute communications package aimed at least partly at Bell Atlantic's existing wireless business.

Separately, AT&T formed a venture to offer local phone service over cable television lines owned by Times Warner Inc., the main cable operator in New York City, the heart of Bell Atlantic's territory. And then, just two days ago, MCI Worldcom Inc. revived its own plan to offer local service in New York. . . .

—Seth Schiesel, *The New York Times* [8]

At many newspapers, if interpretive writing goes much beyond the carefully qualified examples you've seen above, editors "flag" stories to alert readers that personal analysis, though soundly based on strong reporting, is ahead.

The New York Times, for example, "slugs" stories with a "News Analysis" flag when writers really cut loose with behind-the-scenes meaning. An example:

News Analysis

A handful of leading companies will come to dominate cyberspace.

That snippet of rhetoric has become all the analytical underpinning there is to justify the unprecedented stock market values of the prominent Internet companies like Yahoo, American Online and Amazon.com.

On the face of it, that well could be true. On the other hand, the Internet may make it easier for new competitors to constantly challenge the leaders.

Yet one of the byproducts of the irrational exuberance in Internet stock prices is that the prophesied greatness of certain companies becomes self-fulfilling. Their huge market values allow them to grow by acquisitions . . .

—Saul Hansell, *The New York Times*[9]

The *Times* also flags the following:

News Analysis

The thousands of American Airlines pilots who have called in sick as part of a messy labor standoff have adopted a time-honored union tactic—a sort of strike without striking.

For the angry workers, such a tactic has some advantages. For one thing, it enables unions to shut down much of their employers' operations when they would otherwise be barred from striking under an existing contract, as is the case with the American pilots.

And, yes, there is another big advantage: While calling in sick, the pilots, members of the Allied Pilots Association, continue to get paid, something that would not happen if they went on strike . . .

—Steven Greenhouse, *The New York Times*[10]

Two lessons in analytical writing:

- Base your analysis in strong, visible reporting; rest your interpretive language on a strong foundation of authoritative sourcing readers can see.
- Signal readers—with a single word ("seems" or "suggesting") or a flag ("News Analysis")—when you depart from the straight-and-narrow trail of objective hard-news reporting.

Column Writing

In column writing, it's obvious to all that you've crossed the boundary between objective reporting and subjective opinion writing. Often, your photo will accompany your byline; your column will run regularly, in the same spot—and you'll get to use that perpendicular pronoun—"I"—a great deal.

For experienced specialists, opportunities in column writing virtually are unlimited. Columnists range from internationally syndicated writers of global economics to hometown newspaper journalists who cover daily news beats *and* write a column on, say, personal finance at the Main Street level.

What's obviously required of a successful columnist is a high level of expertise that lends credibility, authority, believability to the column. The good ones have that expertise.

George Melloan takes more than 45 years experience as a journalist to his column, "Global View," in *The Wall Street Journal.* His weekly look at international economics and finance is through a viewfinder built on decades of beat reporting, in the United States and abroad. Columnists for *The New York Times, Boston Globe, Los Angeles Times* and other leading newspapers must pass this test: Will their reporting, writing *and their analysis* stand up to scrutiny by nonjournalist experts—bankers, academics, brokers, government specialists—as well as non-expert readers?

Read the following aloud, and ask yourself, "Don't these columnist's *sound* as if they know what they're talking about?"

> With the Dow Jones industrial average confined to a fairly tight trading range for the last 30 days, investors may be starting to wonder where their bull market has gone. It hasn't helped that yields on Treasury bonds have jumped from 5.1 percent in mid-January to 5.42 percent on Friday. Since the Federal Reserve Board has let the bond market take the lead on interest rate policy in recent years, the move in yields may be a sign of higher interest rates in the months ahead—never a plus for stocks.
>
> To be sure, a month of lackluster stock prices does not mean the end of the bull run . . .
>
> —Gretchen Morgenson, "Market Watch," *The New York Times*[11]

It's almost impossible for individual investors to get a square deal in the bond market. Unlike institutional investors with their expensive, real-time databases, individuals don't have transparency—they can't instantaneously see prices across the market. So they put themselves in the hands of brokers, who pad their trading desks' markups.

SEC Chairman Arthur Levitt occasionally gripes about the bond market's unfairness. He hasn't done much about it, but the marketplace finally has. For the first time, individuals can buy bonds at competitive prices. It's happening on the Internet (no surprise), and it is the best deal I have seen in my 22 years in the business. . . .

—Marilyn Cohen, "Capital Markets," *Forbes*[12]

If you run a family-owned business, federal tax law now allows you to set up an employee stock ownership plan, or ESOP, and turn your employees into motivated owners with a stake in the well-being of your company.

Under the correct circumstances, the law even makes it possible for you to use an ESOP to cash yourself out of a family-owned business. . . .

—Juan Hovey, "Financing and Insurance," *The Los Angeles Times*[13]

Project Jupiter, as the secretive folks working for Phil Holden at Microsoft Corp. called it, looks kind of dumb on paper but, I must say it looks great in this gadget-weary writer's trusty red backpack.

I'm touting today the first fruits of Jupiter, namely Mobilon Pro PV-5000 by Sharp Electronics Corp., a 2.7-pound bundle of binary brawn.

Here is a slick, 9-inch by 8-inch by 1.1-inch silver-colored gadget that, in my humble opinion at least, finally delivers on the original laptop promise. . . .

—James Coates, "Binary Beat," *The Chicago Tribune*[14]

Editorial Writing

Editorial writers take a huge step beyond news reporting and analytical writing. They report the news, all right. And they analyze it. But then they suggest, advocate, ***demand*** action.

Reporters use objective, neutral language to reveal that the Fed chairman announces an increase in interest rates.

Columnists analyze what the increase means.

Editorial writers praise or condemn the chairman's action; they express opinion on whether the chairman ***should*** implement the increase and, if not, they call for action to halt it.

Reporters examine their copy to ensure their facts are correct; columnists look back to be certain their analysis is clear; editorial writers ask, "Does this editorial SEA—Stimulate, Explain, Advocate?"

That's the difference—the ***huge*** difference—when you move into editorial writing.

Reporters normally are invited over to the "other side," to write editorials, when they exhibit strong reporting and writing skills **and** profound understanding of current issues.

After years in Main Street business reporting, for example, you might be invited to join a newspaper's editorial page to specialize in writing opinion—yours and the newspaper's—on local business, economic and financial issues.

On large papers, you might stick close to business subjects, ranging only infrequently into other areas—politics, education, for example—where fellow editorialists have established their specialization. On smaller papers, you would write frequently on many subjects outside your specialization.

If writing "institutional" editorials representing the newspaper's position you would take guidance either from the owner or an editorial board established to discuss current issues, then adopt an institutional position. At *The Atlanta Journal,* for example, five editorial writers, headed by Jim Wooten, editor of the editorial page, discuss (and often debate somewhat heatedly) what institutional stance the paper will take. The publisher is not part of the discussion.

Editorial writers carry heavy responsibilities in all this. In communities large and small, newspapers are among the most influential local institutions. They **do** set the agenda for much of the public dialogue in this country; they **do** move, stir and force action.

So, editorial writing should be reasoned yet forceful, balanced yet pointed, thoughtful and responsible while being colorful, engaging and readable.[15]

Editorial writing cannot be limited to heated, contentious attack-dog journalism. Careful reporting—"added value" reporting, the pros call it—must lend understanding for readers, along with your spirited call for action.

A basic structure for an editorial is shown in Figure 10.1.

Figure 10.1.   Example of story structure for an editorial.

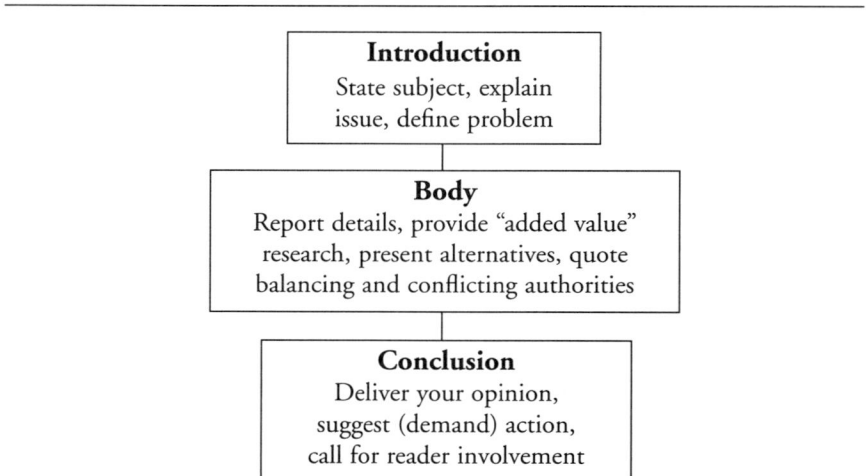

Introduction
State subject, explain
issue, define problem

Body
Report details, provide "added value"
research, present alternatives, quote
balancing and conflicting authorities

Conclusion
Deliver your opinion,
suggest (demand) action,
call for reader involvement

Summary

- Of all sectors of journalism, none is as underdeveloped in campus publications as business news, and that offers you a great opportunity for experience.
- You'll serve campus readers (and build a great clip file) if you focus on the local scene—your campus—and issues pertinent to student readers.
- Conduct your own survey on what news is important to students by listening in class, hallways, on the bus, in the cafeteria line to which dollars-and-cents issues students are discussing.
- Concentrate on core issues such as cost of eating in campus dining halls versus off-campus apartments or how students must work part-time to pay their bills.
- Stay timely, learning to offer stories when editors likely will be receptive and when readers need to know—the availability of jobs for graduates in the spring, for example, not in September, 10 months before graduation.
- Report strongly and authoritatively, interviewing local campus officials who can provide reliable information for your readers.
- As always, write alluringly to pull readers into your story; if you don't, your message is lost.
- Remember to write about and for people, not issues or concepts, which are news only if they affect people.
- Campus journalism offers fertile fields for learning big picture reporting of economics and finance, and especially for how-to stories on such things as buying textbooks or computers or how to obtain student loans.
- In the future, when you're experienced in spot-news reporting, you can move into analytical reporting, columns or editorials.
- Heavy responsibilities attend opinion writing because you must go far beyond reporting facts or analyzing them and into suggesting (or demanding!) action.

Recommended Reading

It's revealing to watch the editorial pages of *The New York Times* and *The Wall Street Journal* cover economic, business and financial issues. Both are among the most influential pages in the world, and their impact on public dialogue and policy is enormous.

Read the columnists who regularly comment on business, economics and finance in the leading metropolitan papers we've discussed in this book—the *Times* and *Journal* among them. No book can give you the "feel" for Big League commentary that you can gain from reading those columnists daily, although I try in Conrad C. Fink, *Writing Opinion for Impact* (Ames: Iowa State University Press, 1999), a detailed discussion of editorial and analytical writing.

Notes

1. "Iowa Farmers Struggle with Dipping Prices," Feb. 15, 1999, p. 1.
2. "Asian Economic Crisis Hits Enrollment," Feb. 9, 1999, p. 1.
3. "Local Banks Provide Many Checking Account Options," March 1, 1999, p. 3.
4. "Credit Cards Can Lead to Distress," Feb. 11, 1999, p. 1.
5. Dispatch for morning papers, Aug. 19, 1988.
6. "Discounted Fees Cure Headaches, Some Doctors Find," Sept. 15, 1998, p. B-1.
7. Dispatch for morning papers, Jan. 2, 1999.
8. "The Bell That Would Be King," Feb. 5, 1999, p. C-1.
9. "Inflated Stocks Cushion Pitfalls of Net Mergers," national edition, Feb. 29, 1999, p. C-1.
10. "Parachute for Pilots," Feb. 12, 1999, national edition, p. C-4.
11. "Market Watch, " national edition, Feb. 14, 1999, section 3, p. 1.
12. "Capital Markets," Jan. 25, 1999, p. 100.
13. "No ESOP Fable: Plan Is Used to Cash Out of Family Firm," March 3, 1999, p. C-6.
14. "Binary Beat," Jan. 31, 1999, section 5, p. 5.
15. This is drawn from my *Writing Opinion for Impact* (Ames: Iowa State University Press, 1999).

Exercises

1. Study five consecutive issues of your campus newspaper (or another paper your instructor designates) and analyze whether economic, business and financial coverage meets the standards of Chapter 10. Does it cover local issues and reveal the writers listened to what campus readers want and need? Does it focus on core issues? Is it timely, and is it reported strongly and authoritatively? Report your findings in about 250 words.

2. Suggest five stories—in about 75 words each—that you could do on campus, covering core issues of compelling interest to students. Three ideas should be for how-to stories; two for broader "big picture" stories covering, say, your university's budget, tuition levels and so forth.

3. With your instructor's approval write one of the five stories you suggested as part of Exercise 2. Do this in 300-350 words. Try for a neck-of-vase intro, using a single individual or anecdotal lead to illustrate a wider story on, say, students working part-time or comparison shopping for the lowest food prices in town.

4. Suggest to your instructor, in about 50 words, a personal bylined column you could do for your campus newspaper's editorial page. Your subject should be a how-to element in the news of compelling interest to students—how to buy a computer at the best price, for example, or where to buy textbooks at the best bargains. Report strongly for this column to provide readers with "added value" and personalize your writing by using the perpendicular pronoun "I."

5. With your instructor's approval, offer to write an institutional editorial for your campus newspaper on a topic of current and compelling interest in economics, business or finance. Investigate, for example, tuition levels at your university over the past three years, or how student fees are allocated by the administration, then write an editorial commenting on that. Try for an editorial that will SEA—Stimulate, Explain, Advocate.

Appendix:
Terms to Learn

Amex. American Stock Exchange, where stock is traded in publicly owned companies. Headquarters and trading floor are in New York City. Smaller than the New York Stock Exchange.

Amortization. Allocation of value of intangible assets (patents, licenses, etc.) over the period of their existence.

Antitrust laws. Designed to prevent monopoly and maintain competition, with aim of ensuring consumers get the best possible goods and services at the lowest prices. Original legislation was Sherman Antitrust Act of 1890.

Arbitrage. Buying in one market while selling in another, thus profiting from price discrepancies. Usually involves currencies, commercial bills, securities.

Assets. Valuables owned by individuals, corporations or estates. *Capital* assets are permanent (buildings) and not normally bought or sold in the course of everyday business. *Current* assets are those normally convertible to cash within 12 months. *Intangible* assets are nonphysical, such as patents, franchises.

Averages. Selected securities averaged to show general market trends. Examples are Dow Jones Industrial Average, S&P 500.

Balance of payments. Total payment to foreign nations minus total receipts from them.

Balance of trade. Difference between monetary value of a country's imports and exports of merchandise (excluding gold).

Balance sheet. "Snapshot" of a company's financial condition (assets balanced by liabilities) on a given day.

Bank reserves. Bank's money available for meeting depositors' demands. U.S. law requires a certain percentage of deposits must be on reserve.

Bear market. When stock prices fall. (Remember: a bear hugs you and drags you *down;* a bull hooks you with his horns and throws you *up*—thus "bull market.") A bear is an investor who anticipates falling prices.

Bellwether stock. A leader watched as an indicator of trends.

Big Board. The New York Stock Exchange.

Blue chip stock. Noted for long record of profits and paying dividends.

Bond. Interest-bearing certificate or evidence of debt, public or private; a promise to repay at a specified time, usually longer than one year. (Debts of less than a year normally are called "notes.")

Break even. Cost equals income.

Bull market. Stock prices are rising. A bull anticipates rising prices.

Bureau of Labor Statistics. Federal agency in Department of Labor; reports statistics on employment, construction, wages; issues consumer price index.

Bureau of the Budget. Unit of the Executive Office of the president; presents federal budget and coordinates statistical reports from various federal agencies.

Bureau of the Census. Department of Commerce unit that conducts censuses of population, housing, agriculture, manufacturing, business.

Buyer's market. Demand is exceeded by supply, so sellers accept lower prices.

Capital. Broadly, property that yields income. Also money invested at interest.

Capital gain (or loss). Difference between cost and sale price of a capital asset (such as land, equipment).

Cash flow. Earnings (profits) plus depreciation and other charges, such as deferred taxes, goodwill amortization.

Central Bank. Government-controlled; exists for public fiscal purposes, such as maintaining adequate reserve against bank credit, and for controlling import/export of money. In the United States, it's the federal reserve system.

Certificate of Deposit. CDs are investment instruments offering interest for fixed periods, usually from six months to five years.

Chicago Board of Trade. CBOT is the main U.S. exchange for trading commodities, such as grain, livestock.

Chief executive officer. CEO is a company's top official.

Closed shop. To be employed, workers must join a union.

Commercial paper. Notes, bills and other short-term obligations sold by firms to raise money.

Commodities. Tangible items, such as wheat, corn, soybeans, traded at exchanges such as those in Chicago and London.

Common stock. Represents ownership of a company; owners normally receive dividends and have voting rights.

Consumer durable goods. Those with general life of over three years.

Consumer goods. Those for direct consumption, such as food, clothing, as opposed to producers' goods, such as machinery.

Consumer price index. Measures purchasing power by noting price changes of typical goods and services.

Convertible bonds. Convertible into shares of common stock.

Cost of living index. Measures price changes for goods and services purchased by households. Important economic indicator.

Council of Economic Advisors. Experts and staff advise U.S. president on economic policy.

Current assets. Assets normally converted to cash within 12 months.

Current liabilities. Obligations that will be paid within 12 months.

Current ratio. Current assets (those convertible to cash within 12 months) divided by current liabilities (those that must be paid within 12 months). Indicates a company's ability to operate independent of short-term borrowing. Generally acceptable ratio is $2 in current assets to every $1 in current liabilities.

Debenture bonds. Debt instruments bearing usually fixed rates of interest, repayable within specified period.

Debt limit. Constitutional or legislative limit on authority of a state or municipal government to borrow funds.

Debt-to-net worth ratio. Liabilities divided by net worth, an indication of amount of borrowed funds being used in a business.

Deficit. Liabilities excess over assets or expenditure excess over revenue.

Deficit financing. Deliberate spending, usually by a government, of more money than it receives in revenue. Often employed to generate business during a recession.

Deflation. Prices decline, usually when supply exceeds demand or consumer spending is curtailed.

Depletion. Gradually exhausting a resource (such as oil) by using it.

Depreciation. Decline in value of a fixed asset, such as buildings, due to wear and tear.

Depression. Rising unemployment, slow investment and consumption due to pessimism in business and consumer circles; creates low end of a business cycle.

Dividend. Portion of profit paid to shareholders, usually in dollars per share. ***Preferred*** shares get a fixed rate of payment; ***ordinary (common)*** shares are paid as the company's board of directors sees fit and according to amount of profits.

"The Dow." The Dow Jones Industrial Average, or DJIA, an average of 30 major industry stocks; viewed by many as a measure of wider market activity.

Earned income. Money from services, trading or business transactions, rather than from property ownership.

Earnings reports. A company's financial results, normally issued every three months, six months, and year.

EBITDA. Earnings before interest, taxes, depreciation and amortization. Like cash flow, it shows pretax income.

Equity. Value of the net assets of a company. "Equities" are ordinary shares owned by shareholders.

Ex-dividend. Company stock dividends are declared payable on a future date. Stock sold between declaration and payment dates is sold ex-dividend, ***without*** the dividend, which will go to the owner of the stock on the date the dividend was declared.

Export-Import Bank of Washington. Independent bank under federal charter that makes loans to finance the flow of imports and exports.

Fair employment practice. Hiring, job and advancement policies based on merit and fitness, not race, color, religion.

Featherbedding. Union tactics designed to increase labor or work time on a particular job force or work time on a particular job; outlawed by Taft-Hartley Act.

Federal Deposit Insurance Corporation. Insures bank deposits against inability of banks to pay.

Federal Home Loan Mortgage Corporation. Freddie Mac promotes secondary market in residential mortgages, buying them for sale.

Federal National Mortgage Association. Fannie Mae is owned by private stockholders and creates a secondary market in mortgages insured by the U.S. Federal Housing Administration.

Federal Reserve System. Twelve banks acting as sources of credit for member banks. This "banker's bank" is a depository of resources and provider of other services for thousands of banks controlling most commercial bank deposits in the United States.

Federal Trade Commission. Charged with preventing unfair business practices and, with the U.S. Justice Department, enforcing antitrust laws.

Fiduciary. Person in position of trust, by law or voluntary act.

Fiscal policy. Government's financial policy, especially regarding the national budget and borrowing.

Fiscal year. A 12-month period, rather than a calendar year, selected as an accounting period.

Free trade. International trade unhindered by protection, such as duties.

General Accounting Office. Federal agency that audits/reviews federal expenditures/appropriations.

Going public. Process of a privately owned company selling shares to the public for the first time. ("Initial Public Offering"—or "IPO"—also is widely used to describe the process.)

Grannie Mae. GNMA, or Government National Mortgage Administration, largest secondary mortgage market in nation.

Gross Domestic Product. Value of all goods and services produced within the United States; *Gross National Product* covers all production by Americans, outside as well as in the United States.

Gross margin. Difference between total cost of goods sold and net sales income.

Income statement (or profit and loss statement or "P&L"). Shows company's financial results, usually over a quarter or year; shows, in dollars, revenue, costs, expenses, taxes, earnings (or profits).

Inflation. Prices of goods and services rise, pushed upward by the increase in volume of money and credit relative to the quantity of goods and services available. Leads to loss of confidence in a nation's money.

Initial public offering (IPO). Process of privately owned company selling shares to public for first time.

Injunction. Court order to cease certain activities.

Insider. In securities trading, an officer or executive of a corporation who also is a shareholder and who thus possesses "inside information" on how the stock price might move.

Interest. Payment for use of money. *Prime rate* is what banks charge their biggest borrowers with the best credit rating. *Treasury bill rate* is paid by the U.S. government on money borrowed for three months.

International Monetary Fund. Member nations supply money to stabilize international exchange and promote orderly and balanced trade.

Junk bonds. High-yield bonds often rated as high-risk by credit-rating agencies because they are issued by companies heavily in debt.

Liability. In finance, what a person/company owes.

Liquidity. Cash or assets easily convertible into cash, as opposed to assets such as buildings or land.

Merger. One corporation buys the property of another (or others) and the buyer continues to exist; the purchased corporation is dissolved. (In a ***consolidation,*** all corporations are dissolved and become equal parts in a new one.)

Monetary policy. Federal measures, by central bank or federal reserve system and treasury, to strengthen the economy and minimize cyclical fluctuations. Tools are regulating credit, the budget, taxes.

Money market fund. Pooled funds controlled by managers; offers investment opportunities with commercial interest-rate returns.

Mortgage bonds. Bonds secured by real property, such as buildings, equipment.

Mutual funds. Provides professional stock portfolio management in diversified securities. Fund sells its shares and redeems them at holders' option, at prices based on its asset values.

National Association of Securities Dealers Automatic Quotations. NASDAQ is an automated system reporting over-the-counter stock trading.

National Labor Relations Board. Government agency that enforces the Wagner Act, the nation's basic labor relations law. Law guarantees workers the right to organize and bargain collectively through unions and forbids unfair labor practices.

Net profit (or "net earnings" or "net income"). The profitability (or "bottom line") of a company after all costs, expenses, taxes are paid.

New York Stock Exchange. NYSE is the "Big Board," the largest of the nation's stock exchanges. Headquarters are in New York City. Most "blue-chip" stocks are traded here.

Note. Written credit instrument (in many forms) that is an unconditional promise to pay a sum of money at some specified future date to a named person or, if unnamed, to the bearer.

Open shop. Union membership is not a condition of employment; workers may decide whether to join.

Operating profit. Sales proceeds minus expense of operating a company and ***before*** taxes and interest expense are deducted.

Options. Contracts giving holders the right (but not obligation) to buy or sell at a set price, particularly securities or commodities.

Over-the-counter market. A securities trading market without a central exchange; traders are linked electronically.

Par value. Face value on a stock certificate or bond; may not be related to actual market value.

Poison pill. Steps companies take to guard against being taken over, usually by making a takeover too expensive.

Prime rate. Interest rate granted by banks to only their best, most creditworthy customers, usually big businesses. Viewed as an important indicator because consumers generally must pay a few interest points above prime.

Preferred stock. Owner gets priority (over common stockholders) in dividend payments or in division of assets when a firm is liquidated.

Pretax profit. Measure of earnings used by most investors.

Recession. Declining business cycle, in which economy's income, output and employment decrease. Business and consumer optimism fades.

Return on investment. ROI is an important indicator for investors. Divide a company's assets into its net income to yield the percentage.

Right-to-work laws. Make it illegal to require union membership as a condition of employment.

Securities. Documents that are evidence of ownership (stock) or debt (bonds).

Securities and Exchange Commission. Federal agency that supervises, regulates securities industry; principal mission is protecting investors against malpractice.

Sell short. Selling borrowed securities and expecting to be able to buy them later at a lower price, then return them—and make a profit.

Stock. Ownership units in a corporation, including ***common, preferred,*** and ***capital*** stock.

Stock split. To lower its share price and increase liquidity in its stock, a company can issue, say, two shares for each one held by shareholders. Total value of shares held remains unchanged. Stocks then are more affordable.

Value-added tax. Successive taxation, as in a sales tax on the sale of a commodity every time it changes hands.

Yields. Difference between purchase price and face value of a commodity or security.

Name Index

Akasie, Jay, 165–6
Akst, Daniel, 99
American Business Editors and Writers, Inc., 184–6
American Editor, 179
American Institute of Accountants, 141
American Society of Newspaper Editors, 191
Anderson (S.C.) *Independent-Mail,* 126, 153
Aristotle, 190
Armour, Stephanie, 130
Associated Press, 9, 10, 11–12, 17–18, 25, 29, 41, 52, 54, 55, 56, 67, 71, 110, 111, 112, 114, 116, 117, 131, 160–1, 210
Associated Press Managing Editors, 154
Athens (Ga.) *Daily News,* 126–8
Atlanta Business Journal, 12
Atlanta Journal and Constitution, 5–7, 26, 94, 97, 98, 160, 214

Banks, Howard, 53
Baltimore Sun, 99
Barron's, 12, 98, 99
Behr, Peter, 15
Belton, Beth, 59
Bergen, Kathy, 99
Berry, John M., 75
Beverage Journal, 12
Biddle, Frederick M., 75
Birt, Arlene, 206
Bloomberg News Service, 9, 16, 29, 41, 50, 51, 54, 55, 59, 67, 69, 77, 112, 115, 116, 209
Borrego, Anne Marie, 93, 156–7
Boston Globe, 71, 72, 78, 125, 153, 155, 212
Bradlee, Ben, 40
Bridge News, 60
Bridis, Ted, 10
Brown, Jeff, 164–5
Buckman, Rebecca, 137–8
Bunker, Matthew D., 174, 180

Business Information Services, 143
Business Week, 38

Carter, Bill, 97
Cassel, Andrew, 91
Chamberlin, Bill F., 174, 180
Chicago Tribune, 99, 111–12, 129–30, 213
CNBC, 154
CNNfn, 28–9, 39, 41, 79, 154, 168
Coates, James, 213
Cohn, Laura, 209
Cohn, Marilyn, 213
Columbus Ledger-Enquirer, 73
Conlin, Michelle, 52, 56
Copple, Brandon, 92
Cox Newspapers, 79, 99
Crain's Cleveland Business, 12
Cronkite, Walter, 89

Dallas Morning News, 17, 70, 93, 155–7, 160–1, 162
Daykin, Tom, 56
Deener, Bill, 70
Deogun, Nikhil, 95
DiStefano, Joseph N., 79
Dockendorf, Randy, 117–8
Dow Jones & Co., 10, 186–9
Dow Jones News Service, 9, 11, 17, 29, 41, 53, 59, 67, 78–9, 85, 112, 117, 138, 167, 189

The Economist, 51, 153
Egodigwe, Laura Sanders, 75
Epstein, Gene, 98
Ernst & Young, 148
Ewing, Terzah, 96
Ezell, Hank, 37, 98

Farhi, Paul, 76

Subject
Index